How it all Vegan!

IRRESISTIBLE RECIPES FOR AN ANIMAL-FREE DIET

How it all Vegan!

IRRESISTIBLE RECIPES FOR AN ANIMAL-FREE DIET

TANYA BARNARD & SARAH KRAMER

ARSENAL
PULP PRESS

VANCOUVER

ARSENAL PULP PRESS
200-341 Water Street
Vancouver, B.C.
Canada V6B 1B8
arsenalpulp.com

The publisher gratefully acknowledges the support of the Government of Canada through the
Book Publishing Industry Development Program and the Government of British Columbia
through Book Publishing Tax Credit Program for its publishing activities.

The author and publisher assert that the information contained in this book is true and complete
to the best of their knowledge. All recommendations are made without guarantee on the part of
the author and publisher. The author and publisher disclaim any liability in connection with the
use of this information. For more information, contact the publisher.

Book design and illustrations by Electra Design Group
Cover photograph by Daniel Collins
Color photographs of Sarah Kramer by Gerry Kramer
Color food photographs by Sarah Kramer (sarahkramerphotography.com)
Selected B&W photographs courtesy of the author and PhotoDisc, Inc.
Pottery provided by VeganDish.net

Printed in China on wood-free paper

Library and Archives Canada Cataloguing in Publication:

Kramer, Sarah, 1968-
How it all vegan! : irresistible recipes for an animal-free diet / Sarah
Kramer and Tanya Barnard. – 10th anniversary ed.

First ed. written by Tanya Barnard & Sarah Kramer.
ISBN 978-1-55152-253-1

1. Vegan cookery. I. Barnard, Tanya, 1972- II. Title.

TX837.B28 2009   641.5'636
C2009-901876-4

CONTENTS

SARAH KRAMER

Welcome to the tenth anniversary edition of *How It All Vegan!* Wowzers, does time ever fly by when you're having fun. Woo hoo! When I think back to how this book started as a little DIY homemade zine—to a decade later and almost a quarter of a million books sold ... it is beyond mind boggling.

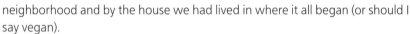

When I sat down to write this new introduction, I found myself at a loss for words. So much has happened to me in the years since *HIAV!* hit the bookshelves, and I couldn't figure out what to write about. With my deadline looming, Fergus (dog), Gerry (husband), and I went for a long walk so I could clear my head. As we walked around town, we found ourselves strolling through our old neighborhood and by the house we had lived in where it all began (or should I say vegan).

How It All Vegan! was lovingly kneaded, given time to rise, and baked to perfection in an old rickety pink-painted house on McClure Street in Victoria, BC. As we walked up the street toward the house, I saw that nothing much had changed. The house was still pink and just as rickety, but as we got closer I was stunned to find out that it was scheduled for demolition the next day. How fortuitous is it that we walked by? As we poked around the property and took some photos for posterity, I was flooded with so many remarkable memories that I couldn't wait to get home and write them down.

The house on McClure Street was one of those amazing vintage homes that gets passed around from friend to friend. The rent was insanely cheap—$325 for a one-bedroom/den with a claw-foot tub and all the charm you can muster in a turn-of-the-century house—but there was a reason for all the charm, and it came in the form of slumlord who didn't care about the property.

Living in a slumlord's house has pros and cons. The benefits are the cheap rent and being able to decorate and paint the walls any color you want. With rent that cheap, my husband and I learned to tolerate the family of raccoons in the attic, the broken windows, dripping taps, and the scary knob-and- tube wiring in the attic. Ahhh. Good times. Good times.

It was there that Tanya Barnard (my co-author) came to me with the idea of making a zine-style cookbook to give to our friends and families for Xmas presents. This was during the height of the '90s zine scene; my friends and I had been making zines for years, so neither Tanya nor I expected that our little homemade zine would turn into an international best-selling book.

I put the book together using a crude desktop publishing program that came with my computer, and then we photocopied all the pages at the local copy store and collated and bound the book in my living room. I think our first run of the zine was maybe 100 copies.

When we handed out the book as Xmas presents, the response from our friends and families was overwhelmingly positive. They loved the book so much that we decided to make another 900 copies to try and sell at punk rock shows and on the Internet. The second run of the *HIAV* zine sold out almost right away and became so popular with our peers that a light bulb went off, and I realized we were on to something. Tanya and I decided to try and go legit and find a publisher.

We started doing research on different Canadian publishers, and Arsenal Pulp Press was our first choice because they were local and seemed to have a similar sensibility to us. I wrote a cheeky book proposal (and included some Tofu Jerky, recipe page 172, for them to try), but to hedge our bets we sent our proposal to five other publishers, just in case. I remember placing our other book proposal envelopes in the mailbox and watching them fall out of sight, but we hung onto our Arsenal Pulp proposal for last because we wanted to give it a big kiss for luck before throwing it into the mailbox. Three days later, we got the call from Brian Lam of Arsenal Pulp asking if we'd like to have a book deal to publish *How It All Vegan!*

What?!!

I'll never forget talking with Brian and trying my best to sound normal and professional— all the while my knees were knocking uncontrollably as I tried not to pass out from excitement. I put down the phone and stared at Gerry in utter shock. Tanya and I had a book deal! I was going to be a published author! For real!

The original *HIAV!* zine was only fifty pages long, so Tanya and I furiously went to work inventing, testing, and adding more recipes as well as adding an introduction that included our story about how we vegan. We also included information for vegan newbies making the transition, and what we ended up with is the book you are holding in your hands.

My kitchen at the house on McClure was incredibly small, and there was almost no counter space, but I made the best of it and used my thrift-store kitchen table as a place to write, bake, chop, test, and re-test every single recipe for *HIAV!*. Gerry and I didn't have a lot of money back then, and I was working with the bare minimum of supplies: a few knives, a food processor (that was a wedding gift), and barely enough money to buy all the food to recipe test. Gerry worked two jobs (in a restaurant and as a tattoo artist) so I could focus on the book. It was a heavy burden to bear, but out of our financial limitations the mantra for the book was born: healthy, delicious recipes that were easy to make, with easy-to-find ingredients.

Our vision was for it to be not just a cookbook but more about how to live a fun and happy life as a vegan. We wanted readers to discover that being vegan was easy once you knew a few tips and tricks. We spent many months recipe testing, editing, and re-editing the book. We poured our hearts and souls into every page, and it was a lot more work than I expected, but once we sent the final draft off to the publishers ... I knew in my heart we had made something special.

I was at Tanya's house the day we got to see the book back from the printers. We eagerly ripped open the envelope, and I stared at the cover in disbelief. Holy shit. We were authors. I thought, "Wow. This is going to end up in a library somewhere." I was incredibly proud of the work we did.

Then I flipped to the back of the book and my heart sank. There was no index. "Where's the index?" I yelled at Tanya. We had both assumed that the publishers would put the index in. I called Brian in a panic, and he said "Does a cookbook need an index?"

Oh my lord.

So the first 2,000 copies of *HIAV!* hit the shelves without an index. For all of you who have that first edition, you can take it up with Brian. *laugh*

Word of mouth really helped boost the sales of *How It All Vegan!* The book did pretty well out of the gate. Arsenal Pulp Press did a great job of promoting it, and because I come from an '80s punk DIY work ethic, I got busy myself, promoting the book via the Internet. The 'net was a fairly new concept back then (can you even remember what life was like before the Internet?), and for the first time I was able to easily communicate with other vegans, not just in my local community but around the world.

The book was flying off the shelves, and I started getting phone calls from friends across the country who'd spotted *HIAV!* in the bookstore or at a friend's house. It was also exciting when we started getting fan mail from places all over Canada, the US, Australia, Germany ... I wrote back to each and every person who wrote to *GoVegan.net* (and I still do). Ten years later, it still blows my mind to think that someone as far away as Greece has my book in their kitchen. I've actually become very good friends with some of the people who wrote fan mail: Josh at *Herbivoreclothing.com*; Rudee at *SecretSocietyofVegans.co.uk;* Sara and Erica at *MooShoes.com*; and the Wimmers at *PlanetWimmer.com*.

I think without the Internet *HIAV!* would have been just another cookbook on the shelves, but people our age were logging onto the web and finding other like-minded people to talk to about animal rights, vegan products, politics, and everything in between. Word of mouth spreads fast on the Internet, and they found us at *GoVegan.net*.

I also think having our photos on the cover helped with sales. Our publisher, Brian, insisted that we be on the cover, and I fought him for a while because I didn't want to be like a cheesy, mainstream Martha Stewart (sorry Martha, I do love you). Thank Tofu he won that argument, because being on the cover was the best thing we could have done. I have countless fan mail from people telling me that they purchased the book without even looking inside because they saw us on the cover and were excited to see someone like themselves reflected back. I also have a few letters from mothers who ripped off the cover, or covered the book with paper so we wouldn't influence their kids with our tattoos and piercings. *laugh*

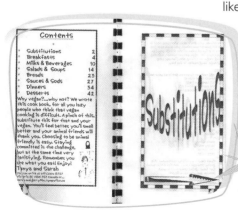

'Why vegan?'...why not? We wrote this cook book, for all you lazy people who think that vegan cooking is difficult. A pinch of this, substitute this for that and your vegan. You'll feel better you'll smell better and your animal friends will thank you. Choosing to be animal friendly is easy. Staying committed is the challenge, but at the same time very satisfying. Remember you are what you eat Enjoy!
Tanya and Sarah

We did every interview request. Every TV show. Every newspaper interview. Whatever came our way ... we did it. We worked hard to get the word out, and it showed in sales. I thought we'd be lucky if we sold a few thousand copies, but when the numbers came back at 30,000 books sold in our first few months of sales ... I was in shock.

What surprised me the most was our first royalty check. I really thought we had hit the big time. Best-selling book. Fame. Where's the fortune? I quickly learned that writing a cookbook is not a way to make quick money. The book sells. The money goes to the store. Who then pays the distributor. Who then pays the publisher, who then splits the royalty portion with each author. Eventually, I would get my check.

It was then that I realized this project was going to be more of a labor of love than a job. A job pays you a regular paycheck. You get medical and dental. You work 9–5. This new job of being a cookbook author was 24/7, and if I added up the hours I worked versus the cash I was bringing in—I was being paid pennies.

But it didn't matter to me because we were receiving so much encouraging fan mail from the readers; they were loving what we were doing, and it was hard to think about walking away to get a real job. I really felt that what we were doing was beneficial for the vegan community, and on a personal level I found the work utterly satisfying, creatively. I love how a little spark of an idea about flavors will turn into a recipe, and even though recipe testing can be frustrating and overwhelming (actually, all the dirty dishes are the worst part), the thrill I get when I finally get the combinations right is intoxicating.

Luckily, we were doing okay. Gerry had started tattooing full-time, and we were able to live off the money he made from that so I could continue with the books. Thank Tofu for Gerry and his support or none of this would have been possible. With a little extra cash in our pockets, we were anxious to get out of the McClure Street house, as it was starting to fall apart, and we were afraid for our safety. We heard later that two months after we moved out, the ceiling in the living room collapsed, so we'd been lucky to move out when we did. But even though that house was a creaky, drafty, mouse-infested dump, my life changed in a way I never expected while I lived there, so that old rickety pink house holds a special place in my heart, and I'm sad that it's now gone.

My hope for How It All Vegan! back in 1999 was to create a book that would make the transition to veganism an easier one for newbies. Ten years later, I hope that those of you then-newbie vegans who are now veterans still love and continue to use the book. For those of you who are picking this book up for the first time, I hope it makes your vegan transition easier and that your new healthy lifestyle makes a positive change in your life and the lives of those around you. Most importantly, I hope that you realize you can have a blast in the kitchen while making yummy healthy food to fuel your body.

As for me now? Writing these books is like baking a cake: I'm so very careful about measuring, mixing, and making sure the oven temperature is perfect, but once the book hits the shelves and I start hearing back from fans, well, that's pure icing. I love the writing. I love the editing. I love traveling to other cities to meet and greet fans of the book. I love visiting with readers at *GoVegan.net*. I love working with the team at Arsenal Pulp. I feel like the luckiest woman in the world to be able to have a career doing what I love. And as for Tanya, we wrote a second book together called *The Garden of Vegan*, and then Tanya decided to leave *GoVegan.net* to pursue a career in nursing.

So here I am in 2009: four cookbooks under my belt, a tattoo shop to run, a loving husband, a snuggly dog, friends and family that I cherish. In 1999, as I sat at my table in that tiny kitchen worrying about every tiny detail of the *HIAV!* manuscript, I don't think I ever could have imagined my life would be as wonderful as it has become.

As for this tenth anniversary edition, some of the information that was current in 1999 is now incorrect, so I've made a few minor tweaks throughout the book and added five new recipes. Thank you to everyone who has supported the books and *GoVegan.net* over the years. You are wicked awesome!

Now enough reminiscing. Start flipping the pages, find a recipe, and start cooking!

Enjoy!

xoxo, SARAH

ACKNOWLEDGMENTS

TANYA:

Firstly, I need to recognize the most important woman in my life, my stepmother Pat. Without her loving support through out my entire life I wouldn't be the person I am today. Her guidance, knowledge, and belief in my abilities has been a crucial inspiration. Thanks to the rest of my family, whose support does not go unnoticed: Kari and Trevor, my beloved siblings; Nana and Papa, for loving support; Bob, Jordan, and Stephanie, for being there. Also, a special thank you to all other family members, of whom there are too many to name.

Chris, whose love, patience and wit has helped me in innumerable ways, especially by providing me with renewed energy sources when I was exhausted beyond belief. I need to thank my patient housemates: Tracy, Dylan, and Pat. Thanks for letting me use your computer for endless hours, and keeping me sane. Appreciation to the Benny's crew: Lisa, Mo, and Ben. These three ladies, who I've shared laughter, knowledge, and inspiration with, have greatly enriched my life.

Thanks to the encouraging Dawn crew, especially Sarah T., Lance, and Noah. Your combined wisdom has provided me with essential motivation and insight. I'm grateful to my friend Jamie. His motivation, integrity, and brilliance leave me constantly in awe. Special thanks to my friend Toni, whose help and encouragement has had a significant impact on me and this project.

Special thanks to all whom are far in miles but not in thoughts. Kyla, Dave, JB, all kids from the Springfield era. The Vic West crew. Chris, Jen, and Kieran. Rob and Todd. Gerry. Sivan. Jana at Earth's Herbal. Again, a list that could go on for miles. All of these people have touched and enriched my life in unimaginable ways.

Recognition to the furry and feathered beings without voice: they provide me with inspiration and drive, especially my sweet, lovable cat, Chicken.

I want to acknowledge all the organizations and businesses who stand for social change. These groups are held together by people who selflessly strive for a more humane world. I thank them for being true to their beliefs.

Sarah, my beautiful friend and co-author, whose friendship means the world to me. Without her encouragement and support through all my endeavours, I don't know where I would be. I have the deepest admiration for her strength, wisdom, and brilliance.

Lastly, thanks to Blaine, Brian, Lisa, and everyone at Arsenal Pulp Press. Due to their vision and expertise, they have taken this dream of mine, and made it into a reality.

ACKNOWLEDGMENTS

SARAH:

There are so many people I need to thank, without them this book would not have been possible. At the risk of forgetting someone, I need to thank those closest to me by name for their support and guidance: Gerry, for his patience, wisdom, and love. My niece Heidi, for filling my heart with joy. My father Ken, for teaching me by example how to be creative, eccentric, and self-confident, and for giving me the space and guidance to discover who I was in my own time. To my mum Sue, for her love, for being the beginning of everything I am now and for leaving a little piece of her spirit in me before she died.

There are two women who have taught me about grace, beauty, and what it means to be a woman: my stepmum Denise and my Auntie Bonnie. I am so thankful to have them as female role models, and I especially need to thank Denise for sticking by me all these years, even when I was a horrible step daughter. Thanks to my brother Ben for his wisdom in the kitchen and his partner Sarah for her laughter. My cousins Stacy and Natasha, for loving and supporting me no matter what. My Zeyda, Art and his wife Lee, for always pushing me to be a better person. Black Bumps, Riley, Sir Douglas Fort, and Chelvin for teaching me about unconditional love. My Grandma Em for making me cardigans, my Aunt Jean, Uncle Geoff and their family for loving and supporting me from so far away. To Corri for her endless love and support. Thanks to Jen, Kieran and Chris, Maureen, JB, Chris, Jana and Korma, Trinity and Steph, and of course, the one and only Larry. Thanks to Pat, Richard, Matthew, Bertha, and Faye. Thanks to Timm, Greg, and Bubba for their integrity. Thank you to Mike and the Stark Raving Tattoo crew, the Capital City Scooter Club, and Earth's Herbal Products. To Cheryl, Leslie, Vanna, Rebecca, Meagan, Shana, Maury, and Graham. The Deverall, Miller, Howard, Ball, Sperling, Cuddington, and Smollett families. Thank you to the Vic West crew and the Springfield roommates who have all moved away, but are still close to my heart. Thanks to my Regina friends, who knew me at my worst and still like me. And of course to Blaine, Brian, and everyone at Arsenal Pulp for their encouragement and support.

I especially need to thank my co-author Tanya. Through good and bad and even worse, she has consistently been the one person I can count on no matter what happens. Her dedication, beauty and strength leave me breathless. Without her, I honestly don't know where I'd be. Her support, frequent pushing, and love make me a better person and for her I am ever so thankful.

A final thanks to everyone who has been so supportive of us and our endeavour. Without your help, suggestions, recipe ideas, excitement, and smiling faces this book would feel hollow. Thank you very much.

Now quit looking for your name and go make something yummy!

Introduction

HOW WE BOTH VEGAN

We vegan in the early 1990s, when we were both lazy vegetarians who occasionally used and consumed animal products. We decided to make the transition to veganism because of our belief in a simple, but important, value: we love and respect animals and the earth. Once we chose to give up eating all animal products, we discovered, with just a little imagination and some good advice, how easy it was to go vegan.

We all choose veganism for different reasons. Maybe it's a fervent belief in animal rights. Perhaps it's a desire to try a healthier diet. Whatever the reason, you can be vegan and still eat wonderful food. And as this book demonstrates, veganism is not something to be afraid of. There is a popular belief that by removing animal products from one's diet, food will become necessarily boring, a life of dining on grass and shrubs. But let us assure you: vegan food is fabulous food, full of flavour and all the nutrients you need.

In the winter of 1996 we came up with the idea of collecting our vegan recipes in a zine-style cookbook that we could share with our families and friends. We slaved over the computer, spending countless hours typing and organizing our recipes, putting great love and care into our project. We printed and bound the books ourselves and went about giving them away as gifts and selling them where we could for cost. This little book then began to snowball, selling like vegan hotcakes wherever we went. Then a light bulb went on: Let's go legit! So we shopped for a publisher and the rest is history.

All the old tried-and-true recipes from our first book are here, as well as a bunch of new ones, and some tips and tricks to living vegan. If you're a curious first-timer, we hope this book will ease your transition to the vegan way. And if you're a full-fledged vegan warrior, you'll probably be pleasantly surprised by some recipes you've never tried before.

Being vegan starts with an open mind. Once you've given these recipes a try, we hope you will adapt them to suit your own individual palate. Just add your own imagination and stir!

We've made these recipes relatively simple to prepare. There are just a few things that you should have that will make your life easier:

- A good kitchen environment. Cooking should be a pleasure!
- The correct ingredients. There's nothing worse than discovering you don't have everything you need in the middle of preparing a recipe.
- A food processor. Your food processor is your best friend. There are models for as little as $40, but you get what you pay for. If you don't have a food processor, a blender will do. But if you can afford one, it's a tool you will use forever.
- The proper equipment. Every kitchen should have:

    food processor or blender
    measuring cups and spoons
    mixing bowls (small, medium, and large)
    mixing spoons
    a good knife or two
    vegetable peeler
    stock pot, sauce pans, steamer
    cookie sheet, loaf pan, 9x13 baking pan, muffin tins, lasagna pan

cooling rack
grater
sifter
whisk
potato masher
colander
rolling pin
wax paper
timer
a good imagination!

Remember, your equipment doesn't have to be brand new or expensive; most of the utensils can be found second-hand – reduce, reuse, and recycle! Once you've assembled your ingredients and your utensils, try one recipe at a time – and don't forget to compost!

We'd love to hear from you. You can write to us c/o Arsenal Pulp Press, or check out our website: www.govegan.net

So make some tea, get out your apron, and let's get cooking. And always remember – you are what you eat!

— SARAH & TANYA

HOW SARAH VEGAN

I have an extraordinarily strong connection to the kitchen – the warmth, the smells, the sounds. No matter whose house I'm in, I always find myself gravitating to this room. I love looking in people's refrigerators, seeing what kind of spices they have, their canned goods, their cooking utensils. A kitchen is a perfect reflection of its owner. You know immediately if they enjoy food, or if they just eat to keep from being hungry. A well-stocked kitchen is a thing of beauty, so if you catch me looking in your cupboards, I'm not snooping . . . I'm just trying to get to know you better.

Why am I vegan? I get that question a lot. My journey into the world of veganism has been a life-long adventure. I was born and raised a vegetarian in Regina, Saskatchewan. My mother believed in the old adage, "You are what you eat," and she raised my little brother and me accordingly. Growing up vegetarian in a prairie town wasn't always easy. There was a tiny health food store called Ina's that was in the basement of a woman's house. I loved going there to visit; I was intrigued by all the different items and it always smelled so exotic. When my mum died, my father continued to raise us as vegetarians. I recently asked my dad why he didn't start serving us meat after she died, since he has always been a meat lover. He told me that as a little girl I was always sickened by the thought of eating meat. We ate dairy and eggs, but animal flesh didn't touch my lips until I was about thirteen years old.

My friends were always trying to get me to try meat. I think I was the only vegetarian in school and I didn't really have a clear reason as to why. It made me feel like a weirdo, an outcast, but the thought of eating meat made me feel sick to my stomach, which pretty much kept me from experimenting. One summer I was camping with my friend Shana and her family. We ended up getting lost on Jan Lake in the fog and had to spend the night on an island in a lean-to her brother Adam built. The next morning there was nothing to eat but a huge stick of pepperoni. Being super-hungry, I took the plunge. It was my first taste of meat. It wasn't so bad. I actually enjoyed how salty it was, and it didn't look anything like an animal, so I managed to get it down.

As a teenager I dabbled in meat occasionally. My stepmum made a mean almond chicken; when I ate it, I'd close my eyes and pretend that it wasn't meat. Or I'd cram down her burgers before my brain would tell my stomach I was eating dead flesh. But after a few bites, I would have to stop. I think I've always felt that eating animals is wrong.

I moved out of my parents' house at seventeen and was on my own for the first time. I couldn't afford anything but Japanese noodles and ketchup. Back then, my roommate Corri and I would spend all of our money on cigarettes, punk shows, beer, and rent. If there was anything left over, we'd buy some food. It seems insane to me now that food was so low on my list of priorities. For a long time, I had a very strange relationship with food. For example, I couldn't eat vegetables that had veins (such as tomatoes or lettuce) and I had no idea how to cook. I lived off noodles and packaged food for years. The crappy food was part of an even crappier lifestyle, and eventually my health deteriorated.

I moved from Regina to Victoria, B.C. in late 1988. I wanted a fresh start, to reinvent myself a little. I found two cookbooks at a garage sale that my mum used to use, *Laurel's Kitchen* and *Diet For a Small Planet.* Slowly I learned how to cook the foods my mum used to make me. I began to really enjoy spending time in the kitchen. I would bake bread every Sunday; while sitting in the quiet of my kitchen waiting for my bread to rise, I would write letters and hang out with my cats. The time I spent in that kitchen on Bay Street was amazing. It was a metamorphosis of sorts. I started buying more cookbooks, became interested in environmental issues, and started stepping away from conventional cleaners and products that were tested on animals.

I would still occasionally dabble in bacon and sandwich meat. Mostly because I'm a saltaholic, and the fact that these products didn't look like anything that used to be alive. It wasn't until I got my first pet that my ideals and beliefs started to really form. I never had a pet growing up (except for a couple of guppies that I accidentally killed and two gerbils who I'm convinced committed suicide). I received Chelvin the cat as a birthday present and soon his brother Black Bumps came to live with us as well. We moved to a new house and with the house came another cat, Riley. After Riley came Sir Douglas Fort. These cats – my experience with them – has changed my life forever. They aren't pets to me anymore; they are part of my family and have taught me more about animals and their rights to a happy life than any book, movie, or conversation ever has.

My appreciation of animals and their emotions has made me a better person. Some people may want to call it anthropomorphism; I call it a wake-up call. When Chelvin died, his brother B.B. was devastated. He would circle the spot where Chelvin's body had been, and would lay in my bed and cry; he wouldn't eat for over a week. It broke my heart. It was then that I realized that these fuzzy little creatures feel emotions like we do.

At the same time my health began to deteriorate. I was still a vegetarian and I believed strongly in animal rights, but was still wearing leather and eating dairy and eggs. I became so ill I couldn't work, could barely function, and was bedridden for over a month. Finally, after seeing more than ten doctors and enduring numerous horrible tests, I was finally diagnosed with chronic fatigue syndrome. I was so weak I could barely feed myself, and relied heavily on my friends for help. I started reading every book on CFS I could and decided that a vegan life-style would be the best for me. I got allergy tests, and cut out all sugars, caffeine, alcohol, and animal products.

I started paying attention to my body. Listening to what it needed. When I'm tired, I rest. When I'm hungry, I eat. My health is not yet up to 100 percent, but I'm getting close. When I think back to how sick I was eight years ago, and the strides I have made in my lifestyle, I am so thankful for all of the support from my friends and family. I think my illness is symptomatic of what happens to a lot of people: we spend too much time ignoring our bodies and pushing ourselves to do more than we are capable of. Our culture teaches us that it is okay to overload on chemicals and waste. We slowly poison ourselves, and eventually our bodies give up.

So . . . why vegan? Out of respect for my mum, my cats, and myself. To be healthy again, and to encourage my family, friends, and community to be healthy, too. I also feel that, for me, using and consuming animal products is wrong. This is my choice, my journey. I am choosing to be the best person I can be, and for me it starts with living vegan and being as environmentally responsible as I can.

There are so many events that have brought me to this point. One of them is my best friend Tanya. Through the nine-plus years that we've been friends, we've somehow seemed to be always on the same page. We've lost friends, and made new ones; we've lived together, lived in different cities, and lived through many demented experiences together. While there have been many changes in my life, the one constant has been Tanya. She took care of me when I was sick, held my hand when I've been scared, and stood side by side with me while we cooked. I couldn't ask for a better friend.

This book reveals just part of what I enjoy about living vegan. I hope that with this book, you will discover how to use your imagination when it comes to cooking and eating – to open your mind, to listen to your tastebuds, and to share what you learn with your loved ones. Food, friends, and family: there is nothing I like better!

—Sarah

HOW TANYA VEGAN

I grew up in a household where it was believed that "meat is the fuel that keep bodies healthy and strong." My father was an adamant meat-eater; he loved the stuff. Throughout my formative years, he would always say to me, "We have to eat at least two servings of meat daily." I never questioned this; I had no reason to because I didn't know any different.

Once when I was eleven, I remember going out for burgers with my family and being disgusted with the amount of vegetables piled on top of my all-beef patty. "If I wanted a salad, I would have ordered one," I said to my fellow diners. They all laughed. Meat – I used to love the stuff.

It wasn't until years later that I began to cultivate my own ideas and beliefs surrounding food. Leasa, my best friend in high school, introduced me to the idea of vegetarianism. She had come back from a family vacation to California, and while driving along the beautiful California coastline, they had passed by a slaughterhouse. The stench emanating from it disgusted her so much that she refrained from eating animals from that day forward. Her passion and convictions intrigued me, but while I was interested in her ideas, I still thought in order to be healthy, I had to eat meat at least twice daily.

Leasa and I moved into our first apartment together after finishing high school. Our interests at the time were in punk rock shows and booze, which is what we spent most of our money on. We bought food from our local 7-11, and ate out in restaurants a lot. We didn't care what we ate, just as long as it was cheap and plentiful. Meat started to become less and less important to me, and after a while, I gave up eating meat for good. That's when I started to call myself a vegetarian.

I maintained my vegetarian lifestyle for about five years until I decided that veganism was the path for me. This transition didn't take place overnight; it was definitely a slow process. I refrained from calling myself an outright vegan for a while, until I was sure I made the right decision. Turning vegan was a much harder transition than becoming vegetarian because there were so many unanswered questions. For example, if I didn't drink milk, where I would get my calcium? And what about iron and protein? Not only that, but I also had to convince my family and friends that my new lifestyle was a healthy one, and that I wouldn't suffer for my choices.

Luckily, I have Sarah. We were sharing a house with some other people during the period when we both decided, at around the same time, to take the plunge into veganism. We were able to adhere to one another's concerns about our lifestyle changes. This made my transition a lot smoother. Through her wisdom and strength, I was able to keep true to my beliefs no matter how hard it seemed.

Now, I believe my decision to go vegan is one of the best decisions I've ever made. I also believe that in order for this planet to survive, we need to take a good look at what we eat and how we act – not only what we put into our mouths, but also what we put on our bodies, what we clean our houses with, and how we live our lives. Most humans selfishly think that we are detached from the rest of the species on Earth. But in truth, we are all part of an integrated whole: humans, animals, plants, all things living. Our actions, no matter how small or large, can have a tremendous impact on the well-being of humans, animals, and eco-systems. It's your choice if you want your life to have a positive or negative effect on the world.

There was a time when we were able to harvest vegetables from our gardens, eat our own chickens' eggs, drink our own cows' milk, and from these sources nourish our bodies. It was also possible to sustain ourselves by saving and using the seeds that our gardens offered. The sacred act of eating – to maintain our bodies' physical, mental, and spiritual well-being – should be so simple. Instead it has evolved into an exploitative act where factory farming, genetic engineering, and the increasing use of pesticides are now the norm. It is a fact that one of the secrets to our health and happiness is right in front of us on a daily basis: food. It's the fuel that our bodies assimilate and turn into energy. If you are eating food that is unhealthy, you yourself will feel unhealthy. It's that simple.

It saddens me that we live in a culture that obsesses over fat. Food is reduced to how many calories and grams of fat it contains. Healthy lifestyles should begin by making conscious decisions about the food we eat and things we do to make it a better world. But don't let me tell you what to do. Get out and read books and magazines and websites to get the facts. Then cultivate your own ideas and philosophies of how to live life. For me, becoming a vegan was not only a decision to make me feel more healthy and alive, but also to save our planet and all who inhabit it.

—Tanya

VEGANISM 101

So you've finally decided to take the plunge to go vegan! At first it may seem overwhelming, maybe even frightening. We are here to make your transition a little easier.

A "true vegan" is someone who does not consume or use any animal products. True veganism can be impractical in today's world. Just remember, the goal of the vegan is to get as close to the ideal as possible. This doesn't mean you can cheat and have a fried egg sandwich or a sausage pizza whenever you feel the need to have a "vegan time-out." This means that you must strive each day to remain "true" to your beliefs. We're not here to judge one another, or monitor others' habits; we're just trying to be the best vegans we can be. As the saying goes, "One vegan day at a time."

We will start off with the most basic facet of veganism:

Food

Food is not just fuel for our bodies. Becoming vegan can open the door to a wonderful culinary journey. Being a lazy vegetarian is easy – just omit the meat, and you're there. Becoming vegan takes a bit more time and energy and a lot more imagination. The first step is always the hardest, but the results are worth it.

1. Dairy
Delete, omit, nix it from your diet. It is not necessary. After all, cow's milk is for baby cows! Experiment. Go to your local health food store and peruse the shelves. There are dozens of dairy substitutes available (soy, rice, barley, etc.). You could also try making some yourself (see the chapter on Milks and Beverages). In the beginning, try spending about a week or so completely dairy-free. Don't cheat by putting cream in your coffee or butter on your toast. After a few days you'll find your sense of taste begins to change. You can slowly introduce your body to one dairy substitute, and then, slowly, to others. By then your tastebuds won't be expecting something that tastes like milk. Alas, omitting dairy also includes removing cheese from your palate. Cheese is a hard one to leave behind, but your colon will thank you.

2. Eggs
Once you've deleted all dairy from your diet, it's time to eliminate the eggs. You probably never really liked the slimy things anyway. And what is that weird, cloudy, chewy stuff all about? There are many substitutions (see page 25), one of the best being tofu. Try it scrambled with veggies, spices, or anything else you can think of. (You'll find plenty of tofu ideas beginning on page 45.)

3. Meat
It goes without saying that you won't be eating anything that used to be an animal, and that includes fish! They have hearts, eyes, and a brain. They count, too!

Know What You're Eating

Food labelling can be tricky, and you should get into the habit of checking the ingredients of all prepared foods before you include them in your shopping basket. See page 208 for a list of ingredients that you should avoid if you want to stay strictly vegan. And remember, buying food can be fun. We're all trying to fit thirty hours into a twenty-four-hour day, and while shopping can be a challenge, it doesn't have to be a chore.

Go Organic

Organic. What does this word mean to you? Overpriced fruits and vegetables? Incredible tasting food? Not sure? Organic foods are rapidly making their way into the mainstream. These foods offer you the healthiest choice possible while at the same time protecting our environment and the health of our planet. The word "organic" is used to describe food whose growth has not been assisted by the use of chemicals. Most commercial crops are sprayed with a wide array of herbicides, pesticides, fungicides, and rodent killers, with over seventy of these being known carcinogens. After spraying, they remain on or in the food and can present long-term health risks.

Organic farmers work to produce crops without harming the consumer, farm workers, soil, water, wildlife, or the environment. Organic farming methods were the norm prior to the 1940s. Since then, with the arrival of chemical agriculture, there has been a dramatic increase in environmental damage, such as water contamination and topsoil erosion. There has also been an increase in illnesses and cancers in humans. Although organic foods cost a little more than conventional food, the taste alone should convince you to switch. You are worth it! What you consume is the fuel that runs your body. Eating hollow, tasteless foods that have been blanketed by chemicals and injected with dyes can do nothing but lessen the enjoyment and nutritional value of your food.

Organic farming is a growing but relatively small industry that cannot survive without our support. Its practices are often labour intensive and most of the farmers' crops don't even make it to neighbourhood organic markets due to the condition of the produce. Without the help of pesticides and herbicides, it is difficult to obtain what most North Americans consider to be "perfect" looking vegetables.

5 reasons to go organic:
1. Organic foods taste better, and may be more nutritious.
2. Organic foods are safer for consumers and farmers.
3. Organic farming protects the environment.
4. Purchasing organic food can help support local farmers.
5. Organic farming works with natural systems rather than seeking to dominate them.

Organic food offers you the healthiest choice possible and protects our environment and the health of our planet. Support local organic farmers and suppliers, or plant your own garden.

Eating Out

Eating out is always difficult for vegans. There is nothing worse than staring into the face of a server who has no clue what vegan means, and having to order just a salad when you had your heart set on a more substantial meal. Choose your resturants wisely. Phone ahead and ask if they can accommodate you. That way, you'll narrow down your options and you won't have to leave starving and grumpy. Carry a card with a list of the foods you won't eat. I find that a brief explanation to your server of what you can't eat helps them to understand your needs so they can point out what you can eat on the menu. Make sure to thank them for providing special service. A nice big tip is a good way to say thank you.

If we're traveling and don't know the town well, the first thing we do is look on *HappyCow.net* or *VegDining.com* to find out where we can eat. If we can't find a place online then we stick to ethnic foods. Asian, Middle Eastern, and Mexican foods can usually accommodate a hungry vegan. Having said all of this, most of the vegans we know prefer to eat at home. You know what you're eating and there is no chance of a mistake.

If Mum Gets Worried

If your family gets worried that you're not getting enough nutrients by becoming vegan, tell them not to sweat it. If you're eating a well-balanced, well-planned meal, you're probably getting all the things you need to stay healthy and happy. If you're concerned about your diet, please consult a registered nutritionist or registered dietician who is well versed in veganism. They can help to guide you in your food planning. But remember, finding a nutritionist, much like a doctor or any other service, is like finding a pair of shoes. You have to try a few on before you find the one you like.

Thanks to jae steele, *domesticaffair.blogspot.com*, for her sage advice in this section

Protein: It has been suggested that we need about 50 to 60 grams of protein a day depending on your activity level. To make a complete protein, combine beans with any grain (rice, quinoa, millet, etc). Combine any grain (rice, quinoa, millet, etc) with beans, nuts, or seeds. Also, soybean products are complete proteins. Consult a nutritionist if you have any concerns about your protein intake.

Calcium: Calcium is found in green, leafy vegetables. Other food sources include almonds, asparagus, blackstrap molasses, bok choy, brewer's yeast, broccoli, cabbage, carob, collards, dandelion greens, dulse, figs, kale, kelp, mustard greens, spinach, and watercress. Herbs and spices that contain calcium include alfalfa, burdock root, cayenne, chamomile, chickweed, chicory, dandelion, fennel seed, flaxseed, kelp, nettle, paprika, parsley, peppermint, plantain, and many more. Consult a nutritionist if you have any concerns about your calcium intake.

Iron: Iron is found in green leafy vegetables, whole grains, almonds, avocados, beets, blackstrap molasses, brewer's yeast, dates, dulse, kelp, kidney and lima beans, millet, peaches, pears, dried prunes, pumpkins, raisins, rice and wheat bran, sesame seeds, soybeans, and watercress. Herbs that contain iron include alfalfa, catnip, cayenne, chamomile, chickweed, dandelion, fennel seed, kelp, lemongrass, paprika, parsley, peppermint, plantain and many more. Consult a nutritionist if you have any concerns about your iron intake.

B12: A B12 supplement is often recommended, but you can find B12 in foods such as brewer's yeast, sea vegetables (dulse, kelp, and nori), as well as in enriched food products. Consult a nutritionist if you have any concerns about your B12 intake.

You Are What You Wear

Veganism encompasses so much more than food, and now that you have mastered the basics of eating, it is time to update your wardrobe. There are many stores and companies who sell vegan clothing. Support and reward local stores who carry vegan clothing.

Thinking about your clothing means every article: shoes, belts, jackets, sweaters. There is nothing worse than expressing your vegan beliefs to someone who then points out your dead cow shoes. Leather is everywhere: the label on your jeans, the collar on your jacket, the watchstrap on your wrist. And don't forget about wool and silk; they're animal products, too. If you choose to remove all animal products from your wardrobe, please donate them to a thrift store or shelter. Remember: reduce, reuse, and recycle. This is where personal choice comes into play.

The Vegan Police

Becoming vegan doesn't mean you are suddenly the vegan police, so don't judge others or try to catch them doing something un-vegan. Pay attention to your own life. What kind of vegan do you want to be? Will you subscribe only to the belief that our animal friends shouldn't be eaten? Will you remove all things from your life that contain animal products? Will you reduce, reuse, and recycle everything you can so that this planet is a clean, healthy place for animals and people? We both wear leather shoes. That's because we're not just pro-animal, we're also pro-Earth. It's our belief that nothing should be wasted. We will never buy new leather products again, but will continue to use the ones we bought before we went vegan. Sarah has had the same leather belt for over eight years, and it will probably last another eight. She wants to use up her possessions rather than litter the garbage dump with discarded leather so that she can buy an animal-friendly replacement. When the time comes for a new belt, she'll opt for the vegan one. That's our personal choice. Our decision to make. What's yours?

Home Is Where the Heart Is

Don't forget about your house. Look around. Is your furniture made from leather? Will you find wool blankets and feather pillows on the bed, animal-tested cleaners and chemicals under the sink? What about your toothpaste, your beauty products? How far are you willing to go? You can follow a few simple steps that just require a little time. Read your labels and support animal-friendly products, companies, and stores. Veganism is an easy choice; everything about it suggests a positive and productive lifestyle.

Educate Yourself

Read a book, talk to people, figure out what you belive. Your local library and the Internet both have a huge source of vegan information that you may or may not agree with. Read it all and decide for yourself.

Ideas to Bring Food, Family, Friends, and Fun Together!

- Host a vegan potluck in which everyone picks a recipe and brings it to the party. Make sure everyone doesn't pick salad!
- Host a vegan potluck birthday party: the best way to celebrate life!
- Make a dish for a friend: if a friend is laid up, just had a baby, or down in the dumps, make them something to eat! Share your favourite recipe and pass on your love and your love of food!
- Make vegan food for a charitable organization. Share the wealth!
- Visit your grandma or someone in a nursing home and bring some vegan cookies!

Enjoy Yourself

Life is a gift. Don't be so serious. Jump in a puddle. Host a potluck meal. Take your neighbour's dog for a walk. Pet a cat. Go to an animal rights meeting. Pick up some trash. Each day offers you a chance to be a better vegan, and a better person. Cherish yourself and the things around you. At first it may seem difficult, but once you take your first step, you'll be well on your way to becoming a vegan warrior.

Alternatives & Substitutions

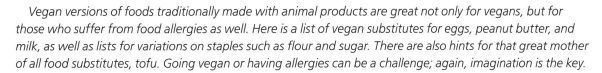

Vegan versions of foods traditionally made with animal products are great not only for vegans, but for those who suffer from food allergies as well. Here is a list of vegan substitutes for eggs, peanut butter, and milk, as well as lists for variations on staples such as flour and sugar. There are also hints for that great mother of all food substitutes, tofu. Going vegan or having allergies can be a challenge; again, imagination is the key.

EGGS

The following are some healthy alternatives to high-cholesterol eggs. Each of these substitutions has a distinct flavour and method of use. Experiment with them all when cooking and baking to see how they can be used.

- Flax Eggs (2 tbsp ground flax + 3 tbsp water = 1 egg) (pg.167)
  Flax is great for pancakes, breads, and other baking.

- Ener-G Egg Replacer (1½ tsp + 2 tbsp water = 1 egg)
  Most health food stores carry egg replacer.

- ½ banana, blended or mashed = 1 egg
  Bananas are great egg substitutes for desserts, or sweet items like pancakes or smoothies.

- ¼ cup tofu = 1 egg
  When using tofu as an egg substitute, ensure you're using soft tofu, and a food processor, so you don't get any grainy bits.

- 3 tbsp apple sauce = 1 egg
  Like bananas, apple sauce is great for sweeter recipes.

- 1 tbsp psyllium husks + 2 tbsp water = 1 egg
  The longer you let the psyllium husks sit in water, the more they become an eggy substance. Terrific in breads and baking.

MILK

Humans consume cow's milk as a beverage but it was designed for baby cows, not humans. There are so many milk substitutes out there on the market, and each brand has its own taste. Try them all and find the ones you like best, or better yet, try making your own.

- Soy milk (pg. 33)

- Rice milk (pg. 34)

- Oatmeal milk (pg. 34)

- Coconut milk (pg. 35)

BUTTER

Butter is made from churning whole milk or cream until the fats separate and form a solid mass. It has a high salt and saturated fat content and is thought to contribute to heart disease. These substitutions offered not only are nutritious, but taste great in baking, too.

- Vegan butter (pg. 89)

- Soy lecithin spread

- Store-bought margarine such as Earth Balance Natural Buttery Spread (which is 100 percent vegan) or other margarine, but make sure you check the ingredient lists of other brands, as they may contain animal products.

- Flax oil
  Don't use this for baking or cooking, but as a topping for potatoes, rice, popcorn, etc.

- Nut butter
  Can be made from almonds, cashews, or other nuts.

- Vegetable shortening
  Use for making pastry.

- Applesauce
  Use for baking only; can replace up to ¾ of butter in a recipe.

CHEESE

There are hundreds of varieties of cheeses offered throughout the world. Sadly, only a few varieties of "mock" cheeses made from rice or soy are available; sadder still, even fewer brands offer vegan versions. (Some brands contain casein, which is an animal by-product.) Check the ingredients before buying your mock cheese, which is available in most health food stores.

- Soy, rice cheese

- Soy, rice Parmesan cheese

- Faux Parmesan cheese (pg. 170)

PEANUT BUTTER

Peanut butter is the most familiar and common nut butter around. But many people are severely allergic to peanuts. It is possible to enjoy the same rich flavouring as peanuts by substituting any of the seed butters located in the list below. Different nuts and seed butters have different tastes, so experiment with them all and choose your favourite. Here are a few examples available in most health food stores.

- Tahini (sesame seed)

- Almond butter

- Cashew butter

- Sunflower seed butter

SUGAR

Here are a few examples of natural alternatives to those white and brown granules found in most homes. Generally found in most health food stores, these alternatives offer a more holistic and healthy approach to sweetening your foodstuffs. Remember that when using a liquid sweetener, you must cut back a little on the other liquid in the recipe.

- Maple syrup

- Cane sugar

- Date sugar

- Barley malt

- Fruit juice concentrate

FLOUR

Wheat is the most popular grain in the North American diet. It is used to make bread products, as a thickening agent – the list goes on and on. Your local health food store probably offers a number of grains that can be used in place of wheat, each one having a different flavour and density. Try them all. In addition to these different kinds of flour, you can make your own in a blender or a food processor. For example, you can make oat flour by blending rolled oat flakes until powdered.

- Spelt flour
  Tends to make your recipes heavier; you can slightly increase the baking powder so that it rises more. Good for bread and baking.

- Kamut flour
  Good for bread and other baking; best if used half and half with other flours.

- Barley flour
  Good for pancakes, cookies.

- Buckwheat flour
  Good for pancakes, but is a heavy flour so use half and half with other flours.

- Oat flour
  Good for breads, cookies.

- Brown rice flour

- Corn flour

- Millet flour
  A dry, coarse flour.

- Potato flour

- Soy flour
  Has a strong flavour.

- Chickpea flour
  Has a strong flavour.

OIL

Oil is an essential part of the daily diet, needed for a variety of purposes to keep the body healthy and strong. Generally, oils are used in baking, cooking, or as a topping on rice or salad. Try to use organic cold-pressed oil, which can be found in most health food stores.

- Olive Oil
  The best oil there is. Splurge a little, because it's worth it! We even use it in our baking, but it does have a distinct flavour, so you may want to use sunflower oil when you bake.

- Sunflower oil, safflower oil, canola oil, vegetable oil
  These are cheaper oils that can be used for basically anything.

- Sesame oil
  Has a strong taste; not good for frying. Excellent oil for salads and Asian recipes.

- Flax oil
  Don't cook with this oil! Use it for salads, or in place of butter on popcorn, potatoes, and rice.

SALT

Increasing levels of salt in the North American diet in the last few decades have led to wide concern. Salt finds its way into our lives by means of flavour enhancers and food preservatives. Instead of reaching for the salt shaker, replace it with these nutritious substitutions.

- Gomashio (pg. 170)
  A condiment made of roasted sesame seeds. Use on cooked vegetables, salads, soups.

- Braggs
  Liquid aminos! Braggs, an all-purpose seasoning brand, is formulated vegetable protein made from pure soybeans and purified water. Great on salads and dressings, soups, veggies, rice and beans, tofu, stir-fries, tempeh, casseroles, potatoes, vegan jerky, popcorn, gravies, and sauces.

T O F U

Tofu is a white, semi-solid product made from soy milk and a curdling agent. Tofu by itself is almost tasteless. It can be used as a filler or substitution or on its own. Think of tofu as a sponge: it will soak up whatever it's surrounded by. Tofu is high in protein and calcium, low in fat and sodium, and cholesterol-free.

There are many kinds of tofu. Which one to use depends on your recipe:

- **Firm:** Good for stir-fries, scrambled tofu, tofu jerky.
- **Medium:** Easily blended; good for stir-fries, scrambled tofu, tofu jerky, sauces, desserts.
- **Soft and silken:** Very easily blended; good for desserts, dips, sauces.
- **Tempeh:** Not a kind of tofu, but a somewhat meat-like substance made from cultured soybeans. It is used in dishes like chicken salad (pg. 71) or in barbecuing, and has a rather strong taste compared to tofu.
- **TVP or Textured Vegetable Protein:** A soy product that comes in granules or chunks. Rehydrate it in water (1 cup of TVP in $\frac{1}{8}$ cup water; add more water if necessary) and use in place of ground meat as in chili. It takes on the flavour (somewhat) of whatever you cook it with.
- **Miso:** Made from fermented soybeans, and usually is found in a paste form. It is used as a flavouring agent and for soup stocks and gravies. There are 3 basic varieties of miso: soybean, barley, and brown rice; each has a different and distinct flavour and colour. Look for this in Japanese food markets or health food stores. Hint: add only at the end of cooking; boiling it will ruin its properties.

BUYING TOFU

When you buy tofu, choose one that has the same consistency as the recipe requires or the ingredient you are replacing. Buying tofu is like buying wine: each brand has a different texture, a different taste. Shop around until you find the one you like.

DRAIN YOUR TOFU

Before using your tofu, place it in a colander over the sink. Let it sit for 5 to 10 minutes so excess water may drain out. You can help it along by giving it a loving squeeze! Note: use this method carefully when working with soft and silken tofu.

MEASURING YOUR TOFU

Here's a trick for measuring tofu in a measuring cup without making a mess. If the recipe calls for a cup of tofu, fill a 4-cup measuring cup with 2 cups of water. Add tofu until it reaches 3 cups. And there you have your 1 cup of tofu!

STORING TOFU

Store your tofu in an air-tight container. Fill the container with water until the tofu is covered. If you are using only part of a package of tofu, recover the remainder with fresh water daily. An open package of tofu will last 4-6 days if stored properly. If it starts to smell "beany" or the water becomes cloudy, then it's time to compost it.

FREEZING TOFU

Freezing tofu will give it a chewy, meaty texture. First, open the tofu package, drain well, and press out any excess water. Seal it in a plastic bag and freeze for at least 8 hours. To thaw quickly, pour hot water over the tofu, then press excess water out before using.

B E A N S

Although there are hundreds of varieties of beans available throughout the world – each one having a unique history and place or origin – only about 10 to 15 varieties are commonly used. Be imaginative and try out different kinds of beans; experiment with different tastes and textures. Beans contain virtually no cholesterol, little fat, and valuable vitamins and minerals. They provide necessary protein and are a great source of carbohydrates.

Dry beans should be pre-soaked in a bowl or jar of water in the refrigerator overnight before using; this shortens the cooking time and helps the body to digest them. Make sure to rinse the beans before and after soaking, and discard any flawed beans, such as those with a lighter colour, or any that contain insect punctures.

Here is a list of readily available beans, and their suggested cooking times:

· Adzuki beans: Combine 1 cup of pre-soaked beans with 4 cups of water, bring to a boil, then simmer on medium heat for 1-1 $\frac{1}{2}$ hours. Stir occasionally.

· Black beans: Combine 1 cup of pre-soaked beans with 4 cups of water, bring to a boil, then simmer on medium heat for 1$\frac{1}{2}$-2 hours. Stir occasionally.

· Chickpeas/Garbanzos: Combine 1 cup of pre-soaked beans with 4 cups of water, bring to boil, then simmer on medium heat for 1 $\frac{1}{2}$-2 hours. Stir occasionally.

· Kidney beans: Combine 1 cup of pre-soaked beans with 3 cups of water, bring to a boil, then simmer on medium heat for 1 $\frac{1}{4}$-1 $\frac{3}{4}$ hours. Stir occasionally.

· Pinto beans: Combine 1 cup of pre-soaked beans with 3 cups of water, bring to a boil, then simmer on medium heat for 1 $\frac{3}{4}$-2 hours. Stir occasionally.

· Navy beans: Combine 1 cup of pre-soaked beans with 2 cups of water, bring to a boil, then simmer on medium heat for 1 $\frac{1}{2}$-2 hours. Stir occasionally.

· Soy beans: Combine with 1 cup of pre-soaked beans with 4 cups of water, bring to a boil, then simmer on medium heat for 3 hours. Stir occasionally.

· Green and brown lentils: Combine 1 cup of dry beans with 3 cups of water, bring to a boil, then simmer on medium heat for 25-35 minutes. Stir occasionally.

· Mung beans: Combine 1 cup of dry beans with 3 cups of water, bring to a boil, then simmer on medium heat for 35-45 minutes. Stir occasionally.

· Split peas: Combine 1 cup of dry beans with 3 $\frac{1}{2}$ cups of water, bring to a boil, then simmer on medium heat for 35-45 minutes. Stir occasionally.

Vegan Milks
& Beverages

MILKS

Really now, what other mammal drinks another species' milk? Only humans carry out this activity. Cow's milk is for baby cows, not for us. Try "milks" made from beans, grains, and nuts. Most supermarkets now carry dairy alternatives. But here are some recipes to try at home.

FRESH MAPLE VANILLA SOY MILK

There is nothing more delicious than a fresh batch of homemade soy milk. The soybean has its origins in China. One of the world's most versatile beans, it is used to make countless items such as faux meats, tofu, tempeh, miso, and soy sauce. Soybeans contain all eight amino acids, and they are very high in vitamin B, protein, and calcium. Soybeans are also a fabulous source of lecithin, which is typically known as brain food. This recipe is a little time consuming...but soooo worth it!

> **1 ½ cups dried soybeans**
> **water**
> **1 tbsp vanilla extract**
> **3-6 tbsp maple syrup**

In a large bowl, cover the soybeans in 6 cups of water. Make sure they are submerged completely. Set aside and leave to soak overnight. When beans have finished soaking (about 8-10 hours), drain out excess water.

In a kettle or small pot, bring 3 cups of water to a boil.

In a blender or food processor, blend one-third of the beans with one cup of boiling water until puréed.

Pour into a large stock pot and set aside. Repeat twice with the remaining two-thirds of the beans and add to stock pot.

Add 7 cups of cold water to the bean purée and slowly bring the mixture to a boil on medium heat, stirring continuously. Once boiled, remove from heat immediately, cover with lid, and set aside to cool.

Once cool enough to handle safely, strain the mixture through a cheesecloth or a metal strainer into a pot. Discard the pulp. Add the vanilla and syrup to the milk and cook for 30 minutes on medium heat, stirring occasionally, in a double boiler. (If you don't have a double boiler, you can use two different-sized pots. Put the milk in the smaller pot and water in the larger one.) Transfer into a pitcher or container and refrigerate. Stays fresh for 5-7 days. Makes 6 cups.

EASY BREEZY RICE MILK

When I lived in Japan I would walk the countryside and was always amazed at the resourcefulness demonstrated by many of the people there. Vacant lots were continuously being transformed into flourishing rice fields. Rice is a staple food for one-half of the world's population. Use brown rice in this recipe if you can, as it contains the most amount of nutrients of all the different varieties of rice. (T)

> **2 cups cooked rice**
> **2 cups hot water**
> **maple syrup (to taste)**
> **vanilla extract (to taste)**

In a blender or food processor, blend all the ingredients until smooth. This will be quite thick and gets thicker as it sets. Thin the mixture with more water if necessary. Strain any lumps and chill. In addition to drinking it as is, it may be used in gravies, sauces, and soups in place of milk. Makes 2 cups.

AMAZING ALMOND MILK

Almond nuts are high in protein, calcium, and good fats, and they help to eliminate bad fats and cholesterol. When making this milk, try to use organic raw nuts, and you will have the most delicious and nutritious milk money can buy.

> **½ cup raw almonds**
> **2 cups water**
> **2 dates, pitted**

In a blender or food processor, blend raw almonds until they become an even meal. Add water and dates and blend again. Strain any lumps and chill. Good for cereal or porridge. Makes 2 cups

OUTRIGHT OATMEAL MILK

Whether in a nutritious breakfast porridge, a tasty flour, or a milk, the oat is a versatile grain. Use oatmeal milk in gravies, sauces, and soups as a healthy thickening agent instead of cornstarch and wheat. Oats contain gluten but are a great alternative to wheat.

> **1 banana**
> **1 cup cooked oatmeal**
> **2 cups water**
> **1 tsp vanilla extract (optional)**

In a blender or food processor, purée all the ingredients until smooth. Place in container with a tight lid and refrigerate. It will keep approximately 4-6 days. Makes 2 cups.

CREAMY COCONUT MILK

It has been suggested that coconut is a good source of saturated fat, something that is necessary and poses no threat in a vegan diet. Use this sweet-tasting milk to thicken soups and curries.

> **1 cup boiling water**
> **½ cup coconut, shredded**

In a blender or food processor, purée the water and coconut until well incorporated. Strain out coconut bits and chill. Makes 1 cup.

SMOOTHIES AND SHAKES

Smoothies and shakes can be made easily and quickly with a bit of imagination and a brave heart. They are great as healthy energy boosters first thing in the morning when you feel like something light, and also midday when you need that extra boost. Bananas are great for their detoxifying qualities. Tip: when your bananas start to go spotty and yucky, just peel them, cut them in half, and place them in a plastic bag with a good seal. Throw them in the freezer and when you need them for a smoothie, they will be waiting for you.

Here are a few smoothie combos to jump-start your imagination and get your mouth watering. The possibilities are endless.

"ANYTHING GOES" VERY BERRY SHAKE

Enjoy double-fruit flavour in this delicious shake. Spirulina is a microalgae high in protein, vitamin B12, and iron. You can get it in health food or vitamin stores.

> **2 cups soy milk**
> **1 ½ cups "Anything Goes" fresh** *or* **frozen berries (your choice)**
> **1 frozen banana**
> **1 tbsp spirulina**

In a blender or food processor, purée all the ingredients until smooth. Makes 2-4 servings.

BANANA DATE SHAKE

A sweet, smooth surprise.

> **1 ½ cups soy milk**
> **6 large dates, pitted**
> **2 frozen bananas**

In a blender or food processor, purée all the ingredients until thick and creamy. If you like a thinner shake, use ½-¾ cup more milk. Makes 2 servings.

HUKI-LA SMOOTHIE

"Oh, we're going, to a Huki-la!" For fun, serve in a coconut and garnish with pineapple and a paper umbrella. This recipe is also great frozen. Pour into popsicle moulds and eat on a hot summer day!

> **2-4 ice cubes**
> **1 cup soft** *or* **silken tofu**
> **4-6 strawberries**
> **1 cup guava** *or* **tropical fruit juice**
> **1 frozen banana**
> **½ cup pineapple** *or* **apple juice**
> **¼ cup pineapple (optional)**

In a blender or food processor, purée all the ingredients until creamy. Makes 2-4 servings.

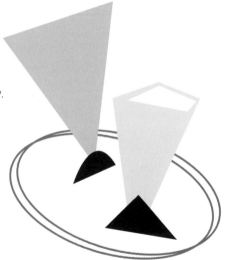

TANGY CITRUS SHAKE

A delightful tropical favourite.

> **1 frozen banana**
> **1 cup orange juice**
> **2 tbsp fresh lime juice**
> **½ cup soft** *or* **silken tofu**
> **1 tsp maple syrup**

In a blender or food processor, purée all the ingredients until smooth. Serve and garnish with a slice of lime. Makes 2 servings.

FRESH 'N' FRUITY ENERGY SMOOTHIE

You can get soy lecithin and spirulina in health food stores.

1 ½ cups apple juice
1 frozen banana
½ cup fresh *or* **frozen blueberries**
1 heaping tsp spirulina
1 heaping tsp soy lecithin

In a blender or food processor, purée all the ingredients until smooth and creamy. Makes 2-4 servings.

IN A HURRY ENERGY SHAKE

Gulp this down and get the hell outta the house.

1 cup apple juice
1 tsp spirulina

Pour ingredients in a large glass and stir. Makes 1 serving.

BAN-INI

Tahini not only enhances this creamy masterpiece with a unique flavour, but adds a nutritional element, too.

1 ½ cups soy milk
2 frozen bananas
3 tbsp tahini
2 tbsp sweetener
1 tsp vanilla extract

In a blender or food processor, purée all the ingredients until smooth and creamy. Makes 2 servings.

TEAS

For centuries teas have been used as a gentle cure for the body's ailments, all the while providing soothing and cozy moments in time. There are hundreds of medicinal herbs that can be used as a daily tonic or for simple pleasure: peppermint for digestion, ginger for fever and nausea, chamomile for relaxation. Many herbs can be grown right outside in your backyard; consult your local herbalist for ideas. The recipes included here are just some ideas of what you can enjoy.

CURE-ALL GINGER TEA

A healthy hot tea that doesn't make you drowsy. Drink when you feel under the weather.

3 cups water	⅛ tsp cayenne pepper
3 tbsp or more fresh ginger, peeled and grated	sweetener to taste

In a medium saucepan on high heat, bring the water to a boil. Add the ginger and cayenne and reduce heat. Simmer for 20 minutes and strain. Add sweetener to taste. Drink and be healthy. Makes 2-4 servings.

JANA'S EARTH'S HERBAL SUN TEA

This is a nice relaxing tea to drink at the end of the day. Also great for children before bedtime. You can get ingredients for the Sun and Moon Teas at health food or herb stores, or pick your own.

1 tsp each of fresh *or* **dried:**
lavender
peppermint
rose
lemon balm

2 cups water

In the morning, place herbs in a glass mason jar. Add water and cap tightly. Set out in the sun in a nice warm spot, and let steep for the entire day. Once the sun goes down, strain and serve. Makes 2 servings.

JANA'S EARTH'S HERBAL MOON TEA

A lovely longevity tonic.

1 tsp each of fresh *or* **dried:**
raspberry leaf
hawthorn berries
chickweed

calendula flowers

2 cups water

In the evening, place ingredients in a glass mason jar. Add water but do not cap. Set jar outside right under the moonlight all night long. Strain and drink first thing in the morning. Makes 2 servings.

SPICED CHAI TEA

A rich, warm tea spiced to perfection. You can find cardamom in South Asian markets. This recipe is also yummy served chilled.

6-8 cups water
1 tbsp dried cardamom
1 tbsp fresh ginger, chopped
¼ tsp whole cloves
1 tsp black peppercorns

1 cinnamon stick
4 tea bags (orange pekoe or peppermint)
sweetener (to taste)
soy milk (to taste)

In a medium saucepan on high heat, add water, cardamom, ginger, cloves, peppercorns, and cinnamon stick and bring to a boil. Immediately reduce heat and simmer for 5 minutes. Remove from heat and add tea bags. Cover pot and let steep for 5-10 minutes. Strain out into a teapot. Add sweetener and milk to taste. Makes 2-4 servings.

QUICK THAI TEA FOR TWO

A delicious and quick version of the popular tea enjoyed in Thailand.

2 cups water
½ tsp dried cardamom
2-4 tbsp sweetener
½ cup soy milk
2 tea bags (orange pekoe or peppermint)

In a small saucepan, add water, cardamom, sweetener, and milk and bring to a boil. Remove from heat and add tea bags. Let steep 3-10 minutes before serving. Makes 2 servings.

QUICK THAI ICED TEA

Sit back, and chill out!

6 cups water
1½ tsp dried cardamom
½-¾ cup sweetener

1½ cups soy milk
4-5 tea bags (orange pekoe or peppermint)
mint sprig (garnish)

In a medium saucepan, add water, cardamom, sweetener, and milk and bring to a boil. Remove from heat and add tea bags. Let steep 3-10 minutes. Remove tea bags and pour into pitcher and chill for 30-60 minutes. Pour tea over ice in large glasses and serve with a sprig of mint. Makes 2-4 servings.

SAVOURY MISO DRINK

This is a delicious and nutritious alternative to coffee or as a pick-me-up if you're feeling spent. Miso, which you can find in most grocery stores or in health food stores, is rich in both vitamin A and B12.

1 tbsp miso (light or dark)
1 mug boiling water

Mix ingredients in a mug until miso dissolves. Drink up! Makes 1 serving.

APPLE CIDER HEALTH DRINK

In 400 B.C. Hippocrates, the Father of Medicine, treated his patients with natural apple cider vinegar for its powerful cleansing, healing, and germ-fighting qualities.

½ fresh lemon, sliced
1 tbsp apple cider vinegar
1-2 tsp liquid sweetener
¼ tsp cayenne pepper
2 cups water

In a small saucepan, add all the ingredients and bring to a slow boil over medium heat. Simmer for 5 minutes. Strain and serve. Makes 1 serving.

EGGLESS EGGNOG

Are you a sad vegan warrior whenever the festive season comes around? Feel outta place with no eggnog in hand? Not a problem. Get out your blender and whip up the best eggless nog on the block. After a couple of spiked cups, no one will be able to tell the difference.

2 ½ cups silken tofu
2 cups soy milk
1 tbsp vanilla extract
½-¾ cup dry sweetener
2 tbsp maple syrup
¼ tsp turmeric
¼-½ tsp nutmeg
½-1 cup rum *or* **brandy (optional)**

In a blender or food processor, purée all the ingredients thoroughly until smooth and creamy. Serve well chilled. Makes 2-4 servings.

SODAS

Enjoy making these refreshing drinks as an alternative to store-bought soda. Surprisingly easy to make, they add just the right amount of sparkle to tickle your tastebuds.

FRESH FRUIT JUICE SPRITZER

Light and lively, you can enjoy this any time of the day.

> **½ cup fresh fruit juice of your choice**
> **½ cup club soda**
> **fruit garnish**

Stir the juice and soda together in a frosty glass. Serve with a fruit garnish. Makes 1 serving.

SPARKLING HOMEMADE GINGER ALE

Begin festivities with this perky ale.

> **3 cups club soda**
> **½ cup fresh ginger, grated (or 1 tsp powdered ginger)**
> **2-4 tbsp sweetener (to taste)**
> **cinnamon stick (optional)**

Mix all ingredients together in a mason jar. (In order to avoid having to strain the ginger ale later, you can place the grated ginger in a "tea ball.") Cap tightly and let it steep in the fridge for about half an hour or more. Strain out ginger and serve with a cinnamon stick if desired. Makes 2 servings.

JUICES

A vegetable or fruit juicer is a great kitchen investment. There is nothing finer than a glass of freshly squeezed juice. It's best to drink immediately after making, so you don't lose any vitamins or nutrients. Here are a few great recipes to get your juices running.

CARROT APPLE GINGER JUICE

Simply the world's greatest juice combination. It tastes great and is nutritious at the same time.

> **8 carrots, peeled and cut into large chunks**
> **4 apples, peeled, cored, and cut into chunks**
> **2-inch piece of fresh ginger**

Run all the ingredients through a juicer. Pour juice into a tall glass over ice and serve. Makes 2 servings.

PEAR APPLE GRAPE JUICE

This fresh triple-fruit juice combination will guarantee a spectacular juice experience.

> **4-6 pears, peeled and cored**
> **2-3 apples, peeled and cored**
> **½ cup grapes**

Run all the ingredients through a juicer. Pour juice into a tall glass over ice and serve. Makes 2 servings.

GERRY'S CHERRY JUICE

Oh my Gerry, he's as sweet as a cherry. (s)

> **1 cup cherries, pitted**
> **¼ fresh lime**
> **1-2 cups green grapes**

Run all the ingredients through a juicer. Pour juice into a tall glass over ice and serve. Makes 2 servings.

HOMEMADE VEGETABLE-8

Are you thinking you should have had something else? Maybe a healthy Vegetable-8 juice? This recipe is an impressive fusion of both fresh vegetables and seasonings.

4 medium carrots, peeled and cut into chunks
2 stalks celery, cut into chunks
3 small tomatoes, cut into chunks
1 cup fresh spinach
¼ cup fresh parsley
1-2 stalks green onion
½ small beet, cut into chunks
1 clove garlic
1 tbsp Braggs
pinch of dried oregano
tomato paste (optional)
Tabasco sauce (optional)

Run all the vegetables through a juicer. Stir in the Braggs and oregano, and a touch of tomato paste if not thick enough, and pour juice into a tall glass over ice and serve. Spike it with a little Tabasco for an added zip. Makes 2 servings.

Vegan Breakfasts

Breakfast! The most important meal of the day. As the recipes in this chapter demonstrate, there are a number of yummy vegan ways to start your morning.

VEGETABLE TOFU SCRAMBLER

Did you know that adding tofu to your diet will protect you against heart disease and some cancers? Tofu is high in protein and calcium, low in fat and sodium, and cholesterol-free. See pg. 30 for more information on tofu. This recipe is great with toast, baked beans (pg. 103), and hashbrowns (pg. 48).

> ½ **medium onion, chopped**
> **4-5 mushrooms, sliced**
> **splash of olive oil**
> **1 pkg firm tofu, crumbled**
> **1-2 tsp curry powder**
> **pepper (to taste)**
> **salsa (to taste)**
> **2 stalks green onions, chopped**

In a large saucepan, add the onions and mushrooms to a splash of oil and sauté on medium-high heat until the onions are translucent. Crumble tofu and add to saucepan. Add the curry and pepper. Sauté 10-12 minutes until moisture has evaporated. Add salsa and green onions and scramble on high heat for 2-4 minutes. Note: you could also add any other veggies you have kicking around. Makes 2 or more servings.

GREEK SCRAMBLED TOFU

A delicious Mediterranean variation on scrambled tofu. Serve with toast and hashbrowns.

> **1 pkg firm tofu, crumbled**
> **1-2 tbsp Braggs** *or* **soy sauce**
> **turmeric (to taste)**
> **pepper (to taste)**
> **dried oregano (to taste)**
> **splash of olive oil**
> **6-8 Greek olives, chopped**
> **handful of sun-dried tomatoes, chopped**
> ½ **cup spinach, chopped**

In a large saucepan, add the tofu, Braggs, turmeric, pepper, and oregano to a splash of oil and sauté on medium-high heat for 10-12 minutes until moisture has evaporated. Add the olives, sundried tomatoes, and spinach. Cover and cook for 2-4 minutes, until spinach is tender. Makes 2 or more servings.

SCRAMBLED EGGLESS EGGS

Light and satisfying.

½ **medium onion, chopped**
3 cloves garlic, minced
splash of olive oil
1 pkg medium tofu, crumbled
½ **tsp turmeric**
⅛ **tsp cumin**
2 tbsp Braggs
gomashio (garnish) (pg. 170)

In a large saucepan, add the onions and garlic to a splash of oil and sauté on medium-high heat until onions are translucent. Add tofu, turmeric, cumin, and Braggs and mix together. Sauté on high heat for 5-10 minutes until tofu is lightly seared on one side. Stir and simmer on medium heat for 5-10 minutes until moisture has evaporated. Garnish with gomashio. Makes 2 or more servings.

BARNARD'S BROWN RICE BREAKFAST

This is a great recipe if you have leftover rice. I love making this one for breakfast. It's fast, easy and oh so delicious. Ⓣ

1 cup cooked brown rice
½ **cup firm tofu**
splash of olive oil

4 tbsp soy mayonnaise (pg. 167)
4 slices bread
flax oil, Braggs, and ketchup (pg. 168) (garnish)

In a medium saucepan, add the rice and tofu to a splash of oil and sauté on medium-high heat until reasonably crisp. Toast bread and spread 1 tablespoon of the mayonnaise on each slice. Spoon the rice and tofu on top of toast and then garnish the way you like it. Eat and be happy. Makes 2 or more servings.

HEARTY 3-GRAIN PORRIDGE

A hot, hardy grain cereal perfect for cold winter mornings. Serve with soy milk, maple syrup, and sliced bananas.

3 cups water
½ **cup rolled oat flakes**
½ **cup barley**
½ **cup rice**

In a medium pot, bring water to a boil. Add all the other ingredients. Lower heat and simmer for 45 minutes to an hour, stirring occasionally. Makes 2 servings.

RACY RAISIN RICE PUDDING

This is a great breakfast recipe if you have leftover rice. Serve hot or cold with soy milk or cream.

2-3 cups soy milk
2 cups cooked rice
1½ tsp cinnamon
1 tbsp vanilla extract
1 cup raisins
½ cup slivered almonds
¼ cup sweetener

In a medium saucepan, add the milk, cooked rice, cinnamon, vanilla, raisins, almonds, and sweetener and bring to a boil. Reduce heat and simmer on low heat for 15-20 minutes until pudding thickens to desired consistency, stirring occasionally. Makes 2 or more servings.

CURRIED PAN-FRIED POTATOES

Don't have any o.j. to accompany your scrambled tofu? No problem: potatoes, eaten with the skins on, are a great source of Vitamin C. Pan-fried potatoes are a great side dish for any breakfast entrée. So eat your spuds! Serve with baked beans (pg. 103) and toast.

1 medium onion, chopped
5 cloves garlic, chopped
1-2 tsp mustard seeds
1-2 tsp curry paste
splash of olive oil
3-6 medium potatoes, chopped
salt and pepper (to taste)

In a large saucepan, add the onions, garlic, mustard seeds, and curry paste to a splash of olive oil and sauté on medium heat until mixed well and onions are translucent. Add the potatoes and fry, flipping occasionally, until potatoes are soft enough to pierce with a fork. Season with salt and pepper to taste. Makes 2 or more servings.

HEAVENLY HASHBROWNS

A delicious take on an old favourite. Pair with Vegetable Tofu Scrambler (pg. 45) and toast!

> **1 small onion, chopped**
> **splash of olive oil**
> **2 large potatoes, diced**
> **6-8 mushrooms, diced**
> **1 medium green pepper, diced**
> **1 tbsp dried dill**
> **pepper & cracked chilies (to taste)**

In a large saucepan, add the onions to splash of oil and sauté on medium high heat until translucent. Add the potatoes, mushrooms, green peppers, dill, pepper, and chilies. Turn down heat and cover until potatoes are soft enough to pierce with a fork. Makes 2 or more servings.

CLASSIC PANCAKES

The best way to make pancakes is with a hot non-stick pan, a plastic spatula, and a lid to cover them while they cook, which hastens the cooking process and ensures that the middle won't end up gooey! Heat your oven to about 200°F and place a heat-resistant plate inside. As you finish making your pancakes, transfer them to the oven so that they'll stay warm until you are ready to serve them.

> **2 cups flour**
> **1 tsp baking soda**
> **1 tsp baking powder**
> **2 cups soy milk**
> **2 tbsp oil**
> **sliced fruit (garnish)**

In a large bowl, sift the flour, baking soda, and baking powder together. Add the milk and oil and mix together carefully until "just mixed" (if you mix too vigorously, the pancakes won't get fluffy!). Portion out about ¾ to 1 cup of batter onto a hot non-stick pan or a lightly oiled frying pan and cover with a lid. Let sit on medium heat until the centre starts to bubble and becomes sturdy. Flip pancake over and cook other side until golden brown. Repeat process until all the batter is gone. Makes 2 or more servings. Garnish with fresh fruit and maple syrup.

BRAINLESS BANANA PANCAKES

So yummy and sweet...you don't even need syrup!

- **1 cup flour**
- **2 tsp baking powder**
- **1 banana, mashed**
- **1¼ cups soy milk**
- **1 tbsp sweetener**
- **sliced fresh fruit (garnish)**

In a large bowl, sift the flour and baking powder together. In a small bowl, mash the banana with a fork and add ¼ cup of the milk, mixing together until there are no lumps. Add the banana, sweetener, and remaining milk to the dry mix and stir together until "just mixed." Portion out about ¾ to 1 cup of batter onto a hot non-stick pan or a lightly oiled frying pan and cover with a lid. Let sit on medium heat until the centre starts to bubble and become sturdy. Flip pancake over and cook other side until golden brown. Repeat process until all the batter is gone. Makes 2 or more servings. Garnish with fresh fruit and maple syrup.

BASIC BUCKWHEAT PANCAKES

- **1 cup buckwheat flour**
- **1 cup all-purpose flour**
- **1 tbsp baking powder**
- **1 tsp cinnamon**
- **1 tsp vanilla extract**
- **egg replacer (to equal 2 eggs)**
- **½ cup apple sauce**
- **2-2½ cups water**

In a large bowl, stir together the flours, baking powder, and cinnamon until evenly blended. Add the vanilla, egg replacer, apple sauce, and water. Stir until "just mixed." Portion out about ¾ to 1 cup of batter onto a hot non-stick pan or a lightly oiled frying pan and cover with a lid. Let sit on medium heat until the centre starts to bubble and become sturdy. Flip pancake over and cook other side until golden brown. Repeat process until all the batter is gone. Makes 2 or more servings.

MONDAY MORNING OATMEAL PANCAKES

To make the oatmeal flour, blend 1¼ cup of rolled oat flakes in a blender or food processor.

> **1 cup oatmeal flour**
> **1¼ cup rolled oat flakes**
> **½ cup flour**
> **1 tsp baking soda**
> **1 tsp salt**
> **1½ cups sour soy milk (add 1 tsp vinegar to soy milk)**
> **egg replacer (to equal 2 eggs)**

In a large bowl, stir together the oatmeal flour, oat flakes, flour, baking soda, and salt until evenly blended. Add the sour milk and egg replacer and stir until "just mixed." Portion out about ¾-1 cup of batter onto a hot non-stick pan or a lightly oiled frying pan and cover with a lid. Let sit on medium heat until the centre starts to bubble and become sturdy. Flip pancake over and cook other side until golden brown. Repeat process until all the batter is gone. Top with maple syrup. Makes 2 or more servings.

APPLE-CINNAMON CORNMEAL PANCAKES

> **½ cup rolled oat flakes**
> **¾ cup cornmeal**
> **¾ cup flour**
> **2 tsp baking powder**
> **1 tsp cinnamon**
> **¼ cup apple sauce**
> **egg replacer (to equal 2 eggs)**
> **2 cups soy milk**

In a large bowl, stir together the oat flakes, cornmeal, flour, baking powder, and cinnamon until evenly blended. Add the apple sauce, egg replacer, milk, and stir until "just mixed." Portion out about ¾-1 cup of batter onto a hot non-stick pan or a lightly oiled frying pan and cover with a lid. Let sit on medium heat until the centre starts to bubble and become sturdy. Flip pancake over and cook other side until golden brown. Repeat process until all the batter is gone. Top with maple syrup. Makes 2 or more servings.

FABULOUS FRENCH TOAST I

What's so French about this toast, anyway? This and the following recipe are both delicious and very easy to prepare. For extra flavour, try using raisin bread (pg. 131).

1 ½ cups soy milk
2 tbsp flour
1 tbsp nutritional yeast
1 tsp sweetener
1 tsp cinnamon
8-10 bread slices, stale or lightly toasted
fruit (garnish)

In a large bowl, whisk together the milk, flour, yeast, sweetener, and cinnamon vigorously. Soak 1 slice of bread in batter until bread is gooey. Fry in a non-stick pan or a lightly oiled frying pan on medium heat until golden. Flip and fry other side. Repeat until batter is gone. Garnish with fruit and maple syrup. Makes 8-10 slices.

FABULOUS FRENCH TOAST II

This French toast is yeast-free for those with yeast allergies.

1 ½ cups soy milk
2 tbsp flour
1 tbsp psyllium husks
1 tsp sweetener
1 tsp cinnamon
8-10 bread slices, stale or lightly toasted
fruit (garnish)

In a large bowl, whisk together the milk, flour, psyllium husks, sweetener, and cinnamon vigorously. Let mixture sit for a spell so the psyllium has a chance to get eggy. Soak 1 slice of bread in batter until bread is gooey. Fry in a non-stick pan or a lightly oiled frying pan on medium heat until golden. Flip and fry other side. Repeat until batter is gone. Garnish with fruit and maple syrup. Makes 8-10 slices.

RISE 'N' SHINE GRANOLA

Enjoy this healthy, crunchy granola for breakfast, or any meal of the day. Once you try this recipe, you'll never go store-bought again.

3-4 cups rolled oat flakes
½ cup raw sunflower seeds
½ cup chopped almonds
¼ cup sesame seeds
¼ cup flax seeds
½ cup oil
1 tbsp carob powder or cocoa (optional)
1 tsp cinnamon
¼-½ cup dry sweetener (you decide how sweet)
½ tsp salt

*Set aside
½ cup shredded coconut
½ cup raisins
½ cup chopped dates
½ cup dried cranberries

Preheat oven to 350°F. In a large bowl, mix together the oat flakes, sunflower seeds, almonds, sesame seeds, and flax seeds. In a medium-sized bowl, whisk together the oil, carob powder, cinnamon, sweetener, and salt. Add this mixture to the large bowl and combine well. In a lasagna pan or on 2 flat cookie sheets, spread mixture evenly and bake for 15-20 minutes, until the top layer is browned (if you use cookie sheets, bake 12-15 minutes). Flip over with spatula and bake for another 8-10 minutes, then remove from oven. The mixture will be moist, but will dry and harden as it cools. Mix in dried fruit ingredients and let cool, stirring every 10 minutes to prevent clumping. Store in air-tight containers. Serve with fresh fruit and soy milk.

*You can throw anything you like into this: e.g., dried apricots, prunes, hemp seeds.

Heaven knows ... anything goes!

2 cups flour
½ tsp salt
3 tsp baking powder
½ cup sweetener
egg replacer (to equal 2 eggs)
¼ cup oil
¾ cup sour soy milk (add 1 tsp vinegar to soy milk)
1 ½ cups "Anything Goes" fresh *or* **frozen fruit (your choice)**

Preheat oven to 350°F. In a large bowl, stir together the flour, salt, and baking powder. Add the sweetener, egg replacer, oil, sour milk, and fruit. Stir together until "just mixed." Scoop into lightly oiled muffin tins and bake for 35-45 minutes (use a fork to see if done). Makes 6 muffins.

Here are some suggestions for fruit combinations for your muffins:

apple, raisin
banana, chocolate chip
raspberry, blackberry
strawberry, apricot
pear, apple
ginger, apple, apricot
See pgs. 135-137 for more muffin ideas.

LIGHT APPLE BRAN MUFFINS

A nutritious way to start your day.

- 1 ¼ cups flour
- ¾ cup bran
- 2 tsp baking powder
- ¼ cup sweetener
- 1 tbsp oil
- ⅔ cup soy milk
- 1½ cups apple sauce
- 1 tsp vanilla extract
- 1 banana

Preheat oven to 350°F. In a large bowl, stir together the flour, bran, and baking powder. In a blender or food processor, blend the sweetener, oil, milk, applesauce, vanilla, and banana. Add this to the flour mixture and stir together until "just mixed." Scoop into lightly oiled muffin tins and bake for 20-30 minutes (use a fork to see if done). Makes 6 muffins.

MAKE YA GO BRAN MUFFINS

This is the perfect way to get the necessary fiber the body needs.

- 3 cups bran
- 2 cups flour
- 1 tsp baking soda
- 1 tsp baking powder
- ½ cup sweetener
- 2 tbsp molasses
- ½ cup oil
- 1½-2 cups water
- 1 tsp vinegar
- ½ cup raisins *or* dates

Preheat oven to 350°F. In a large bowl, stir together the bran, flour, baking soda, and baking powder. Add the sweetener, molasses, oil, water, vinegar, and raisins. Stir together until "just mixed." Spoon into lightly oiled muffin tins and bake for 35-45 minutes (use a fork to see if done). Makes 6-8 muffins.

FAUX EGGS BENNY

A vegan take on an old favourite. This is sure to be a hit.

1 lb medium tofu
¼ cup apple cider vinegar
¼ cup olive oil
¼ tsp salt
4 English muffins *or* **8 slices of bread**
8 slices of veggie back bacon
8 slices of tomato

Sauce:
½ cup nutritional yeast
2 tbsp flour
½ tsp salt
1 cup water
1 tbsp oil
1 tsp Braggs *or* **soy sauce**
2 tsp Dijon mustard

Preheat the oven to 450°F. Drain tofu and cut into 8 slices. In a small bowl, whisk together the vinegar, oil, and salt. Arrange the tofu in a 6x9 baking dish and pour the oil and vinegar mixture over top. Marinate for 15-30 minutes. Make sure to turn the tofu over occasionally so each side gets marinated. Then bake for 20 minutes or until crispy brown.

While tofu is baking, prepare the sauce. In a small sauce pan, whisk the yeast, flour, and salt together. Add the water, oil, and Braggs and stir over medium heat until sauce starts to thicken. Stir in mustard and simmer on low heat until you are ready to serve. Toast the muffins or bread. On each slice of bread, place 1 piece of veggie bacon, 1 tofu piece, and 1 tomato slice, then cover with Benny sauce. Makes 4 servings.

Vegan Soups
& Stews

Soup is a universal meal, enhanced by regional and seasonal flavourings and diverse cooking methods. Here we offer some delicious soup variations. It is suggested that soups be made according to the season or the time of year; for example, hearty bean and grain soups and stews should be reserved for fall and winter, while lighter, vegetable broth-like soups are best made during spring and summer. Enjoy all of our scrumptious soups and feel nourished.

RUSTIC TOMATO LENTIL SOUP

This soup is quick and easy to prepare as lentils tend to cook more quickly than other beans. You can alter the look of this soup depending on your preference, since lentils come in a variety of colours – green, yellow, brown, or red. Cooked lentils are high in calcium, potassium, zinc, and iron.

as much garlic as you can stand, minced
1 medium onion, diced
3 medium carrots, diced
2 tbsp olive oil
2 stalks celery, chopped
6 cups vegetable stock (pg. 169)

1 28-oz can diced tomatoes, including juice *or*
5-8 diced fresh tomatoes + ¼ cup water
2 cups cooked *or* **canned lentils**
pepper (to taste)
cayenne pepper (to taste)
1 cup dry pasta (any short kind)

In a large soup pot, sauté garlic, onions, and carrots in oil on medium-high heat until the onions are translucent. Add the celery, stock, tomatoes, lentils, pepper, and cayenne and bring to a boil. Reduce heat to low and simmer for 20 minutes or until carrots are tender. Add pasta and simmer for 10 more minutes before serving. Makes 4-6 servings.

MIGHTY MISO SOUP

Miso is a fermented bean/grain paste that originated in Asia. There are 3 varieties of miso: soybean, barley, and brown rice; I like to use brown rice miso in this recipe because I find it has the best taste. Combining miso with shiitake mushrooms creates a balanced protein, which of course is a major concern among vegetarians and vegans alike. Shiitakes not only enhance the soup's flavor but also contain all 8 essential amino acids the body needs. A word of caution: NEVER boil or overcook your miso; this kills all of its nutrients. Always add your miso just before removing the soup from the heat. ⓣ

3 ½ cups water
½ cup medium *or* **firm tofu, cubed**
2 large shiitake mushrooms, chopped (or other mushrooms if not available)
3 tbsp dried seaweed, chopped (hijiki is best)
2-3 heaping tbsp miso paste (more or less to taste)
3 stalks green onions, chopped
3 tbsp spinach, chopped (or kale, bok choy, or Swiss chard)

In a medium pot, add the water, tofu, mushrooms and dried seaweed and bring to a boil on medium-high heat. Reduce heat and simmer for 5-8 minutes, until mushrooms are tender. Remove from heat, stir in the miso, onions, and spinach and let sit for another 30 seconds. Makes 4 servings.

SWEET POTATO, SQUASH, & APPLE SOUP

This soup is perfect for those fall days when the sun sets a little earlier than the day before. The squash and apple complement one another quite nicely in this soup. Sweet potatoes and yams are loaded with Vitamins A and C and potassium.

1 medium onion, chopped
1 tbsp olive oil
2 cups vegetable stock (pg. 169)
2 cups butternut squash, peeled & diced
2 cups sweet potatoes *or* **yams, peeled and diced**
2-3 medium apples, cored and diced
½ tsp salt
½ tsp pepper
½ tsp nutmeg
¼ tsp cayenne pepper

In a large soup pot, sauté the onions in oil on medium-high heat until translucent. Add the stock, squash, potatoes, apples, and salt, pepper, nutmeg, and cayenne and bring to a boil. Turn down heat and simmer for 30 minutes. Take 2 ladles' worth of vegetables and 1 ladle of stock and blend in blender or food processor until smooth. Return to soup pot and stir together before serving. Makes 4-6 servings.

GINGER PEANUT SOUP

Did you know that peanuts are not really nuts but are actually a type of bean? Peanuts are sprayed with an array of pesticides and herbicides, so try and use organic peanut butter in this recipe. It will taste better.

1½ cups broccoli, chopped
1½ cups cauliflower, chopped
1 medium onion, chopped
1 tbsp fresh ginger, grated
3 cloves garlic, chopped
¼ tsp Cayenne

½ tsp salt
½ tsp pepper
2 tbsp olive oil
3 cups vegetable stock *or* **water**
1 28-oz can diced tomatoes
5 tbsp of natural peanut butter (*or* **nut butter)**

In a large soup pot, sauté the broccoli, cauliflower, onions, ginger, garlic, cayenne, salt, and pepper in oil on medium heat until vegetables are tender. Add the stock, tomatoes, and nut butter. Reduce heat and simmer for 20 minutes, stirring occasionally. Makes 4-6 servings.

MULLIGATAWNY SOUP

A creamy Indian soup flavored with just the right amount of spices.

1 large onion, chopped	**2 large potatoes, cut in cubes**
3 stalks celery, chopped	**½ cup rice**
3 tbsp olive oil	**1 small red pepper, diced**
½ tsp cayenne pepper	**1 small green pepper, diced**
1 tsp turmeric	**1 small tomato, diced**
1 tsp coriander	**1 cup cauliflower, sliced**
1 tsp curry powder	**¾ cup grated coconut**
2 tbsp Braggs *or* **soy sauce**	**3 tsp lemon juice**
6 cups vegetable stock *or* **water**	**3 tsp cilantro (optional)**
2 medium carrots, sliced	

In a large soup pot, sauté the onions and celery in oil on medium heat until onions are translucent. Add the cayenne, turmeric, coriander, curry, Braggs, stock, carrots, potatoes, and rice. Bring to a boil and reduce heat. Let simmer for 15-20 minutes. Add the peppers, tomato, cauliflower, coconut, lemon juice, and cilantro. Stir together and simmer 5-10 more minutes until vegetables are tender. Remove half of soup and blend in blender or food processor. Return to soup pot and mix together. Makes 4-6 servings.

SPICY CREAMY TOMATO SOUP

Is the tomato a fruit or a vegetable? Most people would say a vegetable, but it's actually a fruit, given that it's a flowering plant containing seeds. Tomatoes are an excellent source of Vitamin C and A. This soup is just like Grandma used to make.

1 medium onion, minced	**1 tbsp sweetener**
6 cloves garlic, minced or crushed	**½ cup soft or silken tofu** *or* **soy milk**
½ tsp salt	**2 medium fresh tomatoes, diced (garnish)**
1 tsp dried dill	
1 tsp pepper *or* **cayenne**	
1 tbsp olive oil	
1 12-oz can crushed tomatoes *or*	
2-4 fresh tomatoes, diced + ¼ cup water	
2 cups vegetable stock *or* **water**	

In a large soup pot, sauté the onions, garlic , salt, dill, and pepper in oil on medium heat until onions are translucent. Add the tomatoes, stock, and sweetener. Cover and simmer over low heat for 20 minutes. In a blender or food processor, blend tofu and 1½ cups of broth until smooth. Add to soup pot and stir in freshly diced tomatoes. Makes 4-6 servings.

HEARTY WINTER POTATO SOUP

Potatoes are highly nutritious, an excellent source of Vitamins B and C as well as minerals like magnesium and iron. Potatoes are also known to be one of the best sources of complex carbohydrates, noted for having a calming effect on the body and mind. This soup is most excellent for that winter funk.

Tip on storing potatoes: cover them with a dark sheet or cloth and store them in a cool, dark, dry place. This prevents light from penetrating the potatoes and causing them to turn green and sprout.

1 medium onion, chopped	½ tsp coriander
3 cloves garlic, chopped	1 tsp cumin
4-6 mushrooms, chopped	1 tsp dried basil
2 tbsp olive oil	¼ tsp pepper
4-5 medium potatoes, cubed	2 tsp Braggs *or* soy sauce
3 cups vegetable stock *or* water	1 cups soy milk
1 red pepper, sliced	2 green onions, sliced (garnish)
pinch of red pepper flakes	croutons (garnish) (pg. 168)

In a large soup pot, sauté the onions, garlic, and mushrooms in oil on medium heat until onions become translucent. Add the potatoes, stock, red pepper, red pepper flakes, coriander, cumin, basil, pepper, and Braggs. Bring to a boil and reduce heat. Simmer on low heat for 10-20 minutes until potatoes are tender. Remove 2 ladles' worth of vegetables and blend in blender or food processor with milk until smooth. Add the mixture back to the soup and simmer for 5 more minutes. Do not boil or it will burn! Garnish with green onions and serve with croutons. Makes 4-6 servings.

AUNTIE BONNIE'S CURRIED APPLE SOUP

My Auntie Bonnie can make a wicked soup out of almost any ingredient. Ⓢ

1 large onion, chopped	2 cups "Anything Goes" vegetables, diced
1 apple, peeled and chopped	(e.g., zucchini, asparagus, broccoli)
2 tbsp olive oil	¼ cup rice
2 tsp curry powder	salt (to taste)
3-4 cups vegetable broth *or* water	pepper (to taste)

In a medium pot, sauté the onions and apple in oil on medium heat until onions become translucent. Sprinkle with curry powder; stir well. Pour in the vegetable stock and bring to a boil. Add the vegetables, rice, salt, and pepper; cover and simmer on low heat for about 30 minutes, until rice and vegetables are tender. In a blender or food processor, blend ½ or all of soup until smooth; return to pot and reheat. Makes 4-6 servings.

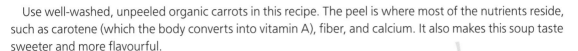

SIMPLY LOVELY CARROT SOUP ✗

Use well-washed, unpeeled organic carrots in this recipe. The peel is where most of the nutrients reside, such as carotene (which the body converts into vitamin A), fiber, and calcium. It also makes this soup taste sweeter and more flavourful.

- **1 small onion, chopped**
- **6-8 large carrots, chopped**
- **2 tbsp olive oil**
- **4 cups vegetable stock** *or* **water**
- **1 tsp salt**
- **1 cup** ~~**soy milk**~~ *oat milk*
- **1 tsp dried dill (***or* **1 tbsp fresh dill)**
- **1 tbsp** <u>Braggs</u> **or soy sauce**
- **½ tsp pepper**

In a large soup pot, sauté the onions and carrots in oil on medium heat until the onions become translucent. Add the stock and salt and simmer over medium heat for about 15 minutes, until carrots are tender. Remove half of the vegetables and blend in a blender or food processor with the milk, dill, Braggs, and pepper, and a small amount of cooking broth until smooth. Return mixture to the pot, mix well, and serve immediately. Makes 4-6 servings.

Alt: process everything for smooth soup!

TORTILLA CHIP SOUP

This soup is deceptively simple. But it's amazing with crumbled tortilla chips and avocado slices!

- **1 small onion, chopped**
- **3 cloves garlic, chopped**
- **2 tbsp olive oil**
- **3 cups vegetable stock** *or* **water**
- **1 28-oz can diced tomatoes** *or*
- **5-8 fresh tomatoes, diced + ¼ cup water**
- **2 tbsp tomato paste**
- **2 jalapeno peppers, seeded and minced**
- **2 tsp cumin**
- **2 tsp chili powder**
- **tortilla chips, crushed (garnish)**
- **avocado slices (garnish)**

In a large soup pot, sauté the onions and garlic in oil on medium heat until onions are translucent. Add the stock, tomatoes, paste, jalapenos, cumin, and chili powder. Simmer for 20-30 minutes. Garnish with crushed chips and avocado slices. Makes 4-6 servings.

Matzo balls can be made before-hand and refrigerated for use later. Just remember not to warm up the matzo balls in your broth; use a separate pot of warm water, and then add them to the soup bowl just before serving. You can use matzo balls in all sorts of different soups. This simple broth is my favourite. It reminds me of the soup my dad used to make me whenever I had a cold. This recipe has been adapted for all of us vegan Jews. (S)

Simple Broth:
2 medium carrots, chopped
splash of olive oil
4 cups vegetable stock
3 stalks green onions, chopped *
½ cup peas *

In a medium pot, sauté the carrots in a splash of oil for 5-8 minutes on medium heat until tender. Add the stock, onions, and peas and simmer for another 5 minutes. Portion out into bowls and then add your matzo balls. Makes 2 servings.

*You can add any other vegetables you like to this broth. When I make this when I'm ill, I like to keep it simple.

Matzo Balls:
½ cup matzo meal
2 tbsp potato starch
1 tsp salt
⅔ cup vegetable stock or water

In a medium bowl, stir together the matzo meal, starch and salt. Add the stock and stir together well. Cover bowl and place in refrigerator for 20-30 minutes. Once chilled, roll about 1 tablespoon of dough into a ball. Set aside and repeat until all the dough is gone. Bring a medium pot of salted water to a brisk boil. Reduce heat to medium-low, drop balls into water, and boil gently for 20 minutes, making sure they don't stick together. Keep an eye on them, because if the water boils too vigorously the balls will fall apart. A good indication that they are done is when they float to the top of the pot. Makes 10-12 balls.

Have broth ready in bowls. Remove matzo balls with a slotted spoon and place in broth.

BUTTERNUT TOMATO SOUP

Autumn captured in a soup. Butternut squash, a variety of winter squash, is spectacular in soups.

4-6 cloves garlic, minced
1 tbsp fresh ginger, grated
1 medium butternut squash, peeled & cubed
1 tbsp olive oil
1 cup vegetable stock or water
1 28-oz can of diced tomatoes *or*
5-8 fresh tomatoes, diced + ¼ cup water
salt (to taste)
pepper (to taste)

1 cup soy milk
croutons (garnish) (pg. 168)
2-3 stalks green onions, chopped
 (garnish)

In a large soup pot, sauté the garlic, ginger, and squash in oil on low-medium heat until the garlic is softened. Add the stock, tomatoes, and salt, and pepper. Simmer on medium heat, stirring frequently, for 15-20 minutes or until squash can be pierced easily with a fork. Blend half of the vegetables with the milk in a blender or food processor. Return to soup and simmer 5 minutes more. Garnish with croutons and green onions. Makes 4-6 servings.

GARDEN VEGETABLE BORSCHT

This bright, eye-catching soup is bursting with fresh vegetable goodness.

1 small red onion, chopped
4 cloves garlic, minced
2 large carrots, chopped
2-4 medium beets, chopped
2 tbsp olive oil
1 cup cabbage, chopped
1 cup spinach, chopped
1 28-oz can diced tomatoes *or*
5-8 fresh tomatoes, diced + ¼ cup water
2½ cups vegetable stock *or* **water**
¼ tsp pepper
¼ tsp prepared horseradish (optional)

In a large stock pot, sauté the onions, garlic, carrots, and beets in oil on medium heat until onions are translucent. Add the cabbage, spinach, tomatoes, stock, pepper, and horseradish. Simmer on medium heat for 20-30 minutes or until carrots and beets can be pierced easily with a fork. Serve with warm fresh biscuits (pg. 128) and tofu sour cream (pg. 168). Makes 4-6 servings.

CHIVE BUTTERNUT SOUP

A colourful and zesty soup. Chives add a subtle flavour that is sure to please.

1 small onion, chopped
1-2 stalks celery, chopped
1½ cups butternut squash, peeled & cubed
2 tbsp olive oil
2 cups stock *or* water
1 cup cooked *or* canned white kidney beans
1 tbsp pepper
½ tsp salt
¼ cup chives, minced

In a medium soup pot, sauté the onions, celery, and squash in oil on medium-high heat until onions are translucent. Add the stock, beans, pepper, and salt. Simmer on medium-low heat for 15 minutes, then remove from heat. Remove half of the vegetables and broth and blend in a blender or food processor until smooth. Return to pot and stir in chives. Makes 2 servings.

JANA'S SPRING GARDEN SOUP

Get outside, plant a garden, and enjoy the fruits of your labour.

8 cups water

2 cups each of as many of the following fresh greens:
nettles
collard greens, sliced into strips
kale, roughly chopped
mustard greens, roughly chopped
Swiss chard, roughly chopped

¼ cup dandelion greens, roughly chopped
2 medium carrots, chopped
3 stalks green onions, chopped
sprig of fresh fennel
2 cups medium tofu, cubed
1 tsp Braggs *or* soy sauce
¼ cup miso

In a large soup pot, bring the water to boil. Add the greens, dandelions, carrots, onions, and fennel and simmer for 20-30 minutes on medium heat. Stir in the tofu, Braggs, and miso and remove from heat. Let stand 10 minutes before serving. Makes 4-6 servings.

When winter has you sniffling and sneezing, strain the broth from this soup and drink as much as you can all day long. If you're not sick but just want a wonderful soup to get you through the winter blahs, Jana's hearty soup will do the trick.

½ **medium butternut squash, peeled & cubed**
4 medium carrots, sliced
½-1 cups burdock roots, sliced
½ dandelion root, chopped
2 tbsp olive oil
½ medium white onion, chopped
4 tbsp fresh ginger, grated
8 cloves fresh garlic, chopped
8 cups vegetable stock *or* **water**

1 tsp cayenne pepper
1 tsp curry powder
pinch of salt
2 tbsp fresh rosemary, chopped
3 lemon slices
4 whole leaves of collard greens, roughly chopped
¼ cup miso
¼ cup green onions, chopped (garnish)

In a large soup pot, sauté the squash, carrots, and burdock and dandelion roots in oil on medium-high heat for 5-10 minutes or until ingredients are tender. Add the onions, ginger, and garlic and cook 5 minutes more. Pour in the stock and add the cayenne, curry, salt, rosemary, lemon, and collard greens and simmer on medium-low heat for 40 minutes. Remove from heat, stir in miso, and let stand 5 minutes before serving. Garnish with green onions. Makes 4-6 servings.

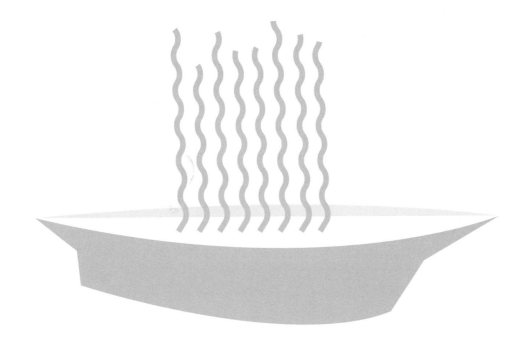

Barley is a rugged grain that has been used for food, barter, and beer for over 4,000 years. It is a nutritionally balanced food high in protein and carbohydrates. It also provides a great deal of bulk by absorbing 2-3 times its volume of the cooking liquid. Having a mild taste but a chewy texture, it is a pleasant addition to this stew.

1 medium carrot, chopped	**½ cup cooked** *or* **canned chickpeas**
½ medium onion, sliced	**(garbanzo beans)**
2 large cloves garlic, crushed	**1 tsp cumin**
½ medium green pepper, chopped	**splash of Tabasco sauce (to taste)**
½ medium red pepper, chopped	**salt (to taste)**
2 tbsp olive oil	**pepper (to taste)**
15-20 small mushrooms, chopped	**1 tbsp Braggs** *or* **soy sauce**
1 cup dry pearl barley	**3-4 cups vegetable stock**

In a large soup pot sauté the carrots, onions, garlic, and peppers in oil on medium heat until onions are translucent. Add the mushrooms and sauté until the mushrooms become tender. Add the barley, chickpeas, cumin, Tabasco, salt, pepper, Braggs, and stock and simmer for 20-30 minutes until barley is cooked.

Serve with warm biscuits (pg. 128). Makes 4-6 servings.

GARDEN MEDLEY VEGETABLE STEW

The most delicious stew ever. Too nutritious to mention all of its wholesome properties, you're just going to have to make this savory stew and find out for yourself. You could also throw in whatever vegetables you have in your fridge – the more, the merrier!

½ medium onion, chopped
3 cloves garlic, crushed
2 medium carrots, chopped
1 tbsp olive oil
½ butternut squash, peeled & cubed
1 medium potato, chopped
½ medium green pepper, cored & chopped

1 28-oz can crushed tomatoes and juice *or*
   5-8 fresh tomatoes, diced + ¼ cup water
1 tsp balsamic vinegar
2 cups vegetable stock *or* water
1 tsp turmeric
1 tsp cumin
1 tsp chili powder

In a large soup pot, sauté the onions, garlic, and carrots in oil on medium heat until onions are translucent. Add the squash, potato, pepper, tomatoes, vinegar, stock, and turmeric, cumin, and chili powder. Simmer for 30-45 minutes until vegetables are tender, and serve. Makes 4-6 servings.

AUNTIE BONNIE'S LIVELY LENTIL STEW

1 large onion, chopped
2 stalks celery, diced
2 medium carrots, chopped
1 tbsp olive oil
1 cup dry green lentils
3 cups vegetable stock *or* water
1 28-oz can diced tomatoes *or*
5-8 fresh tomatoes, diced + ¼ cup water
2 tbsp tomato paste
1 small potato, diced
½ tsp red pepper flakes
½ tsp salt
½ tsp pepper
½ cup spinach, chopped
3 tbsp fresh parsley, chopped

In a large soup pot, sauté the onions, celery, and carrots in oil on medium heat until onions are translucent. Add the lentils, stock, tomatoes, tomato paste, potatoes, red pepper flakes, salt, and pepper. Bring to a boil and simmer gently for 30-45 minutes, stirring frequently until lentils are tender. Stir in spinach and parsley and simmer for 5 minutes more. Makes 4-6 servings.

Vegan Salads & Dressings

Long gone are the days when salads consisted only of iceberg lettuce and tomato slices, slathered with bottled dressing. It's time to welcome a beautiful array of fresh, wholesome salads with tantalizing tastes into your diet. Salads offer the freshest, most wholesome food nutrients available. Raw salad is especially beneficial because our bodies digest nutrients and enzymes more readily than if the ingredients were cooked. These salads are highly nutritious and can be served to accompany meals or as meals on their own.

TANYA'S GARDEN MEDLEY

I just love making this huge salad and feasting on it for days. I combine every vegetable I can find in my refrigerator for this creation. Feel the goodness of all these vegetables racing through your veins, giving you the energy you need to live in this crazy world. Ⓣ

1 head red leaf lettuce, roughly chopped
1 bunch spinach, roughly chopped
1 cup red cabbage, shredded
1 small beet, grated
5-10 mushrooms, sliced
4-5 stalks green onions, sliced

3-4 medium carrots, sliced
1 medium cucumber, sliced
1 cup sunflower sprouts
1 cup broccoli sprouts
1 cup mixed bean sprouts
3 tbsp. gomashio (pg. 170)

Wash and prepare all vegetables. In a large bowl, toss together the lettuce and spinach. Add the other ingredients and toss. Store the uneaten portion in a covered bowl in the refrigerator. Keeps crisp for up to 3 or 4 days. Eat as is or add the dressing of your choice. Makes 4-6 servings.

JANA'S GARDEN KITCHEN SALAD

Our friend Jana from Earth's Herbal Products is an amazing woman. Not only does she have a vast knowledge of herbs and plants and their medicinal qualities, she's also a wiz in the kitchen.

5 whole leaves of Russian purple kale (sweet), roughly chopped
1 handful arugula leaves (including the flowers), roughly chopped
3 whole leaves of mustard greens, roughly chopped
½ head butternut lettuce, roughly chopped
¼ cup cilantro, chopped
¼ cup green onions, minced
2 sprigs of fresh fennel, minced
10 almonds

seasonal edible flowers (throw petals in whole) (optional):
5 rose petals
10 borage flowers (purple)

3 honeysuckle flowers
1 calendula flower

Wash and prepare all vegetables. In a large bowl toss together all the ingredients. Serve with Jana's Famous Herb Dressing (pg. 81). Makes 4-6 servings.

GOURMET GREEK SALAD

Here's a salad of mythological proportions. This combination of vegetables, faux feta, and saucy seasoning would bring a smile even to the face of Zeus.

> **6-8 Roma tomatoes, quartered**
> **1 small cucumber, sliced**
> **1 small red pepper, sliced**
> **1 small green pepper, sliced**
> **1 small yellow pepper, sliced**
> **1 small red onion, sliced**
> **Greek olives (optional)**
> **1 lb Faux Feta (pg. 171)**

Prepare the vegetables and place in a serving bowl. Add the Faux Feta and remaining feta marinade to the salad ingredients just before serving. Toss well. Makes 4-6 servings.

VEGETABLE PASTA SALAD

Simple, cool, and delicious, this salad is refreshing and lively. Perfect picnic food.

> **3-4 cups cooked pasta (e.g., penne, macaroni, fusilli)**
> **3 tbsp flax oil**
> **1 small zucchini, sliced**
> **4 tbsp lemon juice**
> **1 tbsp olive oil**
> **3 stalks green onion, chopped**
> **½ medium green pepper, chopped**
>
> **2 medium tomatoes, chopped**
> **¾ cup snow peas, chopped in half**
> **⅓ cup fresh parsley, chopped**
> **1 tbsp fresh basil**
> **½ tsp salt**
> **pepper (to taste)**
> **½ cup Faux Parmesan cheese (pg. 170)**

In a medium pot, cook noodles until al dente (tender but still firm to bite). Drain and rinse noodles under cold water until cool. Transfer to a large bowl, In a small bowl, whisk together the flax oil and lemon juice. Stir into the pasta and set aside.

In a large saucepan, sauté the zucchini in oil on medium-low heat for 3 minutes. Add the onions, peppers, tomatoes, snow peas, parsley, basil salt, and pepper. Sauté for 3-5 minutes. Add the vegetable mixture and the Parmesan to the pasta and toss well. Chill before serving. Makes 4-6 servings.

FAUX CHICKEN SALAD

The following three "mock" salad recipes are just as impressive alone as they are when served between bread as sandwich fillings.

> **1 cup tempeh, cubed ***
> **½ cup soy mayonnaise (pg. 167)**
> **1 stalk celery, finely chopped**
> **1 medium dill pickle, finely chopped**
> **½ medium onion, chopped**
> **2 tbsp fresh parsley, minced**
> **2 tsp prepared mustard**
> **2 tsp Braggs** *or* **soy sauce**
> **1 garlic clove, crushed and minced**

Steam the cubed tempeh for 15 minutes on medium-high heat. Remove from heat and set aside to cool. In a medium bowl, combine the mayonnaise, celery, pickles, onions, parsley, mustard, Braggs, and garlic with the tempeh and toss lightly. Serve over toast, as a side dish, as a sandwich filling, or alone. (For a variation, add 1-2 tsp. of curry powder to spice it up a bit!) Makes 2-4 servings.

*If you have trouble finding tempeh, you can use firm tofu, but it's not quite as effective.

FAUX TUNA SALAD

You can find kelp powder in health food stores. Serve this on toast or as a side dish.

> **1 lb firm tofu, frozen and then thawed**
> **1 stalk celery, diced**
> **¼ medium red onion, chopped**
> **1 small carrot, finely chopped**
> **½ cup soy mayonnaise (pg. 167)**
> **2 tbsp Braggs** *or* **soy sauce**
> **½ tbsp lemon juice** *or* **vinegar**
> **½ - ¾ tsp kelp powder**

Freezing tofu will give it a chewy, meaty texture. See pg. 30 for instructions. Once thawed, squeeze the excess moisture out and crumble it into small pieces. In a medium bowl, combine the tofu, celery, onion, and carrot. Stir in the mayonnaise, Braggs, lemon juice, and kelp and mix together well. Makes 2-4 servings.

FAUX EGG SALAD

1 lb medium tofu, mashed
½ cup soy mayonnaise (pg. 167)
4 tbsp chopped parsley
1-2 pickles, diced *or*
¼ cup relish
1½ tbsp prepared mustard
1-2 stalks green onion, chopped
2 stalks celery, diced
2 cloves garlic, minced
1½ tsp salt
¼ tsp turmeric

In a medium bowl, mash the tofu with your hands or fork and add the remaining ingredients. Mix together well and chill before serving. Makes 2-4 servings.

EXQUISITE RICE SALAD

A lovely, tangy salad that goes great with any meal.

1 tbsp olive oil	**1 cup long-grain brown rice**
2 tsp mustard seeds	**3 tbsp rice vinegar**
2 tsp cumin seeds	**2 tbsp dark sesame oil**
2-4 garlic cloves, minced	**2 tbsp Braggs** *or* **soy sauce**
1 tsp fresh ginger, grated	**¼ cup flax oil**
1 tsp turmeric	**1 medium carrot, finely chopped**
⅛ tsp cayenne pepper	**½ cup raisins**
2½ cups water	**4 stalks green onion, chopped**
1 cinnamon stick	**½ cup peas**

In a large pot, heat the oil over medium heat. Add the mustard seeds, cumin, garlic, ginger, turmeric, and cayenne. Stir until mustard seeds begin to pop (about 30 seconds), then add water and cinnamon. Cover and bring to a boil.

Add rice to the boiling pot and cover. Reduce heat to low and simmer about 35-40 minutes, until rice is done. Remove the pot from heat and let stand for 10 minutes. Remove the cinnamon stick.

In a small bowl, whisk together the vinegar, sesame oil, Braggs, and flax oil until combined. Pour onto the rice, add the carrots, raisins, onions, and peas. Stir until well mixed. Transfer to bowl and chill before serving.

Makes 4-6 servings.

COUSIN NATASHA'S RICE & BEAN SALAD

This is my cousin's potluck trademark. Our family loves to get together for potlucks; we eat and eat and eat until we bust. My favourite things are: food, family, friends, and fun. (S)

1 cup cooked rice
1 large red onion, diced
2 or more medium tomatoes, diced
1 medium red pepper, diced
½ medium green pepper, diced
1 cup corn
2 cups cooked *or* **canned black** *or* **kidney beans (** *or* **mixture of both)**
1 avocado, diced
6-10 sprigs cilantro, chopped
2 tbsp red wine vinegar
dash of cayenne pepper
juice of one lemon
dash of Tabasco (to taste)

Wash and prepare all the vegetables and place them and the other ingredients in a medium bowl. Stir together well and chill before serving. Makes 4-6 servings.

MUM'S APPLE COLESLAW SALAD

This recipe was adapted from an old recipe of my mum's. When I eat it, I feel like I'm eight years old. (S)

½ small white cabbage, shredded
2-3 apples, grated *or* **chopped**
½ cup raisins
½ cup soy mayonnaise (pg. 167)
1 tsp caraway
dash of lemon juice

Place the cabbage, apples, and raisins in a medium bowl. Add the mayonnaise, caraway, and lemon juice. Mix together well and chill before serving. Makes 4-6 servings.

SESAME NOODLE SALAD

The flavour of sesame oil is the subtle surprise in this tasty creation. An elegant, satisfying salad.

- **buckwheat noodles (to serve 4)**
- **2 tbsp sesame oil**
- **¼ cup Braggs**
- **¼ cup rice vinegar**
- **½ cup cucumber, seeded and shredded**
- **1 cup carrots, peeled and shredded**
- **6 large radishes, sliced**
- **3 stalks green onions, thinly sliced**
- **2-4 tablespoons gomashio (pg. 170) (garnish)**

In a medium pot, cook noodles until al dente (tender but still firm to bite), about 8 minutes. Drain and rinse noodles under cold water until cool. Transfer to a large bowl. In a small bowl, whisk together the sesame oil, Braggs, and vinegar. Toss with the noodles to coat. Add the cucumber, carrots, radishes, and onions, and toss. Garnish with gomashio.

TENACIOUS TABOULI

Bulgur is a dried form of cooked, cracked wheat. Nutritious and delicious, it gives this exquisite salad a chewy texture.

- **3 ½ cups boiling water**
- **2 cups uncooked bulgur** *or* **couscous**
- **3 stalks celery, chopped**
- **4-6 stalks green onions, chopped**
- **2 medium carrots, chopped**
- **3 large tomatoes, chopped**
- **¼ cup flax oil**
- **⅓ cup lemon juice**
- **1 cup fresh parsley, chopped**
- **1 tbsp fresh mint, chopped**
- **1 ½ tsp salt**
- **⅛ tsp cayenne pepper**

- **2-4 cloves garlic, minced**
- **¾ cup cooked** *or* **canned chickpeas (garbanzo beans)**

In a medium bowl, pour boiling water over the bulgur. Set aside and let sit for 30 minutes. Meanwhile, prepare vegetables and set aside. Drain off excess water from the bulgur and add the vegetables, oil, lemon juice, parsley, mint, salt, cayenne, garlic, and chickpeas. Toss together well and chill before serving.

AUNTIE BONNIE'S POTATO CUCUMBER SALAD

This tangy, tart salad will tickle your tastebuds.

2-3 cups new potatoes, cubed
1 tbsp fresh dill, chives *or* **parsley, chopped**
1 tbsp Dijon mustard
2 tbsp red wine vinegar
1 tbsp prepared horseradish
¼ cup flax oil
¼ tsp salt
¼ tsp pepper
2-3 cups cucumber, cubed

In a medium pot, boil the cubed potatoes in water until they can be pierced easily with a fork. In a small bowl, whisk together the chosen herb, mustard, vinegar, horseradish, oil, salt, and pepper. Set aside. Once the potatoes are done, drain and rinse under cold water until cool. In a medium bowl, mix together the potatoes, cucumbers, and dressing just before serving. Makes 4-6 servings.

S & M SPICY SALAD

My cousin Stacy and his partner Molly passed this recipe on to me. This salad rocks! (S)

1 lb firm tofu, cubed
2 medium carrots, chopped
6-8 green beans, cut into 2 inch slices
2 cups butternut squash, peeled and cubed
5-8 mushrooms, chopped
½-1 tsp red pepper flakes *or* **cayenne pepper**
2 tbsp olive oil
1 small red onion, chopped
1 small red pepper, chopped
1 small cucumber, chopped

1 cup spicy Japanese sprouts
1-2 tsp wasabi
¼ cup Faux Parmesan cheese (pg. 170)
3 tbsp rice vinegar

In a medium pot, sauté the tofu, carrots, green beans, squash, mushrooms, and red pepper flakes in oil on medium-high heat for about 8-12 minutes, until the squash can be pierced easily with a fork. Stir occasionally. Set aside.

In a medium bowl, place the onions, peppers, cucumbers, and sprouts. In a small bowl, whisk together the wasabi, Parmesan, and vinegar. Add the cooked ingredients to the fresh vegetables. Toss with the wasabi dressing right before serving. If you want to add some weight to this salad, serve over a bowl of rice.

Makes 4-6 servings.

PERFECT POTATO SALAD

Simple, cool, and delicious – perfect for picnics.

5 cups potatoes, cubed
1 tsp salt
1 tsp sweetener
1 tsp celery seed
2 tsp vinegar
3-5 stalks green onions, chopped

3 stalks celery, chopped
2 pickles, chopped (sweet pickles are great too)
1½ cups soy mayonnaise (pg. 167)
½-1 tsp Dijon mustard
½ cup medium tofu, crumbled

In a large pot, boil the cubed potatoes in water until they can be pierced easily with a fork. Drain and rinse under cold water until cool. Once potatoes are room temperature, place them in a large bowl, and add the rest of the ingredients. Mix well and chill before serving. Makes 4-6 servings.

AMAZING AMBROSIA SALAD

The food of the Gods: need we say more?

1 cup pineapple, chopped
1 cup apples, chopped
1 cup oranges, chopped
1 cup strawberries, sliced
1 cup grapes
½ cup coconut, shredded
1 tbsp cornstarch
6 tbsp lemon juice
3 tbsp dry sweetener
3 tbsp orange juice
½ cup soft tofu, puréed
2 tsp orange rind, grated
1 tsp poppy seeds (optional)

In a large bowl, toss the fruit and coconut until well mixed and refrigerate. In a medium saucepan combine the cornstarch with the lemon juice and stir until well blended. Place the saucepan over low heat and add the sweetener and orange juice. Cook for about 5 to 10 minutes, stirring constantly, until mixture thickens. Remove the saucepan from the heat and allow to cool thoroughly. In a blender or food processor, purée the tofu, then stir in the orange rind and poppy seeds. Add this to the juice mixture and chill for at least 1 hour. Pour the dressing over the fruit immediately before serving. Makes 4-6 servings.

DRESSINGS

Delicious and nutritious dressings depend on the use of the finest ingredients possible. Try to use only cold pressed oil in these recipes, as they contain essential fatty acids needed by the body. Vary your oils by using olive, flax, hemp, canola, sunflower, or sesame; in this way it's possible to get a healthy balance of Omega-3 and Omega-6 in the diet. Some of these dressings have a distinct flavour, so experiment and see which ones you prefer.

PRETTY 'N' PINK CHIVE VINEGAR

My Auntie Bonnie gave me this great idea for a vinegar. When your chives are in full bloom, remove the purple flower tops and cram as many as you can into a clean, dry jar. Pour in white wine vinegar and fill to the top. Cap tightly and let sit in a cool dark spot for 3-5 days. Strain out the flower tops and store the remaining vinegar in a clean, sealable container. Use this lovely, scented, pink vinegar for your salads. Ⓢ

ROASTED GARLIC DRESSING

The perfect topping for enhancing any salad. Also great for dipping veggies!

> **10-12 cloves garlic**
> **1 cup flax oil** *or* **olive oil**
> **½ cup balsamic vinegar**
> **½ cup water**
> **1 tsp salt**
> **½ tbsp pepper**
> **1 tbsp Dijon mustard**

Separate (but don't peel) the cloves of garlic and roast in an un-oiled pan for 10-15 minutes at 350°F, turning occasionally. Set aside and peel garlic when cool. In a blender or food processor, blend together the garlic, oil, vinegar, water, salt, pepper, and mustard until smooth.

BALSAMIC MAPLE DRESSING

Sweet but tart, this dressing is easy to make.

> **½ cup Balsamic vinegar**
> **⅛ cup maple syrup**

In a small bowl, whisk together the vinegar and syrup. Yum!

GREEN GODDESS DRESSING

A colourful dressing with a superb flavour. This is excellent as a dip or dressing.

½ lb soft *or* medium tofu
¼ cup flax oil *or* olive oil
½ tbsp chives
¼ cup fresh parsley
2 tbsp vinegar
½ small onion
1-3 cloves garlic
⅛ tsp pepper
½ tsp salt

In a blender or food processor, blend together all the ingredients until smooth and creamy.

CREAMY ITALIAN DRESSING

A cool, zesty version of this ever so popular dressing.

½ lb soft *or* medium tofu
½ cup flax oil *or* olive oil
3 tbsp vinegar
1 tsp salt
⅛ tsp pepper

4 cloves garlic, minced
2 tbsp sweet pickle relish (or 1 large pickle)
¼ tsp dried oregano
⅛ tsp red pepper flakes

In a blender or food processor, blend together the tofu, oil, vinegar, salt, and pepper until smooth and creamy. Fold in the garlic, relish, oregano, and red pepper flakes. Excellent as a chip dip in addition to a salad dressing.

FABULOUS FRENCH DRESSING

A tangy dressing with superb flavour.

1 garlic clove, minced
½ tsp salt
¼ tsp dry mustard
¼ tsp paprika

¼ tsp pepper
¼ cup flax oil *or* olive oil
2 tbsp vinegar

In a small bowl, whisk together all the ingredients. Serve over a nice green salad.

THOUSAND ISLAND DRESSING

A creamy classic.

½ lb soft *or* medium tofu
½ cup ketchup (pg. 168)
2 tbsp flax oil *or* olive oil
½ small onion, minced
1-2 cloves garlic, crushed
¼ tsp salt
3 tsp sweet pickle relish
3 tsp green olives, minced
6-8 sprigs parsley, chopped

In a blender or food processor, blend together the tofu, ketchup, oil, onions, garlic, and salt until smooth and creamy. Fold in the relish, olives, and parsley.

SWEET GINGER DRESSING

This sophisticated dressing lends its flavour to any vegetable it tops.

½ cup soft *or* medium tofu
2 tbsp gomashio (pg. 170)
2 tbsp sesame oil
¼ cup flax oil *or* olive oil
½ cup rice vinegar
2 tbsp maple syrup
1 tbsp brown rice miso
1 clove garlic
1½ tbsp fresh ginger, grated
½ tsp pepper

In a blender or food processor, blend together all the ingredients until smooth and creamy.

CAESAR SALAD DRESSING

Unique in flavour, this recipe is best when tossed with romaine lettuce and croutons (pg. 168).

- ⅓ cup soft *or* medium tofu
- 1½ tsp Dijon mustard
- ½ tsp kelp powder
- 2 tbsp Faux Parmesan cheese (pg. 170)
- ⅛ tsp sweetener
- 2 tbsp lemon juice *or* vinegar
- 1 clove garlic, minced
- 1 tbsp flax oil *or* olive oil
- ¼ tsp salt
- ¼ tsp pepper

In a blender or food processor, blend together all the ingredients until smooth and creamy.

SARAH'S QUICK & EASY SESAME DRESSING

Quick, hurry, let's eat! You can use this over a salad or in a noodle toss.

- 2 tbsp sesame oil
- ¼ cup Braggs
- ¼ cup rice vinegar

Whisk together all the ingredients.

JANA'S FAMOUS HERB DRESSING

Toss this dressing over Jana's Garden Kitchen Salad (pg. 69) and thank your lucky stars we introduced you to her! You could also use it as a topping for rice.

¼ cup flax oil
4 tbsp nutritional yeast flakes
¼ cup apple cider vinegar
2 tsp pepper
2 tbsp maple syrup
2 cloves garlic, chopped
2 tbsp fresh thyme, chopped
1 tbsp fresh rosemary, chopped
1 tsp fresh oregano, diced
1 tbsp of sesame seeds *or* **gomashio (pg. 170)**

In a small bowl, whisk together all the ingredients. Stir well before serving.

NICE 'N' SPICY AVOCADO DRESSING

This creamy dressing goes great over a fresh green salad or can be used as a veggie dip.

1 avocado
1 tbsp lemon juice *or* **vinegar**
½ cup mock sour cream (pg. 168)
⅓ cup flax oil *or* **olive oil**
1 clove garlic, minced
½ tsp chili powder
¼ tsp salt
¼ tsp Tabasco *or* **other hot sauce**

In a blender or food processor, blend together all the ingredients until smooth and creamy.

Vegan Sauces
& Spreads

SAUCES

Sauces can complement a variety of dishes and grains by adding savory flavours and zest while at the same time providing the body with necessary vitamins and minerals. With these recipes, you can be sure that they will not only add a nutritional note, but will please your palate, too.

MIGHTY MISO GRAVY

This recipe is an addictive topping that partners well with biscuits (pg. 128) or pan-fried potatoes (pg. 47). Use your imagination and discover a dish of your own to use with this delectable sauce.

6-10 mushrooms, chopped
1 medium onion, chopped
1 tbsp olive oil
2-3 tbsp Braggs *or* **soy sauce**
cayenne pepper (to taste)
dried basil (to taste)
dried dill (to taste)
pepper (to taste)

⅓-½ cup flour
1⅓ cups vegetable stock *or* **water**
1 tsp miso

In a medium saucepan, sauté the mushrooms and onions in oil on medium-high heat until onions are translucent and mushrooms are tender. Add the Braggs, cayenne, basil, dill, and pepper and stir together. Remove from heat and slowly stir in the flour, mixing together well. It will become pasty and dry. Slowly start adding the stock a little at a time until everything becomes well mixed and there are no lumps. Place back onto medium heat and simmer until sauce is thickened, stirring often. At the last minute, stir in miso and serve.

Makes 4-6 servings.

EAZY BREEZY CHEEZY SAUCE

A delicious, versatile, and cheesy sauce to serve over burritos, pasta, burgers, or veggies – anything you can think of, really!

½ cup nutritional yeast
3 tbsp flour
4 tsp arrowroot powder *or* **corn starch**
½ tsp salt

1 cup water
1 tbsp olive oil
2 tsp Dijon mustard

In a small saucepan, whisk together the yeast, flour, arrowroot powder, and salt. Add the water and oil and continue to whisk thoroughly. Stir over medium heat until sauce becomes thick, then stir in the mustard. Heat for 30 seconds more and serve. Makes 2-4 servings.

PERFECT PESTO

These next two pesto recipes are delicious favourites that will linger in the hearts and minds of those who try them. Whip up these fabulous sauces and team them with pasta, rice, or veggies.

2 cups fresh basil, chopped
1 cup fresh parsley, chopped
2 tbsp soy Parmesan cheese
3 cloves garlic, minced
2 tbsp pine nuts, toasted
3 tsp miso
¼ - ⅓ cup water

In a blender or food processor, blend together the basil, parsley, parmesan, garlic, nuts, and miso until well minced. With the machine running, slowly add water until you've reach the desired consistency. Heat and serve over pasta or rice, or use in place of tomato sauce on pizza. Makes 2-4 servings.

ZESTY TOMATO PESTO

4 medium tomatoes, chopped
1 bunch spinach, chopped
½ cup green onions, chopped
½ cup olive oil
4 cloves garlic, minced
4-5 tsp fresh basil, chopped
salt (to taste)

In a blender or food processor, blend together the tomatoes, spinach, onions, oil, garlic, and basil until you've reached the desired consistency. Add salt to taste. Heat and serve over pasta or rice, or use in place of tomato sauce on pizza. Makes 2-4 servings.

TRADITIONAL TOMATO SAUCE

Here's a dilly of a sauce that will make Mama weep because she knows it's better than hers.

4 cloves garlic, minced	**¼ tsp pepper**
1 small onion, chopped	**1 tsp salt**
1 small carrot, chopped	**2 tbsp olive oil**
½ cup mixed green & red pepper, chopped	**1 tsp sweetener**
8-10 mushrooms, sliced	**15½-oz can tomato paste**
1 tsp dried oregano	**5-8 fresh tomatoes, diced**
¼ tsp dried basil	**1 28-oz can crushed tomatoes**
¼ tsp dried thyme	

In a large pot, sauté the garlic, onions, carrots, peppers, mushrooms, oregano, basil, thyme, pepper, and salt in oil on medium heat until onions are translucent. Add sweetener, tomato paste and tomatoes. Cover with lid and simmer on medium-low heat for 15-30 minutes, stirring occasionally. Serve with pasta or use for lasagna (pg. 113). This sauce freezes well. Note: this sauce is thick; if you like a thinner sauce, add a little stock or water until you've reach the desired consistency. Makes 4-6 servings.

SUPER EASY TOMATO SAUCE

Great for pizza or when you're in a hurry.

2 tbsp olive oil
½ medium onion, chopped
2 cloves garlic, minced
3 tbsp tomato paste
1 medium *or* large tomato, diced
½ tsp dried basil
½ tsp dried oregano
½ tsp salt
½ tsp pepper

In blender or food processor, blend together all the ingredients until you've reached the desired consistency. Use immediately. Makes 1 cup.

GERRY'S SAUCY CREAMY SAUCE

My Gerry makes a mean cream sauce. He's so saucy! (s)

> **5-8 cloves garlic, minced**
> **8-10 mushrooms, chopped**
> **1 tbsp olive oil**
> **½ cup coconut milk (soy milk works, but not as well)**
> **3 tbsp soy Parmesan cheese**
> **¼ tsp nutmeg**
> **½-1 tsp pepper**

In a medium saucepan, sauté the garlic and mushrooms in oil on medium-low heat, ensuring the garlic doesn't burn. In a small pot, bring the coconut milk to a boil on medium-high heat. When it starts to bubble, add the Parmesan, nutmeg, and pepper and remove from heat. Whisk until smooth and the cheese has melted.

Pour this mixture into the saucepan with the mushrooms and stir together. Simmer on medium-high heat to reduce the liquid by half. Be careful not to burn it! Stir constantly. Once it reaches the desired consistency, pour over pasta or rice and serve. Makes 2-4 servings.

GINGER PEANUT SAUCE

This sure hit, containing a lovely combination of flavours such as ginger, sesame oil, curry, and peanuts, is not only just for stir-fries, but is great with any pasta dish.

> **1 medium onion, chopped**
> **4 cloves garlic, minced**
> **1 tbsp olive oil**
> **1 cup hot water**
> **½ tsp curry powder**
> **1 tbsp fresh ginger, grated**
> **1 cup natural peanut butter (*or* other nut butter)**
> **3 tbsp Braggs *or* soy sauce**
> **1 tbsp sesame oil**
> **dash of cayenne pepper**

In a medium saucepan, sauté the onions and garlic in oil until onions are translucent. Stir in the water, curry, ginger, nut butter, Braggs, sesame oil, and cayenne. Whisk or stir together until smooth. Simmer for 5-7 minutes on medium-high heat, stirring often. Serve over noodles, stir-fries, or vegetables. Makes 2-4 servings.

SPICY GARLIC TOSS FOR NOODLES

A simple sauce that overflows with flavour. A light but lively toss to spark up your noodles.

4-6 cloves garlic, minced *or* **crushed**
2 tbsp olive oil
¼ cup water
2 tsp Braggs *or* **soy sauce**
½ tsp paprika
¼ tsp dried basil
¼ tsp dried thyme
¼ tsp dried pepper
¼ tsp salt
dash of cayenne pepper

In a small saucepan, sauté garlic in 1 tablespoon of oil on medium-low heat until garlic is translucent. Be careful not to burn. Add the water, remaining oil, Braggs, paprika, basil, thyme, pepper, salt, and cayenne and bring to a boil. Simmer for 8-15 minutes. Toss with soba or buckwheat noodles. Serve the noodles with steamed veggies and tofu or eat noodles on their own, right out of the pot, for that bachelor look. Makes 2-4 servings.

FESTIVE CRANBERRY SAUCE

This seductive red sauce will impress and delight your guests come harvest time when presented alongside the tofu turkey (pg. 122). Other possibilities include a topping for vanilla ice cream (pg. 164) or chocolate "cheese" cake (pg. 155).

1½ cups fresh *or* **frozen (thawed) cranberries**
1 cup maple syrup
1 cup cranberry juice
grated zest of orange
1 cup walnuts, chopped (optional)

In a medium saucepan, bring the cranberries, maple syrup, cranberry juice, and orange zest to a boil. Lower heat to medium and simmer for 10 minutes or until the cranberries pop open. Skim off any foam that forms on the surface. Stir in optional walnuts. Chill before using. Makes 4-6 servings.

SPREADS

Spreads can complement sandwiches by adding savoury flavours and zest while at the same time providing the body with necessary nutrients.

EASY GARLIC SPREAD

Relish this spread not only because it's effortless to prepare, but it can be served on a variety of breads or crackers to accompany any salad, soup, or entrée. As you may know, cooked garlic has the strongest aroma of any member of the onion family member. Be sure to have some fresh parsley nearby to chew on in order to curb any nasty garlic breath.

> **½ cup olive oil**
> **6-10 cloves garlic, minced**
> **½ small onion, minced**
> **⅛ tsp salt**

In a blender or food processor, blend all the ingredients together. Spread over bread slices and wrap bread in foil and bake at 350°F for 15-25 minutes. Makes approx. ¾ cup.

FANCY GARLIC SPREAD

This spread is a good companion with crackers, bread, or whatever makes you happy.

> **1 small red onion, chopped**
> **6-10 cloves garlic, minced**
> **3 ½ tbsp olive oil**
> **½ tbsp balsamic vinegar**
> **2 ½ tbsp fresh thyme**
> **salt (to taste)**
> **pepper (to taste)**

In a medium saucepan, sauté the onions and garlic in 1½ tablespoons of the oil on medium-low heat until onions are translucent. In a blender or food processor, blend together the onion mixture, vinegar, thyme, salt, and pepper and remaining oil. Makes approx. ½ cup.

EASY VEGGIE BUTTER

This butter recipe is so easy to prepare, it's a must in all vegan kitchens. It's perfect on toast, muffins, potatoes – whatever butter is good on.

> ¾ cup soft tofu
> 2 tbsp flax oil *or* olive oil
> pinch of salt
> dash of turmeric

In blender or food processor, blend together all the ingredients until well mixed. Store in sealable container. Will keep in the fridge for 4-7 days. Makes approx. 1 cup.

STEPHANIE'S NUMMY YUMMY VEGGIE SPREAD

This veggie spread is to die for! Use in sandwiches or wherever a delicious spread is needed.

> ½ cup veggie butter (pg. 89) (*or* margarine)
> 3 tbsp tomato paste
> 2 cloves garlic, minced
> 1 tsp dried oregano
> 1 tsp dried dill
>
> ½ tsp dried basil
> 1 tbsp fresh parsley
> ½ small green pepper, chopped
> 1-2 stalks green onions, chopped

In a blender or food processor, blend together the veggie butter, tomato paste, garlic, oregano, dill, basil, and parsley. Pour into a bowl and add the chopped pepper and onion. Stir together and place in sealable container. This butter will keep in the fridge for 7-10 days. Makes approx. ¾ cup.

ELEGANT CREAM CHEESE

A nutritious, vegan version of the popular basic cream cheese spread. The velvety smooth texture will make you want to try the following three variations too.

> 1 cup soft *or* medium tofu
> ¼ cup cashew pieces
> 2 tsp sweetener
> 1-2 tbsp water
>
> 1 tsp salt
> ½ tsp pepper

In a blender or food processor, blend together all the ingredients until smooth and thick. Place in sealable container. Will keep in the fridge for 4-7 days. Makes approx. 1 cup.

GARLIC DILL CREAM CHEESE

The garlic combined with the dill gives this tofu cream cheese a perky flavour.

1 cup soft *or* **medium tofu**
¼ cup cashew pieces
2 tsp sweetener
2-5 cloves garlic, minced
1-2 tbsp of water
1 tsp salt
½ tsp pepper
1 tbsp dried dill

In a blender or food processor, blend together all the ingredients until smooth and thick. Place in sealable container. Will keep in the fridge for 4-7 days. Makes approx. 1 cup.

GREEN ONION CREAM CHEESE

The onions make for a colourful spread and a subtle flavour.

1 cup soft *or* **medium tofu**
¼ cup cashew pieces
2 tsp sweetener
1-2 tbsp water
1 tsp salt
½ tsp pepper
4-6 stalks green onion, chopped

In a blender or food processor, blend together all the ingredients until smooth and thick. Place in sealable container. Will keep in the fridge for 4-7 days. Makes approx. 1 cup.

TO-FRUITY CREAM CHEESE

A refreshing fruit-filled version of a classic favourite.

> **1 cup soft** *or* **medium tofu**
> **¼ cup cashew pieces**
> **4 tsp sweetener**
> **½ tsp salt**
> **½ cup fruit (e.g., strawberries, blueberries)**

In a blender or food processor, blend together all the ingredients until smooth and thick. Place in sealable container. Will keep in the fridge 4-7 days. Makes approx. 1 cup.

SUNFLOWER SEED AVOCADO SPREAD

This rich spread is delicious, nutritious, and a snap to make. The avocado ensures a smooth and creamy texture while providing the body with such good things as fiber, Vitamin C, and Vitamin E. The fat found in avocados is monounsaturated and is believed to be a beneficial fat.

> **½ cup raw sunflower seeds**
> **¼ cup soy milk**
> **¼ cup tahini**
> **1 avocado**
> **½ tsp turmeric**
> **¼ tsp mustard seeds**
> **½ tsp pepper**
> **¼ tsp salt**
> **1 tsp lemon juice**

In a blender or food processor, blend together all the ingredients until smooth and thick. Place in sealable container. Will keep in the fridge 4-7 days. Makes approx. 1 cup.

SUN SEED SANDWICH SPREAD

What could satisfy any sandwich more than being smothered with a deliciously seedy sandwich spread?

> **1¼ cups sunflower seeds, toasted**
> **2 tbsp sesame seeds, toasted**
> **3 tbsp flax oil** *or* **olive oil**
> **1-2 cloves garlic, minced**
> **2 tbsp grated soy cheese**
> **1 tbsp light miso**
> **1 tbsp Braggs** *or* **soy sauce**
> **1 stalk celery, diced**
> **1 tomato, roughly chopped**
> **pepper (to taste)**

Toast the sunflower and sesame seeds in an oven at 325°F for 7-10 minutes. In a blender or food processor, coarsely grind 1 cup of the sunflower seeds. Add the oil, garlic, cheese, miso, Braggs, celery, tomatoes, and pepper and blend until you reach desired consistency. Mix in the sesame seeds and remaining ¼ cup sunflower seeds. Store in sealable container. Use as sandwich spread or on crackers.

Makes approx. 1 ½ cups.

ZESTY CHEESE SPREAD

The sautéed red pepper gives this spread a robust flavour. Red peppers, being high in Vitamin C, are a perfect partner for the iron-packed sesame seeds. The combination of these two ingredients is beneficial because iron is absorbed easier when Vitamin C is present.

> **1 small red pepper, chopped**
> **1 tbsp olive oil**
> **1½ cups cashews**
> **¼ cup sesame seeds**
> **½ cup water**
> **⅔ cup nutritional yeast flakes**
> **¼ cup lemon juice** *or* **vinegar**
> **¼ cup flax oil**
> **1 tbsp Braggs** *or* **soy sauce**

In a small saucepan, sauté the peppers in the oil on medium heat until soft. In a blender or food processor, blend the sautéed peppers, cashews, sesame seeds, water, yeast, lemon juice, flax oil, and Braggs until smooth. Place in sealable container. Will keep in the fridge for 7-10 days. Serve on bread, crackers, celery, or mixed into hot rice. Makes approx. 1 cup.

OI-VEY! MOCH CHOPPED LIVER

This spread is best served over matzo.

1 cup mushrooms, roughly chopped
1 large onion, roughly chopped
1 tbsp olive oil
½ cup walnuts
½ tsp salt
½ tsp pepper

In a medium saucepan, sauté the mushrooms and onions in oil on medium heat until onions become translucent. In a blender or food processor, chop the walnuts and add the mushroom/onion mixture and salt and pepper. Blend together for 30 seconds. Serve chilled. Makes approx. ¾ cup.

Vegan
Side Dishes

This section includes mouthwatering recipes that can be served as appetizers, with an accompanying side dish, or teamed up with a entrée. Anyway you choose to serve them, they are guaranteed to please.

HOLY MOLY HUMMUS

Savour this creamy, smooth Mediterranean dip made from chickpeas, one of the most nutritious beans of all, and garlic, known for its medicinal properties and lovely scent. A snap to make, it can be a fantastic accompaniment for your favourite vegetables, crackers, chips, or bread. You can alter the taste of this recipe by changing the beans. Try black beans and sun-dried tomatoes for a treat! Check out the kids' version of hummus on pg. 186.

1 small onion, chopped
5 cloves garlic (more if you dare), minced
splash of olive oil
2 ½ cups cooked or **canned chickpeas**
(garbanzo beans)
¾ cup tahini
1½ tbsp Braggs or **soy sauce**

½ cup lemon juice or
¼ cup water + ¼ cup apple cider vinegar
¼ cup fresh parsley, chopped
¼ cup jalapeno pepper, chopped (optional)
1 tsp cumin
¼ tsp cayenne pepper
1 tsp salt

In a small saucepan, sauté onions and garlic in a splash of oil on medium heat until onions are translucent. In a blender or food processor, blend the sautéed onions, chickpeas, tahini, Braggs, lemon juice, parsley, jalapeno, cumin, cayenne, and salt until you reach the desired consistency. Makes approx. 2 cups.

GORGEOUS GUACAMOLE

A smooth, silky, scrumptious, and spicy spread.

3 avocados
¼ cup lime juice
1 medium tomato, chopped
1-2 cloves garlic, minced
1-2 jalapeno peppers, seeded and chopped
¼ cup chopped hot banana peppers (optional)
½ cup red onion, chopped
1 tsp pepper

Scoop out avocados into a medium bowl. Add lime juice and mash together with a fork. Add the tomatoes, garlic, jalapeno and banana peppers, onions, and pepper. Stir together. Makes approx. 1 ½ cups.

FRESH TOMATO SALSA

Enjoy these three deliciously spiced, addictive salsas. These are essential dips for corn chips; they also make great toppings for burgers, burritos, or even on top of a salad instead of dressing. Luckily, the following recipes are no bother to whip up.

4-6 medium tomatoes, chopped
2-4 cloves garlic
3-6 sprigs cilantro
3 sprigs parsley
1 tbsp red wine vinegar
1 tbsp flax oil

2-4 hot peppers (you decide the heat)
1 6-oz can tomato paste
¼ cup red onion, chopped
½ cup olives, chopped (optional)
1 tsp Paprika (optional)

In a blender or food processor, blend the tomatoes, garlic, cilantro, parsley, vinegar, oil, peppers, and tomato paste until well mixed. Spoon into a small bowl and add onions, olives, and paprika, and stir well. Makes approx. 2 cups.

BEN'S BLACK BEAN SALSA

2 cups cooked *or* canned black beans
1-2 jalapeno peppers, seeded and minced
2-3 medium tomatoes, chopped
1 avocado, chopped
1 cup corn niblets
¼ cup red pepper, chopped

¼ cup yellow pepper, chopped
1-3 tbsp lime juice
1 clove garlic, minced
3-6 sprigs cilantro, minced
salt (to taste)

In a medium bowl, stir together the beans, jalapenos, tomatoes, avocado, corn, peppers, lime juice, garlic, and cilantro. Add salt to taste. Makes approx. 2 cups.

SWEET GINGER-BLACK BEAN SALSA

1 cup cooked *or* canned black beans
½ medium red pepper, roughly chopped
1 jalapeno pepper, roughly chopped
½ small red onion, roughly chopped
2 tbsp lime juice

2 tbsp garlic-chili flax oil
1 tsp fresh ginger, roughly chopped
½ tsp sweetener
½ tsp salt
4-6 sprigs cilantro

In a blender or food processor, blend ¾ cup of the beans, red and jalapeno peppers, onions, lime juice, oil, ginger, sweetener, salt, and cilantro. Blend on high until well mixed. Pour into serving bowl and add remaining ¼ cup of beans. Stir together. Makes approx. 2 cups.

SPINACH & ARTICHOKE DIP

Combine iron-packed spinach with the unique flavour of artichokes to create this elegant dip. This dish will impress the most gourmet of diners at your next soirée. Serve with chips, crackers, or pita bread.

½ **cup fresh spinach**
¾ **cup soy Parmesan cheese**
2 **cups marinated artichoke hearts, drained**
¼ **tsp pepper**
1 **tsp lemon juice**
1 **cup grated soy mozzarella cheese**

Preheat oven to 350°F. In a blender or food processor, blend the spinach, ½ cup of Parmesan, artichokes, pepper, lemon juice, and mozzarella until well mixed. Spoon into a lightly oiled casserole dish and top with the remaining ¼ cup of Parmesan. Cover and bake for 20 minutes, until hot and bubbly. Remove from the oven and let sit 5 minutes before serving. Makes 4-6 servings.

JB'S SWEET DILL CARROTS

In order for JB to lend his moniker to any recipe, it must first reach the highest criteria of sweetness, oranginess, and dill-ectability. These carrots have achieved the highest stature in all of these criteria.

6-10 **medium carrots, sliced**
1 **tbsp dried dill**
1 **tbsp sweetener**
1 **tbsp margarine, flax oil, or olive oil**

In a medium pot or a steamer, steam the carrots until they can be pierced easily with a fork. Place the carrots in a small bowl and add the rest of the ingredients. Stir together until well incorporated. Makes 2-4 servings.

JANA'S HONEY LEMON CARROTS

This side dish is a lovely complement to Jana's Healthy Rice (pg. 119).

½ **cup water**
5 **medium carrots, sliced**
¼ **tsp lemon juice**
2 **tbsp maple syrup**

2 **tbsp fresh rosemary, chopped**
1 **tsp salt**
1 **tsp pepper**

In a medium saucepan, bring the water to a boil. Add the carrots and simmer until carrots are almost cooked. Stir in the lemon juice, honey, rosemary, salt, and pepper and simmer on low heat for 5 more minutes.

Makes 2-4 servings.

ROASTED GARLIC POTATOES

These tasty spuds, spiced with garden herbs, will feel right at home alongside breakfast, lunch, or dinner entrées.

4-5 medium potatoes, cubed
⅛ cup olive oil
8 cloves garlic, minced
2 tsp sage
2 tbsp rosemary
½ tsp salt
1 tsp pepper

Preheat oven to 400°F. Place the cubed potatoes in a medium bowl and add the rest of the ingredients and stir together. Lay evenly onto a cookie sheet or lasagna pan and bake in the oven for 30-40 minutes, until potatoes are golden brown and can be easily pierced with a fork. Makes 4-6 servings.

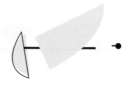

MASHED GARLIC POTATOES WITH KALE

Easy to make and delicious to taste. This side dish is sure to be a hit.

3-4 medium potatoes, roughly chopped
1 medium onion, chopped
4 cloves garlic, minced
2 tbsp olive oil
2 cups kale (about 4-5 stalks), chopped
½ cup soy milk
2 tbsp flax oil
2 tbsp Braggs
pepper (to taste)

In a large pot of water, boil the potatoes until they can be pierced easily with a fork. In a medium saucepan, sauté the onions and garlic in the oil on medium heat until the onion becomes translucent. Add the kale and cover pan with lid. Lower heat and simmer for 5-10 minutes until kale becomes soft. Set aside. When potatoes are ready, drain and place them in a large bowl. Mash together with milk, flax oil, Braggs, and pepper. Stir in the kale mixture and mix together well. Makes 4-6 servings.

TANYA'S SWEET MASH

This mashed delight adds glamour, diversity, and colour to the often-repetitive list of potato dishes. Surprise your guests with a sweet version of a classic favourite.

1 large Kuri squash, peeled and quartered
2 medium potatoes, roughly chopped
2 cloves garlic, minced
1 small onion, chopped
2 tbsp Braggs *or* **soy sauce**
2 tbsp flax oil

In a medium pot of water, boil the squash, potatoes, garlic, and onions until you can pierce the squash and potatoes easily with a fork. Drain the water, then add the Braggs and oil to the pot. Mash together until you reach the desired consistency. Makes 4-6 servings.

DIJON SCALLOPED POTATOES

The rich and flavourful seasoning of this recipe will make leftovers a thing of the past. The addition of the spicy Dijon mustard will delight sophisticated palates.

1 medium onion, chopped
1 tsp turmeric
2 ½ tbsp olive oil
⅓ cup flour
½ cup vegetable stock *or* **water**
¼ cup Dijon mustard
2 cups soy milk
½ tsp salt
⅛ tsp pepper
1 tsp Braggs or soy sauce
3-6 stalks green onions, chopped
6 medium potatoes, sliced into coins

Preheat oven to 375°F. In a medium saucepan, sauté the onions and turmeric in oil on medium-high heat until the onions are translucent. Mix in the flour, stirring constantly for about 2 minutes, resulting in a dry mixture. Slowly stir in stock, mustard, milk, salt, pepper, Braggs, and green onions. Stir until well mixed and there are no flour lumps. Set aside. Place sliced potatoes into a lightly oiled 9x13 inch baking pan. Pour the sauce over the potatoes and bake uncovered for 45-60 minutes. Makes 4-6 servings.

VEGETABLE MEDLEY KUGEL

Kugel is a Jewish baked pudding that can be made out of just about anything – fruit, potatoes, noodles – what-evah. Complete the menu with this unique dish, a delightful medley of vegetables and matzo.

4 matzos
2 cups zucchini, chopped
2 medium carrots, chopped
5-8 mushrooms, chopped
1 cup broccoli, chopped
1 small onion, minced
splash of olive oil
½ cup vegetable stock *or* **water**
egg replacer (to equal 2 eggs)
½ tsp salt
½ tsp pepper

Preheat oven to 375°F. Break matzos into quarters and soak in a bowl of water until soft. Drain, but do not squeeze dry. In a medium saucepan, sauté the zucchini, carrots, mushrooms, broccoli, and onions in a splash of oil on medium-high heat until carrots are tender. Place the vegetables in a large casserole dish and add the stock, egg replacer, salt, and pepper, and mix thoroughly. Stir in the matzo, and bake for 20 minutes. Makes 2-4 servings.

SWEET POTATO & APPLE KUGEL

A tempting dish that will delight all who consume it.

4 cups medium sweet potatoes or yams, peeled and finely chopped
2 green apples, cored and thinly sliced
½ cup raisins
1 cup apple juice or water
1 tsp cinnamon
½ cup matzo meal or bread crumbs
½ cup walnuts (optional)

Preheat oven to 375° F. In a large casserole dish, mix together all the ingredients. Bake uncovered for 45-50 minutes. Makes 4-6 servings.

RUSTIC ROASTED VEGGIES

These bite-sized morsels are so savory and juicy they will explode in your mouth. Roasting them adds a depth and richness that transforms ordinary cooked vegetables into something elegant.

2-4 medium carrots, chopped
2-3 medium potatoes, chopped
8-10 cloves garlic, peeled
6-8 mushrooms, halved
1 small yam, cubed
(plus any other vegetables you want)
½ lb medium tofu, cubed
2-4 tbsp olive oil
1 tbsp dill
2 tbsp rosemary
cracked chilis (to taste)
salt (to taste)
pepper (to taste)

Preheat oven to 350°F. Place the vegetables and tofu on lightly oiled cookie sheet or lasagna pan and drizzle the oil over them. Sprinkle with dill, rosemary, chilies, salt, and pepper and mix together until well incorporated. Bake for 40-60 minutes, stirring every 10 minutes. Remove from oven when potatoes can be pierced easily with a fork. Makes 4-6 servings.

VEGETABLE RICE PILAF

Adding this simply scrumptious rice to sautéed vegetables makes a dish that is sure to please. For variety, use quinoa instead of rice. Quinoa takes half the amount of time to cook and has an interesting nutty flavour.

2 cups brown rice   **½ medium red pepper, diced**
4 cups water   **½ medium green pepper, diced**
½ tsp turmeric   **1 tsp salt**
2-4 cloves garlic, chopped **1 tbsp olive oil**
1 small onion, diced   **1 cup peas**
1 medium carrot, diced   **¼ cup fresh parsley (*or* 2 tbsp dry parsley)**

In a medium pot with a tight-fitting lid, bring rice, water, and turmeric to a boil. Lower heat and simmer for 40 minutes or until rice is done. While the rice is cooking, in a medium saucepan, sauté the garlic, onions, carrots, peppers, and salt in the oil on medium-high heat for 5-7 minutes. Add the peas and parsley and simmer for 5 minutes more, then set aside in a large bowl. When the rice is cooked, add it to the vegetables and stir together. Makes 4-6 servings.

VORACIOUS VEGAN PÂTÉ

I really enjoy this recipe. It's a versatile, tasty spread that can be served with crackers or bread, or done up sandwich-style. If you're really feeling dangerous, spice things up by throwing in a habanero pepper! Ⓣ

1 cup onions, diced
5 mushrooms, diced
4 cloves garlic, diced
splash of olive oil
1 cup raw sunflower seeds, ground
½ cup flour
½ cup nutritional yeast
2 tsp dried basil
1 tsp salt
1 tsp dried thyme
½ tsp dried sage
¼ tsp kelp powder
1½ cups water
3 tbsp Braggs *or* **soy sauce**
1 cup potatoes, grated
⅓ cup olive oil
1 habanero pepper, seeded and minced (optional)

Preheat oven to 350°F. In a medium saucepan, sauté the onions, mushrooms, and garlic in oil on medium-high heat until tender. Meanwhile, in a large bowl, combine the ground sunflower seeds (you can grind them in a blender or a food processor), flour, yeast, basil, salt, thyme, sage, and kelp. Add the water, Braggs, potatoes, and oil and stir together. Stir in the sautéed vegetables and optional pepper and mix well. Spoon mixture into a lightly oiled 9" pie plate. Bake for 45 minutes or until centre is set and browned. Chill thoroughly before serving. Makes 4-6 servings.

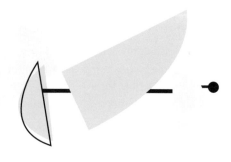

BRILLIANT BAKED BEANS

Beans are an important part of our daily nutritional requirements. The food guide states you should consume 2 servings daily or have them make up 5 to 15 percent of your diet. This bean bake is a savoury, satisfying way to meet your bean quota for the day.

2 cups cooked *or* **canned beans (e.g., pinto, kidney, navy, or soy)**
1½ cups vegetable stock
1 tsp molasses
1 6-oz can tomato paste
1 small onion, chopped
1-2 cloves garlic, minced
4 tbsp Braggs *or* **soy sauce**
1 tbsp dry mustard
1 tsp cumin
½ tsp paprika

Preheat oven to 350° F. In a large baking dish, stir all the ingredients together. Bake uncovered for 40 minutes. Makes 2-4 servings.

LARRY'S RE-FRIED BEANS

Our friend Larry thinks he knows everything there is to know. Well, he sure knows his beans.

2 cups cooked *or* **canned beans (e.g., pinto, kidney, black)**
½ cup vegetable stock *or* **water**
2 cloves garlic, minced
½ cup cilantro, chopped
1 tsp cumin
¼ tsp cayenne pepper
1 Roma tomato, sliced

In a medium pot, cook all the ingredients on medium heat for 10-15 minutes, stirring occasionally. Remove from heat. Mash with a fork and serve as is over rice, or in items such as burritos (pg. 111). Makes 2-4 servings.

Vegan Entrées

Entrées are the focus of all dinner tables. Many people can't imagine a main meal without the presence of a meat dish. These exciting vegan recipes offer nutritious alternatives to that old-fashioned idea. We hope you will be inspired to use vegetables, herbs, and other delicious ingredients in many different new ways. There are both light and filling main dishes here to expand your culinary skills in a healthy direction.

CILANTRO GINGER TEMPEH TOSS

This delightful meal can be served over rice noodles or a grain of your choice.

NEW!

> **1 bunch fresh cilantro (approx. 1 cup, tightly packed)**
> **1 medium tomato, roughly chopped**
> **2 small hot red peppers, seeded and roughly chopped**
> **2-inch piece of fresh ginger, chopped**
> **2 tsp lime juice**
> **½ cup tempeh** *or* **firm tofu, cubed**
> **1 tbsp dark sesame oil**
> **1 13.5-oz (400-ml) can coconut milk**
> **2 cups Chinese eggplant, cubed**
> **1 cup broccoli florets**
> **1 tsp salt**
> **¼ tsp turmeric**
> **¼ cup frozen peas**
> **rice noodles, enough for two people**

In a food processor blend together the cilantro, tomato, hot peppers, ginger, and lime juice. Set aside.

In a large saucepan on medium heat, sauté the tempeh in sesame oil for 3–5 minutes or until tempeh starts to brown. Stir in the coconut milk, eggplant, broccoli, salt, and turmeric and let simmer uncovered for 10–12 minutes or until eggplant is cooked and sauce starts to reduce (stir occasionally). Turn off heat and stir in cilantro mixture and peas, cover with lid, and let sit 5 minutes.

While vegetables are cooking, in a large pot of salted water, boil the rice noodles. Drain, rinse with hot water, and return to pot. Toss noodles with a splash of dark sesame oil and set aside.

Serve vegetables over rice noodles. Makes 2 large or 4 small servings.

LINDA'S GINGER "CHICHEN" NEW!

This recipe has served as comfort food in the Sperling/Cuddington household for many, many years. It is good for colds, stomach aches, and bruised psyches. Enjoy!—Linda

The mock "chicken" can be made in advance to save on time and will keep in fridge for six days or freezer for six months.

Mock "Chicken":
1 cup wheat gluten flour
1 cup water

Broth:
4 cups water
½ cup nutritional yeast
¼ cup soy or tamari sauce
2 tsp onion powder
2 tsp dried sage
1 tsp dried thyme
¼ tsp salt

Ginger Dish:
3 3-inch pieces of fresh ginger, peeled, sliced into paper-thin coins (approx. ¾ cup)
¼ cup vegetable oil
⅓ cup soy or tamari sauce
2 tsp corn starch
¼ cup water
2 green onions, finely chopped (garnish)

In a medium bowl, stir together the wheat gluten flour and water until it becomes elastic. Knead for 5 minutes and set aside.

In a large saucepan, bring all of the broth ingredients to a boil. Slice gluten into 1 inch chunks and drop carefully into broth. Reduce heat, cover with lid, and let simmer for 50–60 minutes, stirring every 10 minutes, until broth has reduced.

In a large pot on medium-high heat, sauté the ginger in oil for 3–4 minutes or until ginger starts to soften and change color. Add "chicken" chunks and sauté 2–3 minutes more, stirring often to prevent sticking. Add the soy sauce, cover pot with lid, and turn down heat to medium. Simmer for 20 minutes, stirring occasionally to make sure the sauce evenly coats the ingredients.

Once "chicken" is cooked, stir together the corn starch and water in a small bowl. Add to pot and stir together well until sauce is thickened. Place "chicken" in a large serving bowl, garnish with green onions, and serve with rice and a side of steamed gai-lan or broccoli. Makes 4–6 servings.

SARAH'S DELICIOUS CHILI

This is one of my favourite recipes. You can whip this up in an instant and feed the masses in a moment's notice! This chili always tastes best the next day and freezes well. (s)

1 medium onion, chopped
2 medium carrots, chopped
1 tbsp olive oil
3 ½ cups cooked *or* **canned kidney beans**
1 28-oz can diced tomatoes (3 ½ cups)
6 oz tomato paste
2 ½ cups cooked *or* **canned chickpeas (garbanzo beans)**
8-12 mushrooms, chopped
1 12-oz can of corn (1 ½ cups)
¾ cup rice
1-3 tbsp chili powder
1 tbsp pepper
2 tbsp curry paste
2 cups vegetable stock *or* **water**

In a large pot, sauté the onions and carrots in oil on medium-high heat until the onions become translucent. Add the remaining ingredients and stir together. Simmer on medium-low heat for 40-60 minutes, stirring occasionally. Serve with fresh bread. Note: you could also add any other veggies you have kicking around; peppers or zucchini work well. Makes 6-8 servings.

TANYA'S ASIAN CREATION

When I was living in Japan, I discovered the art of subtlety in cooking. I used my imagination and came up with masterpieces like this one using only salt and pepper as the spices. I had a hard time in Japan trying to adhere to my vegan lifestyle, but I stuck to my guns and I'm a better vegan warrior for it now. Enjoy this one. If you find it's a little too hot, you can use a little less pepper next time; my feelings won't be hurt. (T)

buckwheat noodles (enough for 4 people)
2 cups cubed squash (e.g., kuri, kabocha, butternut or acorn; don't use spaghetti squash)
2 tbsp olive oil
1 lb medium tofu, cubed
1-3 tsp pepper
1 tsp salt
3 stalks green onions, chopped
4 tbsp flax oil
Braggs (garnish)
gomashio (pg. 170) (garnish)

In a medium pot, boil the noodles in water on high heat. Meanwhile, in a medium saucepan, sauté the squash in the oil on high heat for about 5 minutes, then add the tofu, pepper, and salt. Continue cooking until the squash can be easily pierced with a fork. Add the onions, cover and set aside. When the noodles have finished cooking, rinse in hot water, then place back into the pot and toss with the flax oil to prevent the noodles from sticking. Place them into a bowl or on a plate and top with the squash mixture, then garnish with Braggs and gomashio. Makes 2-4 servings.

RICE PAPER VEGGIE WRAPS

Light, refreshing, and easy to make. Excellent for picnics or hot summer days when cooking seems impossible.

4-6 mushrooms, chopped	2 stalks green onions, chopped
½ cup Braggs *or* soy sauce	1 medium tomato, chopped
1 large carrot, grated	1 cup sunflower sprouts
4 radishes, grated	½ cup hummus (pg. 95)
1½ cups cabbage, grated	6 sheets of rice paper

In a small bowl, marinate the mushrooms in the Braggs for 10-15 minutes. While marinating, prepare the remaining vegetables and set aside. Fill a large bowl with lukewarm water and soak 1 sheet of rice paper until paper becomes soft and pliable. Shake carefully or pat off excess water. Lay the sheet down on a plate or cutting board and fill the centre with a little bit of each vegetable, including the mushrooms, and about 2 tablespoons of hummus. Wrap up like a burrito and lay seam-side down on plate. Repeat process. Use the remaining marinade as a dip. Makes 6 wraps.

NORI SUSHI ROLLS

We're going to have a sushi party tonight! Alright!

4 cups cooked brown rice *or* **sushi rice**
2 tbsp gomashio (pg. 170)
1 tbsp maple syrup
1 tbsp apple cider vinegar
1 cup carrot, grated
1 cup beets, grated
1 small cucumber, sliced like matchsticks
1½ cups sprouts (e.g., sunflower, broccoli, spicy)
2-3 avocados, sliced
3 stalks green onion, chopped
8 nori sushi sheets
Braggs (for dipping)
Wasabi (for dipping)

In a large bowl, combine the cooked rice, gomashio, maple syrup, and vinegar and place in refrigerator to chill for 10-15 minutes. When rice has chilled, place nori sheet on a sushi mat or cutting board and spread ½ cup of the rice mixture over ⅔ of the nori sheet closest to yourself. Add each vegetable, placing it in the middle of the rice mixture. Roll the nori away from you. Dab a little water with your finger to seal up the edges. Slice into two or four pieces. Use Braggs and wasabi for dipping. Try different sorts of vegetable combinations for variation. Makes 16-32 rolls.

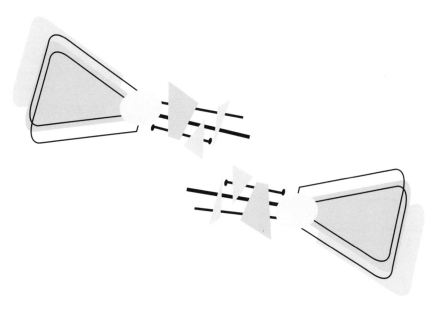

SWEET POLENTA PIE

This mouth-watering dish is just one example of how satisfying a masterful blend of roasted vegetables overtop a colourful bed of polenta can be. It will delight and excite your tastebuds.

Roasted Veggie Topping:

1 medium carrot, chopped
1 small zucchini, chopped
4 mushrooms, quartered
1 small green pepper, sliced
1 small red pepper, sliced
1 small red onion, chopped
2 cloves garlic, minced
½ cup water
1 ½ tbsp tomato paste
1 tsp apple cider vinegar
1 tbsp maple syrup
1 tbsp olive oil
4 leaves fresh basil, finely chopped
4 Roma tomatoes, chopped
salt (to taste)
pepper (to taste)

Preheat oven to 450°F. In a large bowl, combine the carrots, zucchini, mushrooms, peppers, onions, and garlic. Drizzle with a touch of oil and mix well. Lay them out on a cookie sheet or lasagna pan and roast them in the oven for 15-20 minutes, stirring occasionally, until vegetables are browned. When done, place 1/2 a cup of the roasted vegetables into a blender or food processor and blend with the water, tomato paste, vinegar, maple syrup, oil, basil, and tomatoes. Transfer this sauce and the remaining roasted vegetables to a medium saucepan and cook on medium-high heat for 10 minutes. Add salt and pepper to taste. Simmer on low heat.

Pie Crust:

1 cup coarse cornmeal
3 ½ cups water
1 tbsp oil
salt (to taste)
pepper (to taste)

In a medium bowl, whisk together the cornmeal with 1 cup of cold water, then set aside. In a medium pot, bring the remaining 2 1/2 cups of water to a boil. Once boiling, add the cornmeal mixture to the water and turn the heat down to medium-low. Add the oil, salt, and pepper. Continuously stir the mixture for about 10-15 minutes, until the mixture sticks together and becomes very stiff. Pour into a lightly oiled pie shell or a casserole dish. Let set for 5-10 minutes. Pour veggie topping into pie crust. Cut into slices. Makes 4-6 servings.

BURNIN' BUTT BURRITOS

A masterpiece – a tasty and nutritious wrap. Beans and rice make a complementary protein when combined. For variety, add your favourite vegetables to the saucepan.

½ small onion, chopped
2 cloves garlic, minced
½ cup broccoli, chopped
4 mushrooms, chopped
½ medium red pepper, chopped
1-3 jalapeno peppers, seeded and minced

2 tbsp olive oil
4 large tortilla shells
2 cups re-fried beans (pg. 103)
soy cheese (optional)
salsa (pg. 96)
2 cups cooked rice

Preheat oven to 350°F. In a medium saucepan, sauté the onions, garlic, broccoli, mushrooms, peppers, and jalapenos in the oil on medium-high heat until onions become translucent. Set aside. Lay tortilla shells down and spread a thin layer of re-fried beans, cheese, salsa, rice, and the veggie mixture on each. Roll up and lay on cookie sheet. Bake burritos for 15-20 minutes. Serve topped with salsa or guacamole (pg. 95 or 96). Makes 4 burritos.

ARTICHOKE ROTINI PASTA

This unique pasta dish combines capers, artichoke hearts, and sun-dried tomatoes, giving it a tangy, sparkly flavour.

cooked rotini pasta (enough for 4 people)
1 small onion, chopped
1 16-oz jar marinated artichoke hearts, chopped
(don't drain; use the oil to cook with)
4-6 cloves garlic, minced
1 tbsp lemon juice
4-6 sun-dried tomatoes, chopped

3 tbsp capers, drained
1 tsp thyme
2 tsp dried basil
salt (to taste)
pepper (to taste)
Faux Parmesan cheese (garnish)
(pg. 170)

While pasta is cooking, in a medium saucepan sauté the onions in 2 tablespoons of the artichoke oil on medium-high heat until the onions are translucent. Add the artichokes, garlic, and lemon juice. Cook for another 5 minutes, until the sauce has reduced. Scoop out ¼ cup of pasta water and add to the saucepan, along with the sun-dried tomatoes, capers, thyme, basil, salt, and pepper. Cook about 2 minutes, until tomatoes are warmed through. Drain pasta and toss with sauce. Garnish with Parmesan. Makes 4 servings.

FRAGRANT GARLIC PARSLEY PASTA

Simplicity at its finest. A zesty and lively dish that, when teamed with garlic bread (pg. 88), is sure to knock your dinner partners' socks off.

cooked pasta (enough for 2 people)
8-12 cloves garlic, minced
1 tsp red pepper flakes
1 tsp salt
1 tbsp olive oil
2 tbsp flax oil
1 cup fresh parsley, chopped
Faux Parmesan cheese (optional) (pg. 170)

While pasta is cooking, in a small saucepan, sauté the garlic, pepper flakes, and salt in oil on medium-low heat until garlic is tender. Set aside. Drain pasta and toss with flax oil, parsley, and the garlic mixture. Garnish with Parmesan if desired and serve. Makes 2 servings.

CREAMY CURRIED VEGGIES

Rich and full of flavour, this dish is at its best when served over rice.

1 large onion, sliced
2-6 cloves garlic, minced
1-3 large carrots, diced
2 tbsp olive oil
1 medium potato, cubed
1½ cup cauliflower florets, sliced
6-8 mushrooms, sliced

1 tbsp curry powder
½ tsp cumin
½ tsp turmeric
pinch of cayenne pepper
1 cup coconut milk or **soy milk**
1 cup peas
3 tbsp Braggs or **soy sauce**

In a large saucepan, sauté the onions, garlic, and carrots in oil on medium-high heat until the onions become translucent. Add the vegetables, curry, cumin, turmeric, and cayenne, stirring often so they don't stick to the pan, cooking for 2-4 minutes. Add the milk, cover, and reduce the heat to medium-low. Simmer for 10-20 minutes, stirring occasionally, until potatoes can be pierced easily with a fork. Stir in the peas and Braggs, and cook uncovered on medium-high heat stirring constantly until the liquid has thickened. Serve over rice ornoodles. Note: you can use whatever vegetables you have kicking around (e.g., spinach, kale, green onions). Makes 2-4 servings.

CLASSIC SPINACH LASAGNA

Momma mia! A mouthwatering take on an Italian favourite. You can use matzo or tortilla chips in place of noodles if you want to be cheeky!

1 lb medium tofu
¼ cup soy milk
1 tsp dried oregano
3 tsp dried basil
1 tsp salt
2 tbsp lemon juice
4 cloves garlic, minced
1 small onion, chopped
2 cups spinach, chopped
4-6 cups tomato sauce (pg. 85)
cooked lasagna noodles
2 cups soy cheese for topping (optional)

Preheat oven to 350°F. In a blender or food processor, blend the tofu, milk, oregano, basil, salt, lemon juice, garlic, and onions together until it achieves the consistency of cottage cheese. If the mixture is too thick, add a little water. Stir in the chopped spinach and set aside.

Cover the bottom of lasagna pan with a thin layer of tomato sauce, then a layer of noodles. Sprinkle half of the tofu mixture and ½ cup of the optional cheese. Cover this with noodles and a layer of sauce. Add the remaining filling, ½ cup of cheese, and a layer of sauce. Add one more layer of noodles, and cover with sauce. Top with remaining cheese. Bake for 30-45 minutes. Remove from oven and let sit 10 minutes before serving. Makes 4-6 servings.

MUM'S BEAN & CHEESE CASSEROLE

This was my favourite recipe that my mum used to make for my brother and me. Some kids have Kraft Dinner, I had Bean & Cheese Casserole! ⑤

5-6 small potatoes, sliced
1 tbsp prepared mustard
2 cups cooked *or* canned baked beans (pg. 103)
1-2 tsp pepper
1-2 cups soy cheese

Preheat oven to 400° F. In a large pot of water, boil the sliced potatoes until they can be pierced easily with a fork. Meanwhile, in a small bowl, stir together the mustard, beans, and pepper, and set aside. Drain the potatoes and place half of them onto a lightly oiled casserole dish. Add half of the bean mixture on top, then half of cheese. Repeat. Cover and bake for 35-40 minutes. Makes 2-4 servings.

PARMESAN CRUSTED VEGGIE SANDWICHES

Hot and crispy on the outside, cool and fresh on the inside. This secret sandwich recipe will ensure that you never need to visit the corner deli again.

¼ cup margarine
¼ cup soy Parmesan cheese
salt (to taste)
pepper (to taste)
8 thick slices firm bread
1 ¾ tbsp soy mayonnaise (pg. 167)
1 ½ tbsp Dijon mustard
2 avocados, sliced
1 medium tomato, sliced thinly into 12 slices
1 small red onion, sliced
1 ½ cups alfalfa sprouts

In a food processor or small bowl, blend together the margarine, Parmesan, salt, and pepper. Spread a portion of the margarine mixture on one side of each slice of bread. Grill bread slices in batches on a non-stick frying pan on medium-high heat for about 3 minutes, until crisp and deep brown. When done, set toast aside to cool.

In a small bowl, blend the mayonnaise and mustard together. On a piece of toast, spread a layer of the mayo mixture, avocado, tomatoes, onions, and sprouts. Place another toast slice on top. Makes 4 sandwiches.

KIERAN'S FAVOURITE RICE

Our friends Jen and Chris have the most beautiful little girl named Kieran. This is her favourite rice dish. Once you try it, it will be your favourite, too. Note that this recipe makes a huge amount; if you don't have a stock pot, cut the recipe amounts in half.

1 large onion, chopped
2-8 cloves garlic, chopped
½ tsp salt
2 tbsp olive oil
2 ¼ cups tomato juice
1 lb firm tofu, cubed
1 medium green pepper, chopped
1 stalk broccoli, chopped
2 medium carrots, chopped
3-6 mushrooms, chopped
(plus whatever other vegetables you may have)
2 ½ cups cooked *or* **canned kidney beans**
½ tsp dried basil
½ tsp dried oregano
pepper (to taste)
cayenne pepper (to taste)
1 ¾ cups white basmati rice
½-1 cup water (only if you don't have enough liquid to cook the rice)
2 medium tomatoes, chopped
½ cup green *or* **black olives (optional)**

In a large stock pot, sauté the onions, garlic, and salt in the oil on medium-high heat until the onions become translucent. Add the tomato juice, tofu, peppers, broccoli, carrots, mushrooms, and beans. Stir gently, so as not to make the tofu mushy. Add the basil, oregano, pepper, cayenne, and rice. Again, stir gently. If you think there isn't enough liquid to cook the rice, then add a little water.

Cover with a lid, bring to a boil, then reduce heat and let simmer 15-25 minutes or until rice is done. Add the fresh tomatoes and olives. Stir and cover. Let simmer until most of the liquid has been absorbed. Remove from heat, fluff with fork before serving. Makes 4-6 servings.

SAVOURY SHEPHERD'S PIE

This delightful dish is sure to have guests coming back for seconds. It tastes best when topped with miso gravy (pg. 83).

Filling:
1 small *or* medium onion, chopped
3 small carrots, chopped
½ cup spinach, chopped
1 stalk celery, chopped
1 large tomato, chopped
2 tbsp olive oil
½ cup cooked *or* canned green lentils, mashed
½ tsp dried basil
½ tsp salt
1 tbsp Braggs *or* soy sauce

Topping:
3 medium potatoes, roughly chopped
¼ cup soy milk
1 tbsp margarine *or* olive oil
salt to taste

Preheat oven to 350°F. In a medium pot of water, boil the chopped potatoes until they can be pierced easily with a fork. In a medium saucepan, sauté the onions, carrots, spinach, celery, and tomatoes in the oil. Once carrots are tender, add the mashed lentils, basil, salt, and Braggs. Stir and simmer without a lid until the liquid cooks off.

Meanwhile, in a food processor or a medium bowl, mash the potatoes, milk, margarine, and salt with a potato masher or fork. Set aside. Pour the vegetable mixture into a lightly oiled pie plate and then layer the mashed potatoes over top. Bake for 15-20 minutes. Makes 4-6 servings.

BIG BEN'S LENTIL BURGERS

My mum used to make this recipe. We called them Big Ben's burgers because my younger brother Ben was a miniature human garbage disposal with a big appetite. This was his favourite meal as a kid. Ⓢ

¾ cup wheat germ
2 cups cooked *or* canned lentils
1 cup bread crumbs
¼ cup chopped onions

3 tbsp olive oil
½ tsp salt
½ tsp pepper

On a small plate, set aside 2 tablespoons of the wheat germ for coating. In a medium bowl, mash together the remaining ingredients with a potato masher or your hands. Divide and shape into 4 patties. Lay down each patty in wheat germ, coating each side.

Cook on a lightly oiled frying pan on medium-high heat for 5-10 minutes, flipping occasionally. Serve like a regular burger – an all-vegan patty, special sauce, lettuce, soy cheese, pickles, onions on a sesame bun! Makes 4 patties.

Cilantro Ginger Tempeh Toss (pg. 105)

Linda's Ginger "Chicken" (pg. 106)

Better Than Butter Tarts (pg. 139)

Sticky Finger Buns (pg. 140)

SPICY BLACK BEAN BURGERS

These burgers are spiced to perfection. To make them even spicier, you could melt jalapeno soy cheese on each patty and serve topped with salsa (pg. 96).

½ cup flour
1 small onion, diced
2 cloves garlic, minced
½ tsp dried oregano
1 small hot or jalapeno pepper, minced
1 tbsp olive oil
½ medium red pepper, diced
2 cups cooked or canned black beans, mashed

½ cup corn niblets
½ cup bread crumbs
¼ tsp cumin
½ tsp salt
2 tsp chili powder
2 tbsp fresh parsley, minced (optional)

On a small plate, set aside flour for coating. In a medium saucepan, sauté the onion, garlic, oregano, and hot pepper in oil on medium-high heat until the onions are translucent. Add the peppers and sauté another 2 minutes, until pepper is tender. Set aside. In a large bowl, mash the black beans with a potato masher or fork. Stir in the vegetables (including the corn), bread crumbs, cumin, salt, chili powder, and parsley. Mix well. Divide and shape into 5 or 6 patties. Lay down each patty in flour, coating each side. Cook on a lightly oiled frying pan on medium-high heat for 5-10 minutes or until browned on both sides. Makes 4-6 patties.

VEGGIE RICE BURGERS

These make scrumptious and flavourful patties, but they're fragile, so treat them with tender loving care. Serve on a bun or bread with soy cheese, ketchup, and relish.

½ cup flour
1 medium carrot, diced
1 small onion, diced
¼ cup zucchini, diced
1 stalk celery, chopped
2-4 mushrooms, chopped
2 cloves garlic, minced
¼ tsp thyme

¼ tsp dried dill
1 tbsp olive oil
2 cups cooked rice, mashed
¼ tsp salt
1 tbsp Braggs or soy sauce
1 tbsp tahini
1 tbsp psyllium husks

On a small plate, set aside flour for coating. In a medium saucepan, sauté the carrots, onions, zucchini, celery, mushrooms, garlic, thyme, and dill in the oil until vegetables are tender. Remove from heat. In a large bowl, stir together the sautéed vegetables and cooked rice. Add the salt, Braggs, tahini, and psyllium husks. Mix together well. Divide and shape into 6 patties. Lay down each patty in flour, coating each side. Cook on a lightly oiled frying pan on medium-high heat for 5-10 minutes or until browned on both sides. Makes 6 patties.

VEGAN SLOPPY JOES

A truly exceptional vegan dish. Bet you never thought you'd be able to have it again!

Tomato Sauce:
4 tbsp olive oil
1 small onion, chopped
4 cloves garlic, minced
1 6-oz can tomato paste
2 medium *or* **large tomatoes, chopped**
1 tsp salt
1 tsp dried basil
1 tsp dried oregano
1 tsp pepper

1 cup boiling water
1 ½ cups textured vegetable protein (TVP)
1 medium onion, chopped
1 tbsp oil
1 medium green pepper, chopped
1 medium tomato, chopped
1 large pickle, chopped
2 tbsp Braggs *or* **soy sauce**
1 ½ tsp chili powder
dash of cayenne pepper
dash of allspice
dash of salt

In a blender or food processor, blend together the oil, onion, garlic, tomato paste, tomatoes, salt, basil, oregano, and pepper until you reach the desired consistency. Set aside.

In a medium bowl, pour the boiling water over TVP and set aside for 10-15 minutes. In a medium saucepan, sauté the onions in oil on medium-high heat until translucent. Lower heat to medium and add the peppers, tomatoes, pickles, Braggs, chili powder, cayenne, allspice, salt, and tomato sauce. Simmer for 5 minutes. Add TVP to saucepan and stir together. Simmer on medium-low heat for another 20-30 minutes and serve over toast or on a bun. Makes 2-4 servings.

ZUCCHINI DELIGHT

Hard to believe that anything so easy to make could be so delicious.

1 ½ cups soy mozzarella cheese, grated
1 28-oz can diced tomatoes
5 cups zucchini, chopped
½ tsp dried oregano
½ tsp dried basil

½ tsp red pepper flakes
½ tsp salt
1 cup cooked *or* **canned lentils**
½ cup jasmine rice

Preheat oven to 350°F. In a large casserole dish, combine ½ cup of the cheese with the tomatoes, zucchini, oregano, basil, red pepper flakes, salt, lentils, and the rice. Stir together. Top with remaining cheese and bake uncovered for 30-40 minutes or until rice is done. Makes 2-4 servings.

POTATO "CHEESE" PEROGIES

These tasty jewels will explode in your mouth. Serve these up with a green salad or steamed veggies.

Filling:
2 medium *or* large potatoes, cubed
1½ cups soy cheese, grated
1 tbsp lemon juice
1 tsp Dijon mustard
1 tsp dried dill
dash of pepper

Dough:
1½ cups flour
½ tsp salt
⅛ tsp nutmeg
egg replacer (to equal 2 eggs)
4 tbsp margarine *or* vegetable shortening
sour cream (garnish) (pg. 168)
salsa (garnish) (pg. 96)

In a medium pot of water, boil the cubed potatoes until they can be pierced easily with a fork. Drain. In a medium bowl, combine the potatoes, cheese, lemon juice, mustard, dill, and pepper. Mash together well with a potato masher or fork. Set aside.

In a medium bowl, combine the flour, salt, nutmeg, and egg replacer. With your hands or a fork cut the margarine into the flour mixture until well blended. You will want a nice, smooth dough, so you may need to add a touch of water if the dough is dry. Divide the dough evenly into 16 balls. Roll out each ball into a 3-inch circle and put 1 ½ tablespoons of potato mixture in each centre. Fold dough over and press edges down with a fork.

In a large pot of boiling water, add 3-4 perogies at a time and cook for 5 minutes on low boil. Remove perogies with slotted spoon and serve. As an option, you could fry the perogies in a non-stick frying pan until crispy. Top the perogies with sour cream or salsa. Makes 16 perogies.

JANA'S HEALTHY RICE

Try this with honey lemon carrots (pg. 97).

4 cups water
2 cups short-grain brown rice
5 cloves garlic, minced
3 tbsp cilantro, minced
¼ small white onion, chopped

1 tbsp apple cider vinegar
3 tbsp curry paste
1 tsp salt
4 tbsp flax oil
2 cups kale, chopped

In a medium pot, add the water and rice, boil for 30 minutes on medium heat. Stir in the garlic, cilantro, and onion and cook 10 minutes more. Remove from heat and stir in the vinegar, curry paste, salt, oil, and kale. Makes 2-4 servings.

STUFFED SPAGHETTI SQUASH

Warm and homey, this is a perfect harvest-time concoction.

1 medium *or* **large spaghetti squash, halved and cored**
1 medium onion, chopped
4-6 mushrooms, chopped
1 tbsp olive oil
1 tsp salt
1 tsp pepper
½ tsp cumin
1 cup cooked *or* **canned lentils**
½ cup bread crumbs

Preheat oven to 350°F. Cut the squash lengthwise in half and scoop out the seeds, but leave the meat. Lay squash face up on cookie sheet. Set aside. In a medium saucepan, sauté the onions and mushrooms in oil on medium-high heat until onions are translucent. Add the salt, pepper, cumin, lentils, and bread crumbs and cook for 3 minutes more. Spoon the stuffing into each half of squash and bake in oven for 30 minutes or until squash can be pierced easily with a fork. Note: If your squash won't lay flat on your cookie sheet, you can cut a bit off the bottom. Makes 2-4 servings.

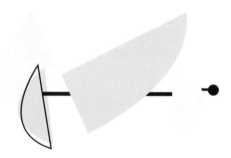

PIZZA

Pizza doesn't have to be about 4 different kinds of cheese or meat. In fact, your pizza doesn't even need cheese or meat at all! The combination possibilities are endless. Here are some of our favourites:

- **tomato sauce, mushrooms, olives, spinach, soy cheese**
- **tomato sauce, artichoke hearts, garlic cloves, soy cheese**
- **tomato pesto sauce (pg. 84), red onion, pine nuts, soy cheese**
- **tomato sauce, sun dried tomatoes, fresh herbs, soy cheese**
- **pesto sauce (pg. 84), red, yellow and green peppers, garlic, fresh herbs**
- **tomato sauce, red onions, black olives, capers, marjoram**

YEAST PIZZA CRUST

1½ cups tepid water
¼ oz packet yeast
1 tsp salt
3 cups flour

Preheat oven to 350°F. In a medium ceramic bowl, whisk together the water and yeast until dissolved. Add the salt and whisk again. Stir in the flour and knead dough for about 3 minutes. Set aside and let dough rise for 20 minutes in a warm, draft-free place. Knead again and if dough is too sticky, add a bit more flour. Let dough rise for another 10-20 minutes. Roll out dough onto a pizza pan and prick dough all over with a fork before adding all your goodies! Bake for 30-40 minutes.

YEAST-FREE PIZZA CRUST

2 cups flour
½ cup soy Parmesan cheese
½ tsp salt
1 tbsp dried oregano
1 tbsp dried basil
4 tbsp margarine
5 tbsp olive oil
⅓ cup cold water

Preheat oven to 400° F. In a food processor or with your hands, mix the flour, Parmesan, salt, oregano, basil, margarine, and oil until "just mixed." Spoon the flour mixture into a medium or large bowl and slowly add the water while you knead the dough. Knead only for a few minutes until dough is pliable. Form into a 6-inch disk and let chill in refrigerator for 20 minutes. Roll out dough onto a pizza pan and prick all over with a fork before adding all your goodies. Bake for 20 minutes.

MATZO PIZZA

4 matzos
1 cup tomato sauce (pg. 85)
toppings (e.g., mushrooms, spinach)
seasoning (e.g., garlic, oregano, basil)
soy cheese

Preheat oven to 350°F. Lay matzos on cookie sheet. Add ¼ cup of sauce on each matzo. Add toppings, seasonings, and cheese. Bake 10-12 minutes or until cheese has melted.

TOFURKY [TOFU TURKEY]

For your vegan festivities. Serve topped with gravy (pg. 83), mashed potatoes (pg. 98), cranberry sauce (pg. 87), and assorted steamed veggies.

Marinade:
1 ½ cups boiling water
½ tbsp dill
½ tsp rosemary
½ tsp thyme

½ tsp marjoram
½ tsp sage
½ tsp pepper
1-4 cloves garlic, thinly sliced
3 tbsp olive oil

1 lb firm tofu, ¼-inch thick

In a large bowl, whisk together the water, dill, rosemary, thyme, marjoram, salt, pepper, garlic, and oil. Set aside. Slice the tofu into desired shapes, about ¼-inch thick. (I usually cut the tofu into 10 ¼-inch squares.) Lay each slice down on a cookie sheet or a lasagna pan, cover with marinade, and let sit for 1 hour or more (the longer the better). Preheat oven to 350°F. Bake for 60 minutes, turning slices over after 30 minutes. To serve, fry tofurky cutlets on a non-stick frying pan until both sides are browned. Makes 10 slices.

"ANYTHING GOES" VEGETABLE STIR-FRY

Using seasonal vegetables will change the character of this fast and easy stirfry. Remember to begin with the denser vegetables first (carrots, squash, etc.) and the more delicate vegetables later (bok choy, kale, peas, etc.).

2 medium carrots, chopped
1 head of broccoli, chopped (including stems)
4-6 mushrooms, chopped
1 lb medium *or* **firm tofu, cubed**
splash of olive oil
2 stalks celery, chopped
2-4 leaves bok choy, roughly chopped
2 cups "Anything Goes" vegetables (e.g., snap peas, kale, bean sprouts)

Braggs (garnish)
flax oil (garnish)
gomashio (garnish) (pg. 170)

In a large wok or frying pan, sauté the carrots, broccoli stems, mushrooms, and tofu in oil on medium-high heat until carrots are tender. Add the broccoli florets, celery, bok choy, and "Anything Goes" vegetables and simmer on medium high heat until al dente. Serve over rice, noodles, or on its own and garnish with Braggs, flax oil, and gomashio. Makes 2-4 servings.

CORRI'S GAGGLE OF GREEN GOO

My friend Corri is just learning the joys of cooking. This is her latest creation. Try serving it over rice or noodles. (S)

- ½ pkg firm tofu, cubed
- ½ medium green pepper, chopped
- 1-2 stalks celery, chopped
- ½ cup mushrooms, chopped
- 1 tbsp olive oil
- 1-2 tbsp coriander chutney (*or* other green chutney)
- 3 cups bok choy, chopped

In a large saucepan or wok, sauté the tofu, peppers, celery, and mushrooms in oil on medium-high heat until the celery turns tender. Stir in the chutney, then add the bok choy (but don't stir it in), cover with a lid, and cook on medium heat for 10-15 minutes. Stir once and then cook for another five minutes without a lid to blend the flavours. Makes 2 servings.

CORRI'S EASY GREEN CHOP SUEY

Corri thinks her recipe tastes like good chop suey. Try it and see! Serve over rice or noodles, and garnish with gomashio (pg. 170).

- ½ pkg firm tofu, cubed
- 2 stalks celery, chopped
- 4-8 mushrooms, chopped
- 1 tbsp olive oil
- 3 cups bok choy, chopped
- 2 tbsp miso
- 2 tbsp water
- 1 tsp fresh ginger, finely grated
- 2 tbsp Braggs
- 3 stalks green onion, chopped
- 2 cups fresh spinach, roughly chopped
- dash of salt

In a large saucepan or wok, sauté the tofu, celery, and mushrooms in oil on medium-high heat until tofu starts to turn golden. Add the bok choy (but don't stir it in), cover with a lid, and cook over medium heat for 10 minutes. In a small bowl, whisk together the miso, water, ginger, and Braggs. Pour over the vegetables and stir together. Add the onions and spinach, but again don't stir them in. Add salt and cover for another 5 minutes. Stir it all together before serving. Makes 2 servings.

Vegan Breads & Muffins

In the How It All Vegan kitchen, we don't like to use baking yeast in our bread or biscuit recipes. To make our loaves light and fluffy, we regularly use sour dough starter, baking powder, baking soda, and vinegar. With a delicate combination of these ingredients, we are able to produce results that we are most happy with.

We believe unyeasted bread is a more holistic and traditional approach to eating. In terms of health benefits, unyeasted bread is easier for the body to digest and also helps to keep disorders like candida away.

It's best if you're able to find/buy/borrow a "bread only" bowl. Try to find a beautiful ceramic or wooden bowl, as they make the best bread palette. A word of caution: never use metal bowls for making bread, as they may deactivate the rising ability of the bread mixture.

An important thing to remember when baking vegan is that you are not using any of the usual things that help to bind your ingredients and make your baked goods fluffy and light. Here are some tips to make your baking work:

SIFT

Using a sifter or a whisk to mix all your dry ingredients together helps to keep things light. Always mix your dry ingredients together before you add any wet!

DON'T OVERMIX

When mixing, use a wooden spoon or your hands to gently mix the dry and wet ingredients together. You want to mix "just" enough to blend all the ingredients together. But avoid mixing too vigorously, as your baking will end up flat and heavy.

KEEP IT MOIST

Place a small pan of cold water in the oven while baking. This will help to keep your baking moist.

DON'T EXPECT STORE-BOUGHT GOODIES

Remember that you're baking vegan now, so your breads, muffins, and treats won't look exactly like those from the local bakery. But don't forget, taste is everything! So before you dismiss your creations, take a bite!

CHECK FOR READINESS

Poke your breads and muffins with a clean knife or fork before taking them out of the oven. If it comes out clean, it's ready; if it's still gooey, wait another 5 minutes, then test again.

OATMEAL BREAD

Due to the wonderful nature of oat flour, this bread is deliciously moist and sweet.

> **3 cups flour**
> **1 cup oatmeal flour (to make oatmeal flour, put 1¼ cups of oatmeal in food processor and blend well)**
> **2 tsp baking powder**
> **1 tsp baking soda**
> **1 tsp salt**
> **2 tbsp sweetener**
> **egg replacer (to equal 1 egg)**
> **2 cups soy milk**
> **1 tsp vinegar**

Preheat oven to 375°F. In a large bowl, sift together the flours, baking powder, baking soda, salt, and sweetener. In a separate smaller bowl, whisk together the egg replacer with the milk and vinegar and add to the flour mixture. Mix together carefully until "just mixed." Place in a lightly oiled loaf pan or shape into an oval loaf and place on a lightly oiled cookie sheet.

Dust top of loaf with oatmeal flakes and bake for 35-45 minutes. Test with a knife to see if done. Makes 1 loaf.

SODA BREAD

This stout, dense loaf is a knockout.

> **2 cups flour**
> **2 cups pastry flour**
> **2 tbsp arrowroot powder or corn starch**
> **2 tsp baking powder**
> **1½ tsp baking soda**
> **1 tsp salt**
>
> **2 tbsp egg replacer**
> **1½ cups water**
> **3-4 tbsp sweetener**
> **3-4 tbsp oil**
> **2 tbsp vinegar**
> **¼ cup ground almonds (optional)**

Preheat oven to 375°F. In a large bowl, sift together the flours, arrowroot powder, baking powder, baking soda, and salt. Add the egg replacer, water, sweetener, oil, vinegar, and optional nuts, and mix together until "just mixed." Spoon into a lightly-oiled loaf pan and brush the top with oil. Bake for 55-60 minutes. Test with a knife to see if done. Makes 1 loaf.

THE ART OF SOURDOUGH BREAD

There is a definite art to making sourdough bread; it requires patience and time. So if your loaves don't turn out the way you feel they should, don't get discouraged, just try again. Here are a few tips if your loaves aren't turning out they way you want them to:

Not rising enough: add a bit more starter
Too gooey: add a bit more flour
Too lumpy: knead the bread a little longer
Cracks: cut some slits in the top of the loaf right before baking

SOURDOUGH STARTER

> **1 cup water**
> **1 cup whole wheat flour**

In a large, clean, dry jar, stir together the water and flour until completely mixed. Cover jar with a cotton cloth and let sit covered for 3-5 days in a warm, draft-free spot (the top of the refrigerator is always a good spot). Stir every 12 hours. On the third day, it's ready to use. You want the starter to be bubbly and smell sour. If it smells rancid, throw it out and start again. After using, store in the fridge with a tight-fitting lid.

As you use your starter for baking, you can keep the rest of it indefinitely by "feeding" it. If you use a ½ cup of starter, for instance, refill it by adding ½ cup of flour and water to the balance. Stir and let sit for 3 hours before returning to storage. If you don't use your starter often, it will become dormant. To revive it, add ⅛ cup of flour and ⅛ cup of warm water, and keep it in a warm place for 10-12 hours before using.

SOURDOUGH BREAD

> **5-7 cups whole-wheat pastry flour ***
> **2 ½ cups water**
> **½- ¾ cup sourdough starter**
> **1 tsp salt**

In a large bowl, stir together 5 cups of flour, water, starter, and salt. Slowly add the remaining flour, ½ cup at a time, while gently kneading the dough until smooth and consistent.

Place dough in a lightly oiled ceramic bowl. Roll the dough around so that it's covered in oil. Cover the bowl with a cotton cloth and let dough rise for 12 hours.

Re-knead dough for 3-5 minutes. Cut it in half and either place in loaf pans or shape into 2 loaves and place on cookie sheet. Cover and let dough rise 6 more hours, until the dough doubles in size.

Preheat oven to 425° F. Bake loaves for 15 minutes, then reduce heat to 350°F and bake for another 45 minutes or until golden brown. Check with knife to see if done. Makes 2 loaves.

*You can vary your flour for different tastes and textures: e.g., 4 cups pastry, 3 cups spelt.

EASY BISCUITS

These tasty jewels are perfect smothered in miso gravy (pg. 83) or simply teamed with any soup.

2 cups flour
3 tsp baking powder
1 tsp salt
¼ cup margarine or vegetable shortening
¾-1 cup sour soy milk (soy milk + 1 tsp vinegar)

Preheat oven to 450° F. In a large bowl, sift together the flour, baking powder, and salt. Add the margarine and sour milk and mix together gently until "just mixed." Spoon into lightly oiled muffin tins, or roll out and cut with biscuit or cookie cutters and place on a lightly oiled cookie sheet. Bake for 12-18 minutes. Makes 6 biscuits.

SOURDOUGH BISCUITS

Enjoy the delicious flavour of sourdough in a biscuit. They stand well on their own or served with a meal.

2 cups flour
½ tsp salt
2 tsp baking soda

1 tbsp sweetener
½ cup margarine
1½ cups sourdough starter (pg. 127)

Preheat oven to 425° F. In a large bowl, sift together the flour, salt, baking soda, and sweetener. Cut in the margarine and mix well. Stir in the sourdough starter. Knead lightly until "just mixed." Spoon into lightly oiled muffin tins, or roll out and cut with biscuit or cookie cutters and place on lightly oiled cookie sheet. Bake for 10-12 minutes. Makes 6-12 biscuits.

FANCY BISCUITS

These scrumptious scrumpets boast a savoury flavour all their own.

2 cups flour
2 tsp baking powder
½ tsp salt
2 tbsp vegetable oil *or* **shortening**

1 cup sour soy milk (soy milk + 1 tsp vinegar)
½ cup green onions, chopped
1 tbsp dried dill
¼ tsp pepper

Preheat oven to 450° F. In a large bowl, sift together the flour, baking powder, and salt. Add the oil, sour milk, onions, dill, and pepper and mix together gently until "just mixed." Spoon into lightly oiled muffin tins. Bake for 12-18 minutes. Makes 6 biscuits.

SWEET BISCUITS

Try serving these biscuits with tea.

> **2 ½ cups flour**
> **¼ cup dry sweetener**
> **2 tsp baking powder**
> **¾ cup margarine**
> **1 cup soy milk**

Preheat oven to 400° F. In a large bowl, sift together the flour, sweetener, and baking powder. Stir in the margarine and milk and mix together until "just mixed." Spoon into lightly oiled muffin tins, or roll out and cut with biscuit or cookie cutters and place on lightly oiled cookie sheet. Bake for 12-18 minutes. Makes 8 biscuits.

CHAPATIS

This flat bread has it origins in India and goes great with curries or exquisite rice salad (pg. 72).

> **1 ½ cups flour**
> **½ tsp salt**
> **2 tbsp oil**
> **¾-1 cup water**

In a large ceramic bowl, stir together the flour, salt, and oil. Slowly add the water to form a soft dough. Knead for 5 minutes. Cover bowl and dough with a tea towel and let stand for 30-60 minutes. Divide dough into 14 equal pieces and shape into balls. With a rolling pin, roll each ball into a 6-inch disk and fry in a dry frying pan over medium heat. Cook each side until browned, and serve warm. Makes 14 chapatis.

FLAX SEED CRACKERS

The flax seed is a nutritious, versatile seed with many proven beneficial properties. For variation, add 1 teaspoon of oregano, onion powder, or dill. You can use hemp seeds instead of flax for this recipe.

½ cup flax seeds
1½ cups flour
½ tsp baking powder
½ tsp salt
4 tsp margarine or vegetable shortening

1 tbsp dried oregano (optional) or
onion powder (optional) or
dried dill (optional)
½ cup soy milk

Preheat oven to 325°F. In a food processor, blend together the flax seeds, flour, baking powder, salt, margarine, and optional spices until well mixed. Place in a medium bowl and slowly add the milk. Mix and knead together until the dough forms a ball. Chill dough for 10-20 minutes.

Divide dough into 4 equal parts. In between 2 sheets of wax paper, roll out the dough very thinly to form a rectangle. Cut into 6 squares, or use cookie cutters. Repeat with remaining dough. Transfer crackers onto a lightly oiled cookie sheet and bake for 15 minutes, then flip them over and bake for 5 minutes more. Makes 24 crackers.

HARVEST HERB BREAD

The classic combination of these herbs bring flavour and life to this delicious bread.

1½ cups flour
½ tsp salt
1½ tsp baking powder
½ tsp baking soda
¼ tsp dried marjoram
⅛ tsp dried oregano
½ tsp dried basil
pinch of dried thyme

½ cup raisins
½ cup chopped nuts (optional)
egg replacer (to equal 1 egg)
2 tbsp sweetener
4 tbsp oil
1 tsp vinegar
¾ cup soy milk

Preheat oven to 400°F. In a large bowl, sift together the flour, salt, baking powder, and baking soda. Add the marjoram, oregano, basil, thyme, raisins, nuts, egg replacer, sweetener, oil, vinegar, and milk. Mix together gently until "just mixed." Spoon into a lightly oiled loaf pan and bake for 20-30 minutes. Test with a knife to see if done. Makes 1 loaf.

SWEET POTATO CORN BREAD

A sweet, savory bread to accompany soups.

1 cup flour	**1 cup sweet potatoes, cooked and mashed**
1 tsp baking powder	**4 tbsp oil**
½ tsp baking soda	**¼ cup sweetener**
½ tsp salt	**egg replacer (to equal 2 eggs)**
⅛ tsp allspice	**½ cup sour soy milk (soy milk + ½ tbsp vinegar)**
½ cup cornmeal	

Preheat oven to 375°F. In a large bowl, sift together the flour, baking powder, baking soda, salt, and allspice. Stir in the cornmeal. Add the mashed sweet potatoes, oil, sweetener, egg replacer, and sour milk. Mix together gently until "just mixed." Spoon into a lightly oiled square or round loaf pan and bake for 30 minutes. Test with a knife to see if done. Makes 1 loaf.

CINNAMON RAISIN BREAD

What could be a more fantastic aroma to wake up to than fresh cinnamon raisin bread hot out of the toaster?

1 cup flour	**¼ tsp nutmeg**
1 cup rye flour	**2 tsp cinnamon**
½ tsp salt	**1 cup sour soy milk (soy milk + 1 tbsp vinegar)**
1½ tsp baking powder	**½ cup sweetener**
1 tsp baking soda	**½ cup raisins**
½ tsp allspice	**½ cup chopped nuts**

Preheat oven to 350°F. In a large bowl, sift together the flours, salt, baking powder, baking soda, allspice, nutmeg and cinnamon. Stir in the sour milk, sweetener, raisins, and nuts. Mix together gently until "just mixed." Spoon into a lightly oiled loaf pan and bake for 45-50 minutes. Test with a knife to see if done. Let the bread sit for 10 minutes before slicing. Makes 1 loaf.

APPLESAUCE BREAD

Be tempted by this fruity-tasting bread. Serve toasted with nut butter and jam.

2 cups flour	egg replacer (to equal 2 eggs)
2 tsp baking powder	1/3 cup maple syrup
1/2 tsp salt	1/3 cup oil
1 tsp cinnamon	1 1/2 cups applesauce
1/4 tsp nutmeg	3/4 cup nuts, chopped
1/4 cup wheat germ	1 tsp vinegar

Preheat oven to 350° F. In a large bowl, stir together the flour, baking powder, salt, cinnamon, nutmeg, and wheat germ. Add the egg replacer, maple syrup, oil, applesauce, nuts, and vinegar. Mix together gently until "just mixed." Spoon the batter into a lightly oiled bread pan and bake for 50-55 minutes. Test with a knife to see if done. Makes 1 loaf.

GINGER BREAD

Ginger is known for its healing properties and spicy taste. It turns this already dynamic loaf into a Spice Capade.

3 cups flour
2 1/2 tsp baking powder
1/2 tsp baking soda
1/2 tsp salt
1 tsp allspice
egg replacer (to equal 2 eggs)
1/2 cup oil
1/2 cup molasses
1 cup soy milk
1 tsp vinegar
3-6 tbsp fresh ginger, grated
1/2 cup crystallized ginger, chopped (optional)
1/2 cup walnuts

Preheat oven to 350° F. In a large bowl, sift together the flour, baking powder, baking soda, salt, and allspice. Add the egg replacer, oil, molasses, milk, vinegar, ginger, optional crystallized ginger, and nuts. Mix together gently until "just mixed." Spoon the batter into a lightly oiled loaf pan and bake for 50 minutes. Test with a knife to see if done. Cool for 10 minutes before slicing and serving. Makes 1 loaf.

ZUCCHINI BREAD

This sweet, summer squash loaf makes an equally good impression as a light, healthy snack or a sensible dessert.

1½ cups flour
2 tsp baking powder
½ tsp salt
1½ tsp cinnamon
egg replacer (to equal 1 egg)
½ cup sweetener
⅓ cup oil

1 tsp vinegar
1 tsp vanilla extract
1½ cups zucchini, grated
½ cup raisins
½ cup nuts, chopped
¼ cup water (optional)

Preheat oven to 350°F. In a large bowl, sift together the flour, baking powder, salt, and cinnamon. Add the egg replacer, sweetener, oil, vinegar, and vanilla, and mix. Stir in the zucchini, raisins, and nuts and mix together gently until "just mixed." Add a little water if the dough seems too dry. Spoon the batter into a lightly oiled loaf pan and bake for 45-50 minutes. Test with a knife to see if done. Cool for 10 minutes before slicing and serving. Makes 1 loaf.

RHUBARB BREAD

This summer spectacular is a classic combination of both sweet and tart.

2½ cups flour
2 tsp baking powder
½ tsp baking soda
½ tsp salt
1 tsp powdered ginger *or*
1 tbsp fresh ginger, grated

egg replacer (to equal 1 egg)
½ cup sweetener
½ cup oil
½ cup orange or apple juice
1½ cups rhubarb, finely chopped
¾ cup nuts, chopped

Preheat oven to 350°F. In a large bowl, sift together the flour, baking powder, baking soda, salt, and ginger. Stir in the egg replacer, sweetener, oil, juice, rhubarb, and nuts. Mix together gently until "just mixed." Spoon into a lightly oiled loaf pan and bake for 35-40 minutes. Test with a knife to see if done. Cool for 10 minutes before slicing and serving. Makes 1 loaf.

APRICOT BREAD

Closely related to the peach, the apricot offers a sweet yet subtle flavour to this loaf.

2 cups flour
2 tsp baking powder
1 tsp baking soda
1 tsp salt
¼ tsp powdered ginger *or*
¾ tbsp fresh ginger, grated

1 cup dried apricots, chopped
egg replacer (to equal 1 egg)
⅔ cup sweetener
2 tbsp oil
1 cup apricot or orange juice
1 tsp vinegar
1 tsp vanilla
½ cup nuts, chopped

Preheat oven to 350°F. In a large bowl, sift together the flour, baking powder, baking soda, salt, and ginger. Stir in the apricots, egg replacer, sweetener, oil, juice, vinegar, vanilla, and nuts. Mix together gently until "just mixed." Spoon the batter into a lightly oiled loaf pan and bake for 50 minutes. Test with a knife to see if done. Cool for 10 minutes before slicing and serving. Makes 1 loaf.

BANANA BREAD

Simply the world's greatest loaf. For added sweetness, add ½ cup of chocolate chips to this recipe.

3 ripe bananas, mashed
1 tbsp lemon juice
½ cup oil
½ cup sweetener
¾ cup chopped dates
1 ½ cups flour
½ cup wheat germ
½ tsp salt
½ tsp baking powder
½ tsp baking soda

Preheat oven to 375°F. In a small bowl, mash the bananas with a fork until very mushy, then add the lemon juice, oil, sweetener, and dates and stir together. In a separate large bowl, stir together the flour, wheat germ, salt, baking powder, and baking soda. Add the banana mixture to the flour mixture and mix together gently until "just mixed." Spoon into a lightly oiled loaf pan and bake for 40-50 minutes. Test with a knife to see if done. Makes 1 loaf.

SPICY SOUP MUFFINS

Warm, spicy, and fragrant, these muffins are sure to please.

1 cup flour	**½ tsp fresh ginger, grated**
1 cup rye flour	**¼ tsp allspice**
2 tsp baking powder	**½ cup raisins**
½ tsp baking soda	**egg replacer (to equal 2 eggs)**
½ tsp salt	**½ cup applesauce**
½ tsp pepper	**¼ cup sweetener**
½ tsp nutmeg	**⅔ cup sour soy milk (soy milk + 1 tsp vinegar)**
¾ tsp cinnamon	**4 tbsp oil**

Preheat oven to 400°F. In a large bowl, stir together the flours, baking powder, baking soda, salt, pepper, nutmeg, cinnamon, ginger, and allspice. Add the raisins, egg replacer, applesauce, sweetener, sour milk, and oil. Mix together gently until "just mixed." Spoon the batter into lightly oiled muffin tins, filling them until about ⅔ full. Bake for 15-20 minutes. Makes 6 muffins.

MAPLE-NUT SOUP MUFFINS

Try these delicious muffins as an accompaniment to any of our hearty soup recipes.

1⅓ cup flour
1½ tsp baking powder
1 tsp baking soda
½ tsp salt
½ tsp cinnamon
¼ cup maple syrup
egg replacer (to equal 2 eggs)
⅔ cup sour soy milk (soy milk + ¾ tsp vinegar)
¼ cup oil
¾ cup pecans, chopped

Preheat oven to 400°F. In a large bowl, sift together the flour, baking powder, baking soda, salt, and cinnamon. Add the maple syrup, egg replacer, sour milk, oil, and pecans. Mix together gently until "just mixed." Spoon the batter into lightly oiled muffin tins, filling them until about ⅔ full. Bake for 15-20 minutes. Makes 6 muffins.

COUNTRY CORN MUFFINS

Perfect alongside a piping hot bowl of quick and easy chili (pg. 107).

¾ cup yellow cornmeal
¾ cup flour
1 tsp baking powder
½ tsp baking soda
¼ tsp salt
egg replacer (to equal 2 eggs)

¼-½ cup soy milk or water
2 tbsp sweetener
2 tbsp oil
½ tsp vinegar
1 cup corn kernels

Preheat oven to 350°F. In a large bowl, stir together cornmeal, flour, baking powder, baking soda, and salt. Add the egg replacer, milk, sweetener, oil, vinegar, and corn. Mix together gently until "just mixed." Spoon mixture into lightly oiled muffin tins, filling cups to the top. Bake for 15 -20 minutes. Test with a knife to see if done. Cool for 5 minutes on a wire rack before serving. Makes 6 muffins.

APPLESAUCE MUFFINS

The aroma of these sweet scented muffins will arouse any tastebud and lead you into the kitchen.

2 cups flour
½ tsp salt
1 tsp baking soda
½ tsp cinnamon
½ cup soy milk
1 tbsp apple cider vinegar
2 tbsp oil
⅓ cup maple syrup
1 cup applesauce
¾ cup raisins

Preheat over to 375° F. In a large bowl, sift together the flour, salt, baking soda, and cinnamon. Add the milk, vinegar, oil, maple syrup, applesauce, and raisins. Mix together gently until "just mixed." Spoon batter into lightly oiled muffin tins and bake for 15-20 minutes. Test with a knife to see if done. Makes 6 muffins.

BLUE BANANA MUFFINS

A true masterpiece. After years of testing and development, we've perfected this muffin! Fearlessly indulge.

3 ½ cups whole wheat pastry flour
2 tsp baking power
½ cup dry sweetener
½ cup oil
1½-2 cups soy milk

2 bananas, mashed
2 tbsp ground flax seed
1 cup blueberries

Preheat oven to 350° F. In a large bowl, stir together the flour, baking powder, and sweetener. Add the oil, milk, mashed bananas, flax seeds, and blueberries. Mix together gently until "just mixed." Spoon into lightly oiled muffin tins and bake for 35-40 minutes. Test with a knife to see if done. Makes 12 muffins.

RASPBERRY CORNMEAL MUFFINS

These are simply scrumptious. An ideal brunch item or mid-day pick-me-up.

1½ cups cornmeal
1 ½ cups flour
dash of salt
¾ cup sweetener
¾ tsp baking soda

¼ cup oil
¾ cup soy milk
¾ cup orange or apple juice
1 tsp vinegar
1 cup raspberries

Preheat oven to 400° F. In a large bowl, stir together the cornmeal, flour, salt, sweetener, and baking soda. Add the oil, milk, juice, vinegar, and berries. Mix together gently until "just mixed." Spoon into lightly oiled muffin tins and bake for 35-45 minutes. Test with a knife to see if done. Makes 6 muffins.

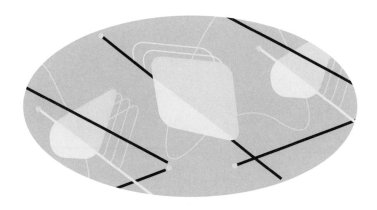

Vegan
Desserts

What could be more satisfying after any meal than a delectable dessert? Some people think that vegan desserts are lackluster and tasteless; au contraire, they're zesty and full of taste. These desserts have been designed to be more nutritious than traditional treats without having to scrimp on flavor or presentation. Use premium ingredients in your baking and dessert-making and you can be guaranteed the tastiest and most gratifying desserts. C'mon, you're worth it!

BETTER THAN BUTTER TARTS **NEW!**

What the croissant is to France, the butter tart is to Canada. Treat your family with this traditional favorite. Whether you're watching a Canada Day parade, spending time with your family around the campsite, or just hanging out on the porch, these gooey yummy treats will be a hit.

1 cup raisins
1 tbsp vegan margarine
¾ cup sugar
2 tbsp ground flax seeds
3 tbsp water
1 tsp vanilla extract
12 unbaked pre-made pastry tart shells (3 inch) *or* **home-made pastry dough**
½ cup walnuts, finely chopped (optional)

Preheat oven to 400°F. Put raisins into a medium bowl and cover with very hot water. Set aside for 10 minutes. Drain hot water off of raisins and add margarine, sugar, flax seeds, water, and vanilla. Stir together well. Spoon 1 tbsp of mixture evenly into each tart shell. Sprinkle each tart with finely chopped walnuts. Bake for 15 minutes and serve at room temperature. Makes 12 tarts.

STICHY FINGER BUNS NEW!

It takes a few hours to make these buns, but you can do other things while you're waiting for your dough to rise (like organize your closet, read a book, or thoroughly wash your hands—because you'll be licking your sticky fingers after you've devoured these buns).

Buns:
2 ½ tsp *or* **one packet dry active yeast**
¼ cup warm water
1 tsp sugar
1 cup vegan milk
¼ cup sugar
¼ cup vegan margarine, room temperature
¼ cup ground flax seeds
1 tsp salt
3 ½–4 cups all purpose flour

Topping:
¾ cup vegan margarine
¾ cup sugar
½ cup pecans *or* **walnuts, finely chopped**

Center:
¼ cup vegan margarine
¾ cup sugar
½ cup walnuts *or* **pecans, finely chopped**
1 tbsp ground cinnamon

Buns

In a small bowl, stir together the yeast with warm water and 1 tsp sugar. Set aside for 10 minutes (if your yeast mixture is not foamy, your yeast is dead).

In a mixer or a large bowl, blend together the yeast mixture, milk, sugar, margarine, flax seeds, salt, and 1 cup of flour. Stir in the remaining flour, 1 cup at a time, kneading dough until smooth and elastic (add a little extra flour if the dough is too sticky).

Knead dough into a ball for 3–5 minutes, before transferring to a large, lightly oiled bowl. Turn dough until covered with oil, cover the bowl with cloth, and set aside in a warm, non-drafty spot and let rise for 1 hour or until doubled in volume.

Topping

When dough is almost done rising, in a small saucepan on medium heat, melt the margarine, stir in the sugar, and whisk until sugar is dissolved. Pour topping evenly into the bottom of a lightly oiled 9 inch x 13 inch pan. Sprinkle evenly with pecans. Set aside.

Center

In a small saucepan, melt the ¼ cup of margarine. Set aside to cool.

Punch down dough and knead out air bubbles. On a lightly floured surface, roll dough into a large rectangle (18 by 9 inches). Brush the surface of the rolled dough with 2 tbsp of melted margarine (leaving a 1 inch border around the edge). Sprinkle margarine area evenly with sugar, pecans, and cinnamon. Starting at the long edge, tightly roll up dough into a log and pinch the seam to seal. Brush the outside of the log with remaining 2 tbsp of melted margarine. With a bread knife, cut log into 16 pieces and place cut side down in pan with topping. Cover with cloth and set aside in a warm, non-drafty spot and let dough rise for 1 hour.

Preheat oven to 375°F. Bake for 25–30 minutes. Remove pan from oven and let sit for 5 minutes and then remove buns by flipping them over onto another pan or serving tray. Spoon any remaining topping back over the buns. Serve warm. Makes 16 buns.

For added yummy, you can drizzle with the tops of your buns with "Cream Cheese" Frosting or Quick Cake Glaze (recipes below), but wait until buns are completely cooled before you frost.

CREAM CHEESE FROSTING

½ cup vegan "cream cheese"
2 tbsp vegan margarine
½ tsp vanilla extract
1 cup vegan icing sugar

In a food processor, blend all ingredients together until smooth. Makes approx. 1 ½ cups.

QUICK CAKE GLAZE

1 cup icing sugar
1 tbsp vegan "milk"

In a small bowl, stir together all ingredients until smooth. Makes approx. 1 cup.

PEPPERMINT PATTIES   **NEW!**

Is there anything better then the sweet marriage of mint and chocolate? Wrap these treats in candy foil for a great home-made gift.

Center:
2 cups powdered icing sugar
1 tbsp vegan margarine
2 tsp peppermint extract
2 tbsp vegan milk

Coating:
1½ tsp vegan margarine
4 1-oz squares (28-g) unsweetened or semi-sweet chocolate

Line the bottom of a cookie sheet with wax paper. Set aside. In a food processor (using the dough blade), pulse together sugar, margarine, extract, and milk. Turn up speed and mix for another minute until it attains a creamy dough-like consistency.

Spoon out 1 tsp of dough and drop onto prepared cookie sheet. Continue until all dough is on sheet (approx. 24 small patties) and place in freezer for 15 minutes. (Alternately, use 2 tsp per patty to make 12 larger patties. If you would like to make differently shaped patties, you can roll the dough out onto a lightly powdered icing sugar surface and then cut with small cookie cutters before next step.)

Remove cookie sheet from freezer and quickly roll each candy into a ball shape (be careful not to handle the patties too much), and gently flatten each one with palm of hand and set back on sheet. Place cookie sheet back into the freezer for 15 more minutes.

While dough is in freezer, in a small saucepan on medium-low heat, melt the margarine. Add the chocolate and melt, stirring constantly to prevent burning. Once melted, remove from heat and set aside to cool down a little.

Using a dinner fork like a spatula, lift a patty off the cookie sheet and *quickly* dip into the melted chocolate until fully covered. Holding the fork over the pot, allow chocolate to run off through the tines of the fork before dragging the back of the fork on the side of the saucepan to remove excess chocolate. Lay coated patty back on wax paper by pushing gently off fork with your finger or another fork. Repeat for remaining candies. Tap the top of each dipped candy with the back of the fork to add a little decorative touch.

Place cookie sheet into refrigerator and let chill for 1 hour before serving. Makes 24 small or 12 large patties.

CHARMING CHOCOLATE CUPCAKES

Cupcakes are great. They're easy to make, portable, and take the formality out of cake. It doesn't matter whether you serve them out of a plastic container or off a silver platter – your guests will love them.

1 cup molasses
1 cup soy milk
2 cups chocolate *or* **carob chips**
6 tbsp oil

1 tsp vanilla extract
4 tbsp cornstarch
2 cups flour
1 tsp baking soda
6 cupcake paper liners

Preheat oven to 375° F. In a small saucepan, whisk together the molasses, $\frac{1}{2}$ cup of the milk, and the chips. Cook on medium heat until chips have melted, stirring constantly with a spoon. Add the oil, vanilla, cornstarch and stir until well mixed. Remove from heat and set aside. In a medium bowl, sift the flour and baking soda together. Add the remaining milk and the chocolate mixture and stir. Spoon into cupcake paper liners and bake for 15-20 minutes. Test with a knife to see if done. Once cooled, you can frost with icing (pg. 159). Makes 6 cupcakes.

CHOCOLATE PECAN BROWNIES

Whoever thought a vegan dessert could ever be so rich and decadent? Try these tantalizing confections and chide yourself for ever thinking vegan baking was dull. There are two brownie recipes here to test the most critical sweet-tooth's palate.

1 cup soft *or* **medium tofu**
1 cup dry sweetener
2 tsp vanilla extract
4 tbsp oil

4 tbsp cocoa *or* **carob powder**
1 ⅓ cup whole-wheat pastry flour
2 tsp baking powder
¾ cup pecans, chopped

Preheat oven to 350° F. In a blender or food processor, blend the tofu, sweetener, vanilla, oil, and cocoa powder until smooth and creamy. In a large bowl, sift together the flour and baking powder. Add the pecans and tofu mixture, and mix together gently until "just mixed." If the batter is too dry, add a splash of water. Spoon the batter into a lightly oiled 8x8 cake pan and bake for 20-25 minutes. Test with a knife to see if done. Let cool in pan for 5 minutes before icing (pg. 159) and cutting into squares. Makes 6 large brownies.

MAPLE WALNUT BROWNIES

1⅓ cup flour	¼ cup apple juice *or* water
⅓ cup cocoa *or* carob powder	⅓ cup oil
1½ tsp baking powder	2 tsp vanilla extract
½ tsp salt	½ cup walnuts, chopped (optional)
¾ cup maple syrup	

Preheat oven to 350° F. In a large bowl, sift together the flour, cocoa powder, baking powder, and salt. Add the maple syrup, juice, oil, vanilla, and walnuts and mix together gently until "just mixed." Spoon into a lightly oiled 8x8 pan and bake for 25-30 minutes. Test with a knife to see if done. Makes 6 large brownies.

CHOCOLATE PEANUT BUTTER CUPS

For years, the idea of making your own peanut butter cups seemed a laborious task. Now thanks to the efforts of vegan pioneers, recipes like this are only a little harder than making ice cubes.

½ cup margarine	1 cup chocolate *or* carob chips
¾ cup peanut butter *or* other nut butter (e.g., cashew)	¼ cup soy milk
¾ cup graham wafer crumbs	¼ cup nuts, chopped
¼ cup dry sweetener	12 cupcake paper liners

In a small saucepan on medium heat, melt the margarine. Once liquefied, stir in the peanut butter, graham crumbs, and sweetener until well incorporated. Spoon about 2 tablespoons of the peanut mixture into muffin tins lined with cupcake paper liners (the liners are important). In a different small saucepan on medium heat, melt the chocolate and milk together until completely melted, stirring often. Spoon over top of the peanut butter cups. Garnish with nuts and allow to set in the fridge for 6-8 hours before serving. Makes 12 cupcakes.

CHOCOLATE RICE CRISPY SQUARES

Children and adults of all ages will appreciate this crispy, sticky, taste sensation. Bask in the nostalgia of your childhood.

1 cup dry sweetener	6 cups puffed rice *or*
1 cup corn syrup	other puffed grain
1 cup peanut butter *or* nut butter	2 cups chocolate or carob chips

In small saucepan on medium heat, mix together the sweetener and corn syrup until hot and bubbly. Remove from heat and add the nut butter, stirring together until well mixed. In a large bowl, add the puffed rice and chips. Stir in the nut butter mixture and mix together well. Pour mixture into a 9x13 pan, press flat, and let cool for 1 hour before cutting into squares. Makes 6 large or 12 small squares.

CHOCOLATE CHIP BARS

Please, oh please lock me up so I can eat my way to freedom, straight through these fantastic chocolate chip bars. (T)

3 ½ cups flour	1 cup oil
1 ½ tsp baking powder	1 tsp vanilla extract
½ tsp baking soda	1 cup soy milk *or* water
½ tsp salt	1 cup chocolate *or* carob chips
1 ½ cups dry sweetener	

Preheat oven to 350°F. In a large bowl, stir together the flour, baking powder, baking soda, salt, and sweetener. Add the oil, vanilla, milk, and chocolate chips and mix together gently until "just mixed." Pour mixture into a 9x13 pan and bake for 25-30 minutes. Test with a knife to see if done. Let cool 10 minutes before cutting into bars. Makes 12 bars.

DELIGHTFUL DATE SQUARES

Also known as the "matrimonial square," this recipe overflows with wholesome goodness, given the oats and the dates, which are full of iron. Date squares are a prestigious confection perfect for those unexpected occasions when royalty comes a knocking.

Filling:	Crust:	
1 cup water	4 cups rolled oat flakes	½ tsp baking soda
2 cups pitted dates, chopped	2 cups flour	1 tsp cinnamon
½ tsp salt	1 cup dry sweetener	1 cup margarine
	½ tsp salt	¼ cup oil
	½ tsp baking powder	¼ cup water (optional)

Preheat oven to 350°F. In a small saucepan, bring the water to boil, then reduce to medium heat and add the dates and ½ a teaspoon of the salt, and simmer until the dates are soft and will mix easily with the water. Remove from heat and set aside to cool.

In a large bowl, stir together the oat flakes, flour, sweetener, salt, baking powder, baking soda, and cinnamon. Add the margarine and oil and stir together until well combined. If the crust is too dry, add the optional water.

Press half of the crust mixture into the bottom of a 9x13 pan. Spread the date mixture over top, spreading out with the back of a large spoon. Sprinkle the remaining crust mixture over top. Bake for 25-40 minutes, until the top is lightly browned and tender. Crust will harden when it cools, so cut into squares before it gets too difficult! Makes 12 bars.

GRANOLA BARS

1 cup granola (pg. 48)
1 cup coconut, shredded
1 cup rolled oat flakes
1 cup flour
¾ tsp baking powder

pinch of salt
½ cup sweetener
½ cup raisins
flax or psyllium egg replacer (to equal 1 egg)
½ cup oil
2 tbsp sesame seeds

Preheat oven to 350°F. In a large bowl stir together the granola, coconut, oat flakes, flour, baking powder, and salt. Stir in the sweetener, raisins, egg replacer, and oil. Mix together well. Spread mixture into a 8x8 pan. Sprinkle top evenly with sesame seeds. Bake for 18-20 minutes.

MAPLE NUT ORBS

Absolutely delicious. A healthy treat requiring only a few ingredients. You'll make these often! For chocolate orbs, add ½ cup cocoa powder to the dough.

1 cup nut butter (e.g., peanut, cashew, tahini)
⅓-½ cup maple syrup
1 cup oat bran
½ cup wheat germ

1 cup sesame seeds
½ cup coconut, shredded

In a food processor, blend together the nut butter and maple syrup. Add the oat bran, wheat germ, and sesame seeds and blend until it has a stiff, dough-like consistency. You can either roll the dough into 14 individual orbs, and then roll them in coconut and chill, or spread the dough onto a square pan and sprinkle with coconut, chill, and cut into squares. Makes 14 orbs.

GINGER SNAPS

This temptation was Hansel and Gretel's downfall. But fear not, these snaps hold no hidden traps. No need to proceed gingerly!

2½ cups flour
1 tsp baking powder
1 tsp baking soda
½ tsp salt

¾ cup maple syrup
¼ cup molasses
½ cup oil
5 tbsp fresh ginger, grated

Preheat oven to 350°F. In a large bowl, stir together the flour, baking powder, baking soda, and salt. Add the maple syrup, molasses, oil, and ginger. Stir together gently until "just mixed." Scoop spoon-sized portions onto a lightly oiled cookie sheet and bake for 12-15 minutes. Makes 6 large or 12 small cookies.

CLASSIC CHOCOLATE CHIP COOKIES

A vegan version of the kind of cookies that Grandma used to make. Serve with a big cold glass of soy milk.

- ¾ cup dry sweetener
- ½ cup margarine
- ½ cup oil
- 3 tbsp water
- 2 tsp vanilla extract
- 2 ¼ cups flour
- 1 tsp baking soda
- ½ tsp salt
- 1-1 ½ cups chocolate chips

Preheat oven to 375°F. In a small bowl, stir together the sweetener, margarine, oil, water, and vanilla. In a large bowl, mix together the flour, baking soda, and salt. Add the margarine mixture and the chocolate chips and mix together well. Scoop spoon-sized portions onto an unoiled cookie sheet and bake for 8-10 minutes or until the edges are browned. Let cool before removing from cookie sheet. Makes 6 large or 12 small cookies.

BANANA OATMEAL COOKIES

These oatmeal cookies are no plain jane treats. In fact, their sensation is in their subtlety.

- 2 bananas, mashed
- ½ cup applesauce
- ¾ cup dry sweetener
- 1 tsp vanilla extract
- 2 ½ cups flour
- 2 ½ cups rolled oat flakes
- 1 tsp cinnamon
- 1 tsp baking soda
- 1 cup raisins
- ½ cup chocolate *or* carob chips

Preheat oven to 350°F. In a food processor or small bowl, mix together the bananas, applesauce, sweetener, and vanilla. In large bowl, stir together the flour, oat flakes, cinnamon, and baking soda. Add the banana mixture and mix together well. Add the raisins and chips and mix together again. Scoop spoon-sized portions onto a lightly oiled cookie sheet and bake for 12-15 minutes. Makes 6 large or 12 small cookies.

SPICY OATMEAL RAISIN COOKIES

Delicately flavoured with herbs and spices, the uniqueness of these cookies intrigues all.

3 cups rolled oat flakes
1 cup flour
½ tsp salt
1 tsp baking soda
1 tsp cinnamon
1 tsp nutmeg
1 tsp ground ginger
1 tsp cumin
½ tsp dried cardamom

½ tsp pepper
dash of cayenne pepper
1 banana, mashed
½ cup dry sweetener
2 tbsp oil
1 cup sour soy milk (soy milk + 1 tsp vinegar)
¾ cup raisins
½ cup chocolate *or* carob chips (optional)

Preheat oven to 375° F. In a large bowl, stir together the oat flakes, flour, salt, baking soda, cinnamon, nutmeg, ginger, cumin, cardamom, pepper, and cayenne. Add the mashed banana, sweetener, oil, sour milk, raisins, and chocolate chips to the oat mixture and mix together gently until "just mixed." Scoop spoon-sized portions onto a lightly oiled cookie sheet and bake for 8-10 minutes. Makes 6 large or 12 small cookies.

COOTIE'S COCONUT COOKIES

These are best straight from the oven, but they're nice and chewy when cold, too.

2 bananas, mashed
1 tsp vanilla extract
½ cup sweetener
½ cup oil
3 tsp coconut *or* soy milk
1 cup flour
1 tsp baking soda
1 tsp cinnamon
1 cup rolled oat flakes
1 cup coconut, shredded

Preheat oven to 350° F. In a blender or food processor, blend together the mashed bananas, vanilla, sweetener, oil, and milk. In a large bowl, sift together the flour, baking soda, and cinnamon. Stir in the oat flakes and then fold in the banana mixture, stirring well. Mix in the shredded coconut. Scoop spoon-sized portions onto a lightly oiled cookie sheet and bake for 15-20 minutes. Makes 12 large or 24 small cookies.

APRICOT & ALMOND TEA COOKIES

Truly delectable. An elegant cookie suitable for all occasions.

2 cups flour	**1 cup almonds, chopped**
¾ tsp baking powder	**1 cup dried apricots, chopped**
½ tsp baking soda	**½ cup oil**
½ tsp salt	**¼ cup soy milk**
1 ¼ cups rolled oat flakes	**1 tbsp vanilla extract**
½ cup sweetener	

Preheat oven to 350° F. In a large bowl, sift together the flour, baking powder, baking soda, and salt. Add the oat flakes, sweetener, almonds, apricots, oil, milk, and vanilla. If the mixture is too dry, add a splash of water (but you don't want them gooey). Scoop spoon-sized portions onto a lightly oiled cookie sheet and bake for 12-15 minutes. Makes 12 large or 24 small cookies.

AUNTIE BONNIE'S HAMISH BREAD COOKIES

These cookies are a Kramer family favourite that we've adapted. They freeze well and are great for tea parties or munching when you're feeling nibbly. Ⓢ

6 tbsp cane sugar	**¾ cup applesauce** *or*
½ tsp cinnamon	**egg replacer (to equal 3 eggs)**
3 ½ cups flour	**¼ cup oil**
½ cup dry sweetener	**1 tsp vanilla extract**
1 tsp baking powder	**1 cup almonds, chopped**
dash of salt	**¼ cup coconut, shredded**
	¼ cup chocolate *or* **carob chips**

Preheat oven to 350° F. In a small bowl, mix together the cane sugar and cinnamon and set aside. In a large bowl, whisk together the flour, sweetener, baking powder, and salt. Add in the applesauce, oil, vanilla, almonds, coconut, and chips and mix together gently until "just mixed." Separate the dough into 3 balls. Cover your cookie sheet with tin foil, then roll each ball into a snake shape the length of the cookie sheet. Press down a little so the dough is about an inch thick. Repeat with the remaining balls of dough. Sprinkle each log with the cinnamon-sugar mixture. Bake for 35-40 minutes. Before cookies cool, cut each log into 24 slices. Place cookies back on the cookie sheet and bake for another hour at 200° F. Makes 72 small cookies.

HOT WATER PIE CRUST

Does the filling make the pie, or is it the crust? After all, the crust is the foundation that holds this classic dessert together. Without it, it's just jam.

> **1 cup vegetable shortening**
> **1 tsp margarine**
> **¾ cup boiling water**
> **3 ½ cups pastry flour** *or* **3 cups all-purpose flour***
> **2 tbsp baking powder**
> **¼ tsp salt**

In a large bowl, mix together the shortening, margarine, and water until creamy. Add the flour, baking powder, and salt and mix together until a dough forms. Knead for a minute or two. Wrap the dough in wax paper and chill for about 3 hours before rolling it out (not overnight). Roll the dough into individual pie crusts. Makes 2 crusts.

If you want to freeze the dough to use later, roll out to the size you want and place in an airtight container, placing a sheet of wax paper between the sheets of dough. Fold the sheets as necessary to fit in the container, but thaw completely before unfolding and using for pie. When ready to use, bake at 350° F for 15 minutes and let cool before adding filling.

Note: white flour works better than whole-wheat flour for pie crusts. You lose some nutrition, but live a little!

SOURDOUGH PIE CRUST

This is a versatile crust. Use with your favourite fruit filling.

> **1 cup flour**
> **½ tsp salt**
> **¼ tsp baking soda**
> **⅓ cup vegetable shortening** *or* **margarine**
> **⅓ cup sourdough starter (pg. 127)**

In a large bowl, sift together the flour, salt, and baking soda. Cut the shortening into the flour mixture and, once well-mixed, add the sourdough starter and stir together well. Set bowl aside and let dough rise, covered, for about half an hour. Roll the dough into a pie crust. Makes 1 crust.

GRAHAM CRACKER CRUST

Use this with the "cheese" cake recipes (pg. 155-156).

> **1½ cups graham cracker crumbs**
> **2-3 tbsp oil**
> **3 tbsp water**
> **dash of salt**

In a medium bowl, mix together all the ingredients. Press the mixture evenly onto the bottom of a pie plate or cheesecake pan, using your fingers or the back of spoon. Makes 1 crust.

ROLLED OAT PIE CRUST

This crust is good for apple pie, or in place of the graham cracker crust.

> **2 cups rolled oat flakes**
> **¼ cup vegetable shortening** *or* **margarine**
> **½ cup sweetener**
> **¼ tsp cinnamon**

In a medium bowl, mix together all the ingredients. Press the mixture evenly onto the bottom of a pie plate or cheesecake pan, using your fingers or the back of spoon. Bake at 350° F for 10 minutes before using. Makes 1 crust.

AMAZING APPLE PIE

Just imagine this hot pie cooling on your window sill, brimming with raisins and apples, with a slight hint of maple. It makes a fabulous team with vanilla ice cream (pg. 164) when served oven-hot. You can add any other fruit combinations. Just subtract 1 apple for each cup of fruit.

6-8 large baking apples (Granny Smith are best), cored and sliced
½ cup raisins (optional)
¾ cup maple syrup
1-2 tbsp lemon juice
2 tsp cinnamon
2 ½ tbsp cornstarch *or* **arrowroot powder**
1 pie crust (pg. 150)

Preheat oven to 350° F. Core and slice apples into bite-sized pieces. Bring a medium pot of water to boil, then reduce heat to medium and add the apples and optional raisins to simmer for 8-10 minutes. Save ¼ cup of "apple water" for use later. Drain apples and place in a large bowl. Mix carefully together the cooked apples, maple syrup, lemon juice, and cinnamon. Set aside. In a small saucepan, mix the ¼ cup "apple water" with the cornstarch over medium heat, stirring constantly until the mixture turns very thick. Add the cornstarch mixture to the rest of the ingredients, stirring until mixed well. Pour into a pie crust and bake for 30-40 minutes.

Note: If you're too busy to make a pie crust, there are store-bought crusts available that are vegan! Just check the ingredients.

PERFECT PUMPKIN PIE

Pumpkin, or winter squash, is usually harvested in the fall, just in time for winter solstice and other seasonal holidays. Which is why this pie always makes its way to the table alongside the tofu turkey (pg. 122). This delicious old favourite is sure to be a hit, especially when topped with whipped cream (pg. 161).

1½ cups soy milk
egg replacer (to equal 2 eggs)
1 16-oz can of pumpkin
½ cup sweetener
1 tsp cinnamon
½ tsp powdered ginger
1 pie crust (pg. 150)

Preheat oven to 350° F. In a large bowl, whisk together the milk and the egg replacer. Add the pumpkin, sweetener, cinnamon, and ginger, and mix together well. Pour into a pie crust and bake for 30-40 minutes, until centre is firm.

CREAMY COCONUT PIE

Classically creamy and light as a cloud, this is the kind of pie dreams are made of.

> **2 cups soft tofu**
> **½ cup oil**
> **2 tsp vanilla extract**
> **½ tsp salt**
> **1 ½ cups dry sweetener**
> **2 ¼ cups coconut, shredded**
> **1 graham cracker pie crust (pg. 151)**

Preheat oven to 350° F. In a blender or food processor, blend together the tofu, oil, vanilla, salt, and sweetener. Pour into a large bowl and fold in 2 cups of the coconut. Pour into a graham cracker pie crust and bake for 15 minutes. Sprinkle the remaining ¼ cup of coconut on top and bake for another 10 minutes, until filling looks set and centre is firm. Serve chilled.

CHOCOLATE BOURBON PECAN PIE

Formally referred to as the "orgasm pie." One bite and you will understand. This pie is so elegant and rich, it has a reputation. Three words describe it: "better than sex!"

> **egg replacer (to equal two eggs)**
> **2 tbsp molasses**
> **½ cup corn syrup**
> **2 tbsp Jack Daniels bourbon (optional)**
> **1 tsp vanilla extract**
> **⅛ tsp salt**
> **1 ½ cups pecans, chopped**
> **1 cup chocolate chips**
> **4 whole pecans**
> **1 pie crust (pg. 150)**

Preheat oven to 350°F. In a large bowl, mix together the egg replacer, molasses, corn syrup, bourbon, vanilla, and salt. Add the chopped pecans and chocolate chips and mix together well. Pour into a pie crust and arrange the 4 whole pecans in the centre of the pie as decoration. Bake for 40-45 minutes.

CHOCOLATE-BANANA NO-BAKE PIE

No-bake pie! Sounds crazy, you say? Try it, we say.

1 cup chocolate chips
splash of soy milk
1 ½ cups applesauce
½ cup dry sweetener
4 bananas, chopped
1 pie crust (pg. 150)

In a small double boiler, melt the chocolate chips with a splash of milk over hot water, stirring until smooth. In a blender or food processor, blend together the applesauce, sweetener, bananas, and melted chocolate until well mixed. Pour into the pie crust of your choice. Chill for at least 12 hours before eating.

ANGELIC APPLE CRISP

If there is a heaven, it will have the aroma of baked apples. If heaven has a restaurant, it will serve this apple crisp recipe. Since we're not in heaven yet, we might as well eat as if we are. This recipe is best with ice cream (pg. 164).

6-8 apples, cored and chopped
¼-½ cup raisins (optional)
⅓ cup apple juice
½ cup maple syrup

Topping:
1 cup rolled oat flakes
½ cup flour
¼ cup margarine
¼ cup sweetener
½-1 tsp cinnamon
½ tsp powdered ginger
dash of salt
dash of nutmeg
¼-½ cup chopped nuts (optional)

Preheat oven to 350°F. Core and chop the apples into bite-sized pieces. Place onto a lightly oiled baking dish and mix in the optional raisins. In a small bowl, mix together the juice and maple syrup. Pour the juice mixture over the apples and raisins evenly. In a medium bowl, mix together the oat flakes, flour, margarine, sweetener, cinnamon, ginger, salt, nutmeg, and optional nuts. Sprinkle the oat mixture over top of apples and bake for 30-40 minutes. Makes 4-6 servings.

A lovely variation on an old favourite. Imagine small morsels of apple flawlessly baked, combined with fragments of pecans, raisins, and matzos. Serve with banana vanilla ice cream (pg. 164).

4 matzos
¼ cup oil
egg replacer (to equal 3 eggs)
½ cup sweetener
½ tsp salt
1 tsp cinnamon
½ cup pecans, chopped
½ cup raisins
2-3 apples, cored and chopped

Preheat oven to 350°F. Break matzos into quarters and soak in a medium bowl of water until soft. Drain, but do not squeeze dry. In a medium casserole dish, mix together the oil, egg replacer, sweetener, salt, and cinnamon. Stir in the matzos, pecans, raisins, and apples. Bake for 45 minutes. Makes 4-6 servings.

C H O C O L A T E   " C H E E S E "   C A K E

Chocolate lovers beware. This dessert is truly magical.

3 cups medium tofu
1 cup margarine, melted
1-1½ cups dry sweetener
¾ cup cocoa powder
2 tsp vanilla extract
¼ tsp salt
½ cup soy milk
1 graham cracker pie crust (pg. 151)

In a blender or food processor, blend all the ingredients until smooth. Pour into a cheesecake pan that has been lined with a graham cracker crust. Chill for at least 12 hours before eating.

PINEAPPLE "CHEESE" CAKE

This cheesecake has just the right amount of pineapple zing. Garnish with Fresh fruit sauce (pg. 162) or fresh fruit slices.

2 ½ cups silken tofu
2 cups medium tofu
lemon zest from 1 lemon
1 ½ tsp lemon juice
½ cup corn syrup
½ cup dry sweetener
2 tbsp oil
2 ½ tsp vanilla extract
dash of salt
1 cup pineapple, finely chopped
1 graham cracker pie crust (pg. 151)

Preheat oven to 325° F. In a blender or food processor, blend the tofus, lemon zest, lemon juice, corn syrup, sweetener, oil, vanilla, and salt until very smooth. Stir in the pineapple and pour into cheesecake pan that has been lined with a graham cracker crust. Bake for 45-60 minutes until centre is well-set and a knife inserted into the centre comes out clean. Serve chilled.

JEN'S CHOCOLATE CAKE

Cake making has never been so easy. Crown with any delicious icing recipe from pgs. 159-160.

3 cups flour
2 tsp baking soda
½ tsp salt
¾ cup cocoa powder
¾ cup margarine
1 ½ cups dry sweetener
¼ cup water
2 cups soy milk
2 tsp vanilla extract

Preheat oven to 350°F. In a large bowl, stir together the flour, baking soda, salt, and cocoa powder. In a blender or food processor, blend together the margarine, sweetener, and water. Add this to flour mixture along with the milk and vanilla, and mix together gently until "just mixed." Pour into a lightly oiled cake pan and bake for 30 minutes. Test with a fork to see if done. When cooled, ice and serve.

AUNTIE BONNIE'S WACKY CAKE

A mouth-watering surprise. Perfect for birthdays, anniversaries, or any special occasion. And yup, that's vinegar in the list of ingredients.

1½ cups flour	1 cup dry sweetener
4 tbsp cocoa *or* carob powder	1½ tsp vanilla extract
1 tsp baking powder	1 tbsp vinegar
1 tsp baking soda	5 tbsp oil
½ tsp salt	1 cup cold water

Preheat oven to 325°F. In a large bowl, stir together the flour, cocoa powder, baking powder, baking soda, and salt. Add the sweetener, vanilla, vinegar, oil, and water and mix together gently until "just mixed." Pour into a lightly oiled cake pan and bake for 45-50 minutes. Test with a fork to see if done. When cooled, ice (pgs. 159-160) and serve.

VANILLA CAKE

These next two cakes are just the right dessert to top off a great meal. A light, airy cake with the essence of vanilla or lemon.

1½ cups flour	¾ cup soy milk
2 tsp baking powder	2 tsp vanilla extract
¼ tsp salt	¼ cup oil
¾ cup dry sweetener	egg replacer (to equal 1 egg)

Preheat oven to 350° F. In a large bowl, stir together the flour, baking powder, and salt. Add the sweetener, milk, vanilla, oil, and egg replacer and mix together gently until "just mixed." Pour into a lightly oiled cake pan and bake for 25-30 minutes. Check with a knife to see if done. When cooled, ice (pgs. 159-160) and serve.

LEMON CAKE

1½ cups flour	2 tsp lemon extract
2 tsp baking powder	zest of 1 lemon
¼ tsp salt	¼ cup oil
¾ cup dry sweetener	egg replacer (to equal 1 egg)
¾ cup soy milk	

Preheat oven to 350°F. In a large bowl, stir together the flour, baking powder, and salt. Add the sweetener, milk, lemon extract, lemon zest, oil, and egg replacer and mix together gently until "just mixed." Pour into a lightly oiled cake pan and bake for 25-30 minutes. Check with a knife to see if done. When cooled, ice (pgs. 159-160) and serve.

COUNTRY CARROT CAKE

No one will ever know that this vegan version of an all-time classic is so easy to prepare.

1½ cups flour
¾ cup dry sweetener
2 tsp baking powder
1 tsp cinnamon
¼ tsp salt
¾ cup soy milk

2 tsp vanilla extract
¼ cup oil
egg replacer (to equal 1 egg)
½ cup carrot, finely shredded
1 tsp fresh ginger, grated

Preheat oven to 350°F. In a large bowl, stir together the flour, sweetener, baking powder, cinnamon, and salt. Add the milk, vanilla, oil, egg replacer, carrot, and ginger and mix together gently until "just mixed." Pour into a lightly oiled cake pan and bake for 25-30 minutes. Check with a knife to see if done. When cooled, ice with To-Fruity Cream Cheese (pg. 91) and serve.

CHOCOLATE UPSIDE DOWN PUDDING CAKE

Don't let the name fool you. Is it a cake, is it pudding? It's just good!

1 cup flour
1 tbsp baking powder
¼ cup cocoa powder
¼ tsp salt
½ cup dry sweetener
½ cup margarine
½ cup soy milk
1 tsp vanilla extract

Sauce:
¾ cup dry sweetener
¼ cup cocoa powder
2 cups boiling water

Preheat oven to 350°F. In a large bowl, stir together the flour, baking powder, cocoa, and salt. Add the sweetener, margarine, milk, and vanilla and mix together gently until "just mixed." Spread in a lightly oiled casserole dish or loaf pan. Set aside.

In a medium bowl, mix together the sweetener and cocoa. Sprinkle evenly on top of the cake mixture. Carefully pour the boiling water over top. *Note: DO NOT MIX THIS!* It will do its own thing in the oven. Bake for 40 minutes. To serve, scoop out portions and serve in a bowl with ice cream (pg. 164).

The recipes for these icings are enough to frost 1 layer of a cake or 6 cupcakes.

CHOCOLATE ICING

This icing is the perfect finishing touch – velvety and oh-so-smooth.

1 cup cold water
5 tbsp flour
1 cup dry sweetener
1 tsp vanilla extract
6 tbsp margarine
3 tbsp cocoa powder

In a small saucepan, whisk together the water and flour constantly over medium heat until thick (about the consistency of glue). Be careful not to burn it! Once thick, remove from heat and cool off completely by setting the pot in a slightly larger pan of cold water, or a sink with a bit of cold water. While it's cooling, in a medium bowl, mix together the sweetener, vanilla, margarine, and cocoa powder until well mixed. Add the cooled flour mixture to the bowl and stir together until there are no lumps. Let cool in the fridge for 30-60 minutes – before using.

COFFEE ICING

A grown-up tasting sweet treat.

2 cups medium tofu
½ cup dry sweetener
¼ cup oil
2 tsp vanilla extract
2-3 tbsp coffee *or* **Inka**
dash of salt

In a blender or food processor blend all the ingredients together until well mixed. Pour into a medium bowl and chill for at least 2 hours before using.

NUT BUTTER ICING

A scrumptious topping that is Sarah's favourite.

3 tbsp margarine
½ cup dry sweetener
⅓ cup peanut butter (or other nut butter)
2 tbsp soy milk
⅓ cup nuts, chopped (optional)

In a medium bowl or food processor, mix together the margarine, sweetener, and nut butter. Add the milk and mix well. Stir in nuts before using.

MAPLE BUTTERESQUE ICING

This icing is a dazzler. A decadent way to top any cake.

> ½ **cup margarine**
> **3 cup powdered sugar***
> **6 tbsp maple syrup**
> ¼ **cup walnuts or pecans, chopped**

In a medium bowl, thoroughly mix together the margarine and sugar. Stir in the maple syrup until consistency is light and spreadable. Stir in nuts before using.

*You can powder sugar yourself by blending sugar in a dry blender or food processor until powdered.

MARVELOUS MAPLE ICING

A perfect icing for your perfect cake.

> ¼ **cup margarine**
> **2 ¼ cups powdered sugar***
> **2 tbsp soy milk**
> **1 tsp maple syrup**

In a food processor or medium bowl, mix together the margarine and 1 cup of the powdered sugar. Add remaining sugar alternately with milk, mixing until smooth. Stir in the maple syrup until consistency is light and spreadable.

"ANYTHING GOES" ICING

A versatile classic. Vary the colour for each occasion.

> ¼ **cup margarine**
> **2 ¼ cups powdered sugar***
> **2 tbsp soy milk**
> **1 tsp "Anything Goes" extract (lemon, peppermint, or maple extract)**

In a food processor or medium bowl, mix together the margarine with 1 cup of the powdered sugar. Add remaining sugar alternately with milk, mixing until smooth. Stir in the extract until consistency is light and spreadable.

* You can powder sugar yourself in a blender or food processor.

SOY MILK WHIPPED CREAM

And you thought you'd never get to eat anything this scrumptious again.

- **¼ cup soy milk**
- **2-4 tbsp sweetener**
- **½ tsp vanilla extract**
- **1 tsp cornstarch**
- **½ cup oil**

In a blender or food processor, blend together the milk, sweetener, vanilla, and cornstarch. Slowly drizzle in the oil while the blender is running. Blend until smooth and creamy. Chill for 1 hour before using. Makes approx. ¾ cup.

TOFU WHIPPED CREAM

A light and satisfying dessert topping.

- **1½ cups soft tofu**
- **2-4 tbsp sweetener**
- **2 tsp vanilla extract**
- **2 tsp cornstarch**

In a blender or food processor, blend all the ingredients well. Chill for 1 hour before using. Makes approx. 1 cup.

BANANA-RAMA CREAM

Enjoy this rich, creamy sauce over fruit salad, oatmeal, even pancakes.

- **1 banana, chopped**
- **2 tbsp oil**
- **1 tsp vanilla extract**
- **½ tsp lemon juice**

In a blender or food processor, blend together the banana, oil, vanilla, and lemon juice until smooth and creamy. Use immediately. Add a little water if you want to thin it out a little. Makes approx. ¾ cup.

CASHEW CREAM

Use this as a creamy topping for fruit, puddings, or cake.

> **½ cup raw cashews**
> **1 cup white grape juice**
> **¼ tsp vanilla extract**

In a blender or food processor, grind the cashew nuts into an even meal. Add the grape juice and vanilla and blend together until smooth and creamy. Strain out any lumps and chill. Makes approx. ¾ cup.

FRESH FRUIT SAUCE

A fruit-filled version of a cool favourite.

> **2 cups fresh fruit (e.g., blueberries, strawberries)**
> **¼ cup maple syrup**

In a blender or food processor, blend together 1 ½ cups of the fruit and maple syrup until saucy. Pour into a medium bowl and stir in the remaining fruit. Spoon over dessert. Makes approx. ½ cup.

SINFUL CHOCOLATE PUDDING

Chocolate lovers take note. Bask in the most delicious of chocolate treats.

> **1 cup soft tofu**
> **¼ cup oil**
> **½ cup sweetener**
> **4 tbsp cocoa powder**
> **¼ tsp salt**
> **1½ tsp vanilla extract**

In a blender or food processor, blend together all the ingredients until smooth and creamy. Chill well before serving. Makes 2-4 servings.

CREAMY BANANA PUDDING

Delicate banana flavouring accents this creamy dessert.

1 cup soft tofu
2 bananas, chopped
3 tbsp dates, chopped (optional)
2 ½ tbsp oil
¼ cup sweetener
1 tsp lemon juice
dash of salt
½ tbsp vanilla extract

In a blender or food processor, blend together all the ingredients until smooth and creamy. Chill well before serving. Makes 2-4 servings.

"ANYTHING GOES" FRUIT PUDDING

A dessert spectacular. Creat any combination you wish.

1 cup soft tofu
2 ½ tbsp oil
¼ cup sweetener
dash of salt

¾ cup "Anything Goes" fresh *or* **frozen fruit (your choice)**
½ tsp vanilla extract
½ tbsp lemon juice

In a blender or food processor, blend together all the ingredients until smooth and creamy. Chill well before serving. Makes 2-4 servings.

RACY RAISIN RICE PUDDING

This is a great recipe if you have leftover rice. Serve hot or cold with soy milk or cream.

2-3 cups soy milk
2 cups cooked rice
1 ½ tsp cinnamon
1 tbsp vanilla extract

1 cup raisins
½ cup slivered almonds
¼ cup sweetener

In a medium saucepan, add the milk, cooked rice, cinnamon, vanilla, raisins, almonds, and sweetener and bring to a boil. Reduce heat and simmer on low heat for 15-20 minutes until pudding thickens to desired consistency, stirring occasionally. Makes 2 or more servings.

CHOCOLATE ICE CREAM

Enjoy this old time favourite, then watch how everyone screams for more ice cream.

2 cups soft tofu
1 cup soy milk
½ cup oil
½-1 cup dry sweetener
¼ cup cocoa powder
1 tbsp vanilla extract
dash of salt

In a food processor, blend together all the ingredients until very smooth and creamy. Place in a sealable container and freeze. Remove from freezer and defrost for 20-40 minutes. Place back in food processor and blend again. Spoon back into container (at this point, you may add chocolate chips or crumbled cookies if you like), then re-freeze. Remove from freezer 5 minutes before serving. Makes 4-6 servings.

VANILLA BANANA ICE CREAM

Rich, flavourful, and easy to make.

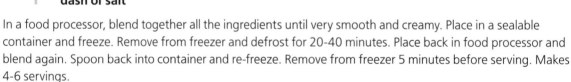

1 cup soft tofu
1 cup soy milk
½ cup oil
2 bananas, chopped
⅓ cup dry sweetener
2 tbsp lemon juice
1 ½ tbsp vanilla extract
dash of salt

In a food processor, blend together all the ingredients until very smooth and creamy. Place in a sealable container and freeze. Remove from freezer and defrost for 20-40 minutes. Place back in food processor and blend again. Spoon back into container and re-freeze. Remove from freezer 5 minutes before serving. Makes 4-6 servings.

"ANYTHING GOES" FRUITY ICE CREAM

Use whatever fruit you'd like with this — strawberries, blueberries, peaches. . . .

> **2 cups soft tofu**
> **½ cup soy milk**
> **½ cup oil**
> **1 cup dry sweetener**
> **1 tbsp lemon juice**
> **1½ cups "Anything Goes" fresh** *or* **frozen fruit (your choice)**
> **1 tbsp vanilla extract**
> **dash of salt**

In a food processor, combine all the ingredients except for ½ a cup of the fruit, and blend together until very smooth and creamy. Place in a sealable container and freeze. Remove from freezer and defrost for 20-40 minutes. Place back in food processor and blend again. Spoon back into container and add the remaining fruit. Re-freeze. Remove from freezer 5 minutes before serving. Makes 4-6 servings.

COFFEE ICE CREAM

A creamy, delicous blend.

> **¼ cup soy milk**
> **5 tbsp oil**
> **1 banana, chopped**
> **¼ cup sweetener**
> **2-3 tsp instant coffee powder** *or* **Inka**

In a food processor, blend together all the ingredients until very smooth and creamy. Place in a sealable container and freeze. Remove from freezer and defrost for 20-40 minutes. Place back in food processor and blend again. Spoon back into container and re-freeze. Remove from freezer 5 minutes before serving. Makes 4-6 servings.

Check out pages 189-190 for other fantastic frozen treats!

Vegan
Odds & Sods

This is a collection of wonderful and flavourful recipes that just didn't seem to fit anywhere else in this book, but that doesn't make them any less great. Included here are condiments, dips, spicy and savoury toppings, and healthy snacks. Fearlessly indulge yourself in the exotica of vegan miscellany!

FLAX EGGS

Purchase an inexpensive coffee grinder to use for grinding flax seeds or spices. Don't use your regular coffee grinder unless you want everything to taste like coffee. This recipe makes enough ground flax seeds for four "eggs" (see below for proportions).

- **¹/₂ cup flax seeds**

In a coffee grinder, process the flax seeds until powdered. Keep powder stored in refrigerator in a container with a tight-fitting lid. 2 tbsp ground flax seeds + 3 tbsp water = 1 egg.

In a small bowl, combine all ingredients and allow to sit for 2–3 minutes before adding to baking.

SOY MILK MAYONNAISE

One of the greatest challenges facing vegans is having to abstain from that fantastic creamy condiment known as mayonnaise. But fear not: it's time to welcome mayonnaise back into your life.

- **¾ cup soy milk**
- **1½ tbsp lemon juice** *or* **vinegar**
- **¾ tsp salt**
- **dash of pepper**
- **¾ cup oil**

In a blender or food processor, blend together (on high) the milk, lemon juice, salt, and pepper for 1 minute. Add the oil gradually while the blender is running until mayonnaise becomes thick. Store in the refrigerator in a clean, dry container with a tight-fitting lid. Will keep for 7-10 days. Makes approx. 1 ½ cups.

TOFU MAYONNAISE

- **¾ cup soft** *or* **medium tofu**
- **2 tbsp lemon juice** *or* **vinegar**
- **½ tsp salt**
- **dash of pepper**
- **2 tbsp oil**

In a blender or food processor, blend together (on high) the tofu, lemon juice, salt, pepper, and oil until thick and creamy. Store in the refrigerator in a clean, dry container with a tight-fitting lid. Will keep for 7-10 days. Makes approx. 1 ½ cups.

FAUX SOUR CREAM

Since you cut sour cream out of your diet, have baked potatoes, perogies, and burritos not tasted the same? Bask again in the rapturous tang of this soy-based topping.

> **2 cups soft** *or* **medium tofu**
> **¼ cup oil**
> **3 tbsp lemon juice** *or* **vinegar**
> **1 tsp sweetener**
> **1 tbsp Braggs** *or* **soy sauce**

In a blender or food processor, blend together all the ingredients until smooth and creamy. Store in the refrigerator in a clean, dry container with a tight-fitting lid. Will keep up to 5 days. *Note: This may separate upon refrigeration and may need to be re-mixed before using.* Makes approx. 1 ½ cups.

KLASSIC KETCHUP

After trying this sweet, savoury recipe you'll realize that store-bought ketchup is nothing more than a pale impostor compared to the way "real" ketchup is supposed to taste.

> **1 6-oz can of tomato paste**
> **1½ tbsp vinegar**
> **1 tbsp sweetener**
> **1 tsp Braggs or soy sauce**
>
> **⅛ tsp dried basil**
> **⅛ tsp paprika**
> **⅛ tsp salt**
> **2½ tbsp water**

In a medium saucepan, simmer all the ingredients on medium-low heat for about 10-15 minutes, stirring often. Set aside to cool and store in the refrigerator in a clean, dry container with a tight-fitting lid. This will keep for about 2 weeks, but make sure the lid is tight or it will go bad! Makes approx. ¾ cup.

CRISPY CROUTONS

Sure, lettuce and other assorted vegetables are crispy enough on their own, but your salad will shine when served up with these crunchy, toasted delights.

> **2 cups sourdough bread, cubed (pg. 127)**
> **1 tbsp olive oil**
>
> **1 tsp thyme**
> **½ tsp pepper**

Preheat the oven to 375°F. In a large bowl, toss together all of the ingredients. Spread out evenly on a baking sheet and bake for about 10-15 minutes, until golden brown. Set aside to cool and store in a clean, dry container with a tight-fitting lid. Makes 2 cups.

VERSATILE VEGETABLE STOCK

A flavourful stock is an important and crucial ingredient for soups and sauces. A helpful tip to ensure a delicious stock: if you won't eat what's rotting in your fridge, then don't put it into your stock. You could include vegetables that are just past their prime, or even vegetable trimmings, in this recipe, but try to add at least 3 or more of the veggies listed here. Use this stock for your soups and sauces. It also freezes well.

> **assorted vegetables (e.g., onions, celery, carrots, potatoes, garlic), roughly chopped**
> **10 cups water**
> **½ tsp salt**
> **⅛ tsp peppercorns**

Wash, cut, and prepare vegetables. Place all the ingredients into a large soup pot and bring to a boil. Turn heat down and let simmer until stock has reduced to half the original amount. Remove all the vegetables with a slotted spoon. Remove pot from heat and let the stock cool. Pour into clean, dry containers with a tight-fitting lid and store in the freezer or refrigerator. Makes approx. 8 cups.

If you're not freezing the stock, use it within 5 days. If freezing, make sure you leave a little room for the stock to expand in the container.

I like to store my stock in 4-cup containers so that if I'm going to make soup, I can pull the stock out of the freezer the night before and it will be ready for me by dinnertime. No muss, no fuss! (S)

CAJUN SPICE

This spicy condiment sparkles up any dish that it's matched with. Use cajun spice in place of salt and pepper to season burgers, fried tofu, or tofu jerky. You can even try it to spice up your popcorn.

> **1 tbsp dried onion flakes**   **1 tsp salt**
> **1 tsp fennel seeds**   **1 tsp dried oregano**
> **1 tsp coriander seeds**   **¼ tsp pepper**
> **¼ cup chili powder**   **dash of cayenne pepper**
> **2 tsp garlic powder**

In a blender, food processor, or coffee grinder, grind the onion flakes, fennel seeds, and coriander seeds until powdered. You can also use a rolling pin to grind the spices between 2 sheets of wax paper. In a small bowl, stir together the chili and garlic powders, salt, oregano, pepper, and cayenne. Combine both mixtures and store in a clean, dry container with a tight-fitting lid. Makes approx. ½ cup.

GOMASHIO

A simple yet wonderful Japanese condiment. Very addictive and satisfying, use it as a topping for any recipe or in place of salt on cooked vegetables or in salads or soups.

1 cup raw sesame seeds
1-2 tsp sea salt
1 tsp kelp powder

In a dry frying pan, heat the sesame seeds, salt, and kelp on medium-high for 3-5 minutes, stirring constantly until seeds start to pop and brown. Remove from heat and set aside to cool. Place in a blender, food processor, or coffee grinder and grind for 3 seconds. You don't want the seeds to become powdered, just lightly ground up. Store in a sealable container. Makes 1 cup.

BALSAMIC ONIONS

This recipe can be used in a variety of ways. It's a great addition to any sauce or stir-fry, or simply delicious atop salads.

1 large onion, peeled, cut, and separated
1 tsp salt
½ tsp pepper

1½ tsp sweetener
1 tbsp oil
2 tbsp balsamic vinegar

In a medium saucepan, sauté the onion, salt, pepper, and sweetener in oil on medium heat until onions are a dark golden brown, stirring often. Transfer to a medium bowl and stir onions together with the vinegar. Set aside and let sit for 10 or more minutes. Makes 1 to 1 ½ cups, depending on size of onion.

FAUX PARMESAN CHEESE

Simply the world's greatest faux cheese topping. Enjoy.

¼ cup nutritional yeast flakes
¼ cup sesame seeds, toasted
¼ tsp salt

In a blender, food processor, or coffee grinder, grind the yeast, sesame seeds, and salt until completely milled. Store in a clean, dry container with a tight-fitting lid. Makes ½ a cup.

FAUX FETA

A delightfully tangy tofu masterpiece. Use in Gourmet Greek salad (pg. 70) or atop pizza.

> ¼ cup olive oil
> ¼ cup water
> ½ cup red wine vinegar
> 2 tsp salt
> 1 tbsp dried basil
> ½ tsp pepper
> ½ tsp dried oregano
> 1 pkg firm herb tofu, cubed *or* crumbled

In a large bowl, mix together the oil, water, vinegar, salt, basil, pepper, and oregano. Marinade the tofu in the mixture for at least an hour or more. Makes approx. 1 ½ cups.

BAKED SESAME FRIES

Serve these yummy fries with homemade ketchup (pg. 168) or some other yummy dipping sauce. If you like to spice things up, use cajun spice (pg. 169) instead of gomashio.

> 4-6 large potatoes, sliced
> 3 tbsp olive oil
> 2 tbsp gomashio (pg. 170)

Preheat oven to 400°F. Slice the potatoes to the desired width and place them in a medium bowl with some cold water. Let sit for 5 minutes. Drain potatoes and toss together with the oil and gomashio. Lay potatoes on a non-stick cookie sheet and bake for 30 minutes. Flip fries after 15 minutes. Makes 2-4 servings.

DRY-ROASTED SOY SNACKS

A delicious snack for any occasion.

> 2 cups dry soybeans
> 1-2 tsp seasoning (e.g., salt, cajun spice, pepper, red pepper flakes, cumin, curry)

In a large bowl filled with water, soak soybeans overnight. Preheat oven to 250°F. Drain beans well and pour back into the empty large bowl. Add your desired seasoning, stirring together well, and spread out onto a large baking sheet. Bake for 3-4 hours. Let cool before serving. Makes 2 cups.

CHICKPEA NIBBLES

A great nibbly snack.

2 cups cooked *or* **canned chickpeas (garbanzo beans)**
1-2 tsp seasoning (e.g., cajun spice, pepper, red pepper flakes, cumin, garlic, curry)
1 tbsp oil

Preheat oven to 400°F. In a medium bowl, toss together the chickpeas and desired seasoning in the oil. Stir together well and spread out onto a large baking sheet. Bake for 45-60 minutes, flipping after 20 minutes. Let cool before serving. Makes 2 cups.

ORIGINAL PEPPER TOFU JERKY

Another amazing tofu transformation. The cries of shock and pleasure should be enough to convince you that this is truly a great recipe.

1 lb extra-firm tofu
½ cup Braggs *or* **soy sauce**
3-4 tbsp liquid smoke
⅛ cup water
1 tbsp onion powder
1 tsp garlic powder *or* **1 clove garlic, crushed**
1 tbsp pepper
1 tsp sweetener

Cut the drained tofu into long narrow strips (about ¼ inch thickness). They may look big, but they will shrink during baking. In a small bowl, whisk together the Braggs, liquid smoke, water, onion powder, garlic, pepper, and sweetener. Place the tofu strips in a shallow baking pan or on a cookie sheet and pour the marinade over them. Let them marinate for several hours or overnight for best results.

Cook the tofu in a food dehydrator (follow directions) or bake in the oven for about 4-6 hours at 200°F. Turn the tofu over once every hour so it bakes evenly. Continue until the texture is very chewy, but not crispy. Tofu jerky will keep indefinitely. Store in a container with a tight-fitting lid.

CAJUN JERKY

1 lb extra-firm tofu
½ cup Braggs *or* **soy sauce**
3 tbsp liquid smoke
⅛ cup water
1 tbsp cajun spice (pg. 169)
1 tsp sweetener

Cut the drained tofu into long narrow strips (about ¼ inch thickness). They may look big, but they will shrink during baking. In a small bowl, whisk together the Braggs, liquid smoke, water, cajun spice, and sweetener. Place the tofu strips in a shallow baking pan or cookie sheet and pour the marinade over them. Let them marinate for several hours or overnight for best results.

Cook the tofu in a food dehydrator (follow directions) or bake in the oven for about 4-6 hours at 200°F. Turn the tofu over once every hour so it bakes evenly. Continue until the texture is very chewy, but not crispy. Tofu jerky will keep indefinitely. Store in a container with a tight-fitting lid.

HAWAIIAN JERKY

1 lb extra-firm tofu
⅛ cup Braggs *or* **soy sauce**
½ cup pineapple juice
1 tsp powdered ginger
¼ tsp pepper
⅛ tsp cayenne
1 tsp garlic powder
1 tbsp sweetener

Cut the drained tofu into long narrow strips (about ¼ inch thickness). They may look big, but they will shrink during baking. In a small bowl, whisk together the Braggs, pineapple juice, ginger, pepper, cayenne, garlic powder, and sweetener. Place the tofu strips in a shallow baking pan or on a cookie sheet and pour the marinade over them. Let them marinate for several hours or overnight for best results.

Cook the tofu in a food dehydrator (follow directions) or bake in the oven for about 4-6 hours at 200°F. Turn the tofu over once every hour so it bakes evenly. Continue until the texture is very chewy, but not crispy. Tofu jerky will keep indefinitely. Store in a container with a tight-fitting lid.

Vegan Kids Stuff

Some of my fondest childhood memories come from the kitchen. The smells, sounds, and tastes that surrounded me as a child helped me to become the vegan food-lover I am today. I remember sitting on the kitchen table in an apron that covered my feet, food all over my hands and face, helping to pour ingredients into my Mum's big beige mixing bowl. I felt terribly important and was proud to help. (S)

Children love to lend a hand in the kitchen. We're all busy trying to do too much in too little time; when it comes to food, we grab a quick bite, order in, or make something that requires only water and a microwave. But that's not really eating. We need to take the time to slow down and teach ourselves and our children to savour the food we eat, to appreciate what we put into our bodies.

In this chapter we have included recipes that the children in your life can help with and some they can do on their own, as well as activities to keep them busy. We've also included tried and true, nummy-yummy recipes to please even the pickiest eater.

Our wish is that you pass on an appreciation for healthy food and spend some time with your kids in the kitchen making memories to last a lifetime.

TIPS FOR FEEDING KIDS

EAT TOGETHER

We're all busy. Do you occasionally find yourself eating in front of the TV or standing over the stove picking out of a pot? We grab meals when we can. But the single most important thing you can to do to give your kids healthy attitudes toward food is to sit down at the table and eat with them. It's also important to eat what they're eating instead of serving separate "grown-up food" and "kid food." Talk about your meal, how it tastes and smells. Create eating experiences that are significant, happy times that involve conversation and laughter as well as nourishment. Above all, keep your meal free of stressful nagging and criticism.

MONKEY SEE, MONKEY DO

While considering your child's eating habits, take a good look at your own. Children learn from your example, so you owe it to them, and to yourself, to improve your own eating habits.

- Eat a good, hearty breakfast. A full belly makes for a happy and attentive child.

- Eat your veggies! Let your children see you eating and enjoying raw vegetables.

- Eat healthy snacks. Instead of junk food, nibble on fresh and dried fruit, vegetable sticks, soy yoghurt, and air-popped popcorn. Check pgs. 181-185 for some good snack ideas.

OFFER HEALTHY FOODS

Children won't crave or beg for cookies and candies if they are never around or offered. Keep around only the foods you want your kids to eat. Have fresh fruit, celery and carrot sticks, radishes, cucumbers, and other vegetables washed, cut, and available in the fridge. In the summer, try juice popsicles (pg. 190) or to fudge-sicles (pg. 189).

DON'T FORBID ANY FOODS

This may sound like a contradiction, but it's best not to make a big deal out of "bad" foods. Even though we wish our kids never touched junk food, let them have it once in awhile, perhaps on special occasions. By allowing kids to eat what they want at birthday parties and school outings, they'll learn that junk food is something to be eaten sporadically. They'll also learn the important lesson that these foods can occasionally fit into an overall healthy diet.

HOW MUCH TO EAT

Many parents agonize over how little or how much their children consume. Children whose parents aren't overly controlling of their food intake are in a better position to regulate how much they eat themselves. Remember that your child is much smaller than you and requires smaller portions. He or she also needs to eat more frequently. A good rule for children under six is to serve one tablespoon of each food item for each year at each meal. For example, serve three tablespoons of applesauce to a three-year-old. Kids' food intake will vary as their growth speeds up and slows down. Some days they may seem to eat very little, but they will make up for it by eating more the next day or the day after. By letting kids decide when to have more and when they've had enough, you are helping them to recognize the internal cues of hunger and fullness. These cues will help them regulate their food intake and weight for life.

Limit fruit juice intake to half a cup per day. Offer juice after meals, and not before when it may curb a child's appetite for more wholesome foods. Some children may better tolerate white grape juice than apple juice. Offer fresh filtered water at all times. Clean, clear water is the best way to a healthy body.

WHAT TO EAT

Encourage your child to help plan meals and select veggies at the market. Get them involved in meal preparation. Even a two-year-old can tear lettuce for a salad and help wash produce. You can ease tensions at the table by including them in decisions on what to make for dinner. Children will take pride in a meal they've helped to plan and prepare. Encourage your children to try everything you offer, but don't force them to eat what they don't want. Don't make a fuss if they refuse a certain dish. Eventually they'll come around. We've heard too many horror stories about parents who force their kids to eat foods they don't want. Food is not about power; it's about nourishment. If your child is picky, take a deep breath and be patient.

DON'T USE FOOD AS A WEAPON

Never use food as a bribe or a reward. And never send kids to bed without supper, or keep them at the table until they've cleared their plates. Let food be what it is – a source of nourishment and enjoyment.

TEACH THEM TO LOVE VEGETABLES

Some vegetables have strong flavours and many kids will refuse to try them. Introduce a variety of different vegetables into your child's diet as soon as possible. They'll quickly become accustomed to the tastes. Don't force anything on your child; just offer and encourage. Always keep fruits and vegetables in the fridge, washed, cut, and ready to eat. Remember that calories, not protein, are the main issue with young children. While it's important to have raw fruits and vegetables in any child's diet, don't forget about high-density foods such as tofu, nut and seed butters, avocados, and olives.

Let kids grow their own food. They will be fascinated by the process of seeds turning into plants. Even if you only have a flowerpot on the kitchen window sill, it's easy to grow vegetables such as sprouts, parsley, and radishes.

RAISING HEALTHY EATERS

Ours is an obsessed, sick, and sad culture! Children, especially girls, as young as nine and even younger are dieting and worrying about their figures. It has got to stop. You can help by teaching your children to love their bodies, their imaginations, and the food they eat. It all starts in the kitchen.

FUN IN THE KITCHEN

Have you ever noticed that kids are at their brattiest just as you're working on making that perfect vegan cream sauce? Here are some ideas to keep them busy and out of your hair while you're cooking meals:

Doing Their Own Thing

Get a plastic storage container and fill it with items such as a kids-sized apron, plastic utensils, wooden spoons, small bowls, measuring cups, measuring spoons, empty spice jars, and a small rolling pin. Let them pretend they're making dinner when you are. Or allow them to help when you're baking or cooking, using their own kitchen utensils.

Edible Necklace

This is a good project to bring along before heading to the grocery store with your kids. They can munch on the necklace while shopping. Get some healthy cereal and/or candy with holes, as well as some healthy shoestring licorice. Have your kids thread the candy or cereal on the licorice. When complete, tie the ends together. This will keep them busy noshing while you do other things!

Flour Fun

Sprinkle flour over a baking sheet. They can draw letters, numbers, shapes. Play hangman or other common games in the flour.

Painting with Pudding

This makes clean-up a lot of fun because it's lickable! Prepare the pudding recipe on page 162 ahead of time. When it's ready, let your kids fingerpaint with the pudding on waxed paper (or a clean table, if you dare!).

Personal Place Mats

Personal place mats make eating special. They also make excellent gifts! Get some heavy construction paper or card stock, crayons, glue, sparkles, and anything else you can think of. Let the kids draw their own pictures on the paper, adding whatever other elements they have. Use clear Mac-Tac to cover the front and back of the drawing or have it laminated.

Macaroni Pictures and Sculptures

Use various shapes of pasta for different looks. Let your kids glue these onto coloured paper for imaginative 3-D pictures.

Taste Testing

Clean and cut up various food items. Blindfold your child and have them taste and smell different foods. Get them to describe the various tastes, smells, and textures before they try to guess what it is. For fun, tell them that olives are eyeballs and spaghetti noodles are brains and watch the looks on their faces!

PLAY DOUGH

Every kid deserves to play with play dough, especially if it's home-made.

1 cup flour
½ cup salt
2 tbsp oil
2 tbsp cream of tartar
1 cup water
food colouring

In a medium saucepan, cook the flour, salt, oil, tartar, and water over medium-high heat, stirring constantly until stiff. Cool and knead out lumps while kneading in the food colouring. Store in a container with a tight-fitting lid. Makes 1 cup of dough.

ORNAMENTS

1 cup cornstarch
2 cups baking soda
1¼ cups cold water

In a medium saucepan, cook the cornstarch, baking soda, and water over medium-high heat, stirring constantly, for about 4 minutes or until mixture thickens into a moist, mashed potato-like consistency. Place in a bowl and cover with a cloth until its cool enough to knead. Knead well and roll out the dough to cut into shapes. Use a straw to place a small hole in the top for a ribbon or string so you can hang the ornament somewhere special. Allow to dry for 24 hours before painting with paints.

You can also use this recipe for making sculptures. Form clay into desired shapes and let dry for 36 hours before painting.

GLUE / PASTE

Use a paint brush, popsicle stick, or even your fingers to spread this paste!

½ cup flour
⅔ cup water
1 tbsp salt

In a small bowl, mix the flour, water and salt together. Stir until paste is creamy. You can store left-over glue in a clean, dry jar with a tight-fitting lid. Makes approximately 1 cup of paste.

PAPIER-MÂCHÉ

1 cup flour
2 tbsp salt (prevents moulding)
1 cup water
newspaper strips

In a large bowl, mix the flour, salt, and water together until smooth. Cut newspaper into strips and soak them in the mixture. Use your fingers to squeeze off excess paste and layer on to whatever base you are using (balloon, wire rim, etc.). Allow to dry for 24 hours before painting. Makes approximately 1½ cups of paste.

BUBBLE SOLUTION

You can make your own bubble wands by twisting one end of a pipe cleaner into a large loop, or use a straw as a bubble pipe.

¾ cup dish soap
1 cup water
¼ cup white corn syrup

Place soap, water, and corn syrup in clean, dry jar. Stir together with a large spoon. Makes approximately 2 cups of solution.

FUN SNACKS FOR KIDS

Let your children have some control over when and how much they eat. Even toddlers can have their own personal snack shelf stocked with bread sticks, dried fruit, and other nutritious snacks. Snacking is an important way for young children to get the calories they need. Spend some time getting messy, and exploring different taste combinations. Your kids will love to make these recipes with you!

MELON BOWL

watermelon
various other melons
melon baller *or* **spoon**

Cut a watermelon in half. If your kids are old enough, have them help scoop out the inside using a small spoon or melon baller. Set aside in a separate bowl. Cut the other melons and have the kids scoop them out, then fill the watermelon bowl with the various melon balls. Serve with fruit sauce (pg. 162) or apple dip (pg. 183).

ANTS ON A LOG

Munch away on these little ants.

celery sticks, washed
peanut butter *or* **nut butter**
raisins

If your kids are old enough, let them use a dull knife to fill up the centre cavity of the celery sticks with the nut butter. Top with raisins.

ANTS ON A RAFT

crackers
peanut butter *or* **nut butter**
raisins

If your kids are old enough, let them use a dull knife to spread the nut butter on the crackers. Top with raisins. If you like, you can use jam or some other spread for your creations.

DROWNING ANTS

> **bowl of soy yoghurt** *or* **pudding (pgs. 162-163)**
> **raisins**

Mix the raisins in the bowl of yoghurt or pudding. Get your kids to try to fish out the ants and eat them!

APPLE VOLCANO

> **apple, top removed**
> **peanut butter** *or* **nut spread**
> **raisins**

Using a teaspoon, help your child scoop out the inside of the apple. Fill it with peanut butter and top with raisins. If this is to be eaten later, brush apple edges with lemon juice to prevent browning and wrap in foil.

BANANA CREAM PIE

Super messy but that's what being in the kitchen is all about!

> **banana**
> **graham crackers**
> **whipped cream (pg. 161)**

Have your kids tear up the banana into bite-size pieces. Place on graham crackers, then add a glob of whipped cream. Place another graham cracker on top and then squish it down.

ICE CREAM COOKIES

> **graham crackers** *or* **cookies**
> **ice cream (pgs. 164-165) or whipped cream (pg. 161)**

Spread ½ a teaspoon of ice cream or whipped cream between 2 crackers. Freeze for 30-60 minutes.

MAPLE APPLE DIP

A great after-school snack.

1 cup silken tofu
½ tsp cinnamon
½ tsp vanilla extract
¼ cup maple syrup
1-2 medium apples, sliced

In a blender or food processor, blend together the tofu, cinnamon, vanilla, and maple syrup until smooth. Spoon into a small bowl and use as a dip for the slices of apple and other fruits. Makes approximately 1 ½ cups.

HUKI-LA SMOOTHIE

This recipe is also great frozen. Pour into popsicle moulds and eat on a hot summer day!

2-4 ice cubes
1 cup silken *or* **soft tofu**
4-6 strawberries
1 cup guava *or* **tropical fruit juice**
1 banana, frozen
½ cup pineapple *or* **apple juice**
¼ cup pineapple (optional)

In a blender or food processor, blend together all the ingredients until creamy. Garnish with more pineapple. Makes 2 servings.

FRESH FRUIT KABOBS

wooden skewers (1 per person)
bananas, chopped
apples (e.g., red, golden delicious), chopped
green, red, and purple grapes
pineapple chunks
melon, chopped
apple dip (pg. 183) *or* soy yoghurt
coconut, shredded

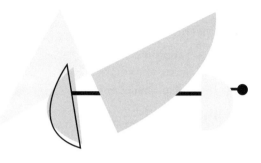

Cut the fruit into bite-sized chunks. Pour dip onto a large plate, and the shredded coconut onto another plate. Slide pieces of fruit onto each skewer, making sure to include a piece of each kind of fruit, and leaving enough room for your fingers to grab. Hold the kabob at each end and roll it in the dip, and then in the coconut. If you like, you can roll the kabobs in something other than coconut; try granola, nuts, or raisins.

TRAVELLERS' TRAIL MIX

When you're hungry for a snack, reach in and munch away!

granola (pg. 52)
nuts and seeds (e.g., peanuts, cashews, almonds, sunflower seeds)
dried fruit (e.g., raisins, apricots, cranberries)
cereal rings
carob chips

Add all the ingredients in a small plastic bag or clean, dry jar. Seal it tight and then shake until well-mixed.

VEGGIES IN A BLANKET

You can add any veggies you want to this recipe. The more the merrier!

2 flour tortillas
2 tbsp cream cheese (pg. 89)
1 carrot, grated
2 lettuce leaves

Warm the tortillas in a dry pan on low heat. Lay each one on a plate and lightly spread the cream cheese over each. Add carrots and lettuce (or whatever vegetables you choose), and roll. Makes 2 servings.

A portable, totally edible veggie treat! After you've eaten the veggies, you can eat the bowl!

> **green, yellow, *or* red pepper, cored**
> **celery, chopped**
> **carrots, chopped**
> **broccoli, chopped**
> **snow peas, chopped**
> **creamy salad dressing (pgs. 77-81)**

Cut the pepper in half width-wise. Remove the seeds and the white veins from the inside. Now you have two pieces, one of which will be your bowl. Cut the other half of the pepper into thin slices. Cut the celery, carrots, broccoli, and snow peas into bite-size pieces and add to the pepper slices. Spoon a little salad dressing into the bottom of your pepper bowl and place the assorted veggies inside.

MEALS FOR THE PICKY

When it comes to making meals for kids, let go of any rigid ideas you may have about what goes into a meal and experiment with ingredients to come up with recipes they will love. Even better, let them in on the process and help with making the meal! These recipes have been tested on some of the pickiest eaters out there. Let's hope they work on yours.

ALPHABET LENTILS

ABCDEFG, eat your lentils 1-2-3!

> **¾ cup dry lentils**
> **1 small onion, minced**
> **1 carrot, finely diced**
> **4 mushrooms, finely chopped**
> **1 cup tomato sauce (pg. 85)**
> **2½ cups vegetable stock**
> **2 tbsp Braggs *or* soy sauce**
> **½ cup dry alphabet pasta**

In a medium saucepan, combine the lentils, onions, carrots, mushrooms, tomato sauce, stock, and Braggs. Cover and simmer for 20-30 minutes, or until lentils are tender. Add the dry pasta. Cover and simmer for 10 more minutes, or until the pasta is tender, stirring occasionally. Makes 2 servings.

Serve this and watch with amazement as they gobble it up.

2 tbsp peanut butter or **nut butter**
1 tbsp Braggs or **soy sauce**
1 tbsp orange or **apple juice**
4 cups broccoli, chopped

In a small saucepan on medium heat, stir together the nut butter, Braggs, and orange juice. Heat until warmed through. Meanwhile, steam broccoli for about 3 minutes until it is tender but not fragile. Drain and toss with the sauce. Makes 1-2 servings.

Serve with an assortment of vegetables sticks, fruit slices, and crackers.

¾ cup cooked or **canned chickpeas (garbanzo beans)**
¼ cup peanut butter or **nut butter**
¼ cup apple juice
½ tsp cinnamon
¼ cup any jam or **fruit spread**

In a blender or food processor, blend together the chickpeas, nut butter, apple juice, and cinnamon until smooth. Spoon into a medium serving bowl, and top with a layer of jam or fruit spread. Makes 2-4 servings.

You can heat this sauce up if need be, or just stir into warm rice and serve.

1 cup carrot, grated
¼ cup water
¼ cup soft tofu
2 tsp Braggs or **soy sauce**
1 tsp toasted sesame oil
⅛ tsp fresh ginger, grated
raisins (garnish)

In a blender or food processor, blend together the carrots, water, tofu, Braggs, sesame oil, and ginger. Garnish with raisins. Makes 1 serving.

ORANGE RAISIN SAUCE

You can also heat up this sauce or add to warm rice or pasta.

> ¾ cup cooked *or* canned chickpeas (garbanzo beans)
> 1 tsp Braggs *or* soy sauce
> ⅓-¼ cup orange juice
> ½ tsp mild curry powder
> ¼ cup raisins

In a blender or food processor, blend together the chickpeas, Braggs, orange juice, and curry until smooth. Stir in the raisins. You may add peas, carrots, or any other vegetables. Makes 1 serving.

FART SANDWICH

The best part about being a vegan kid is the vegan farts!

> ¼ cup re-fried black beans (pg. 103)
> 2 slices of bread
> cucumber slices
> mild salsa (pg. 96)
> soy cheese (optional)

Spread the beans on a slice of bread. Add the cucumbers, salsa, and cheese on top. Cover with other slice of bread.

FART ROLL

You can add salsa to this if your kids are feeling spicy!

> ½-¼ cup re-fried black beans (pg. 103)
> tortilla shell
> tomatoes, sliced
> cucumbers, sliced
> lettuce, shredded
> sprouts

Spread the beans on the tortilla. Add the tomato, cucumber, lettuce, and sprouts in a thin layer on top, then roll up the tortilla.

Check out our other faux egg salad on pg. 72.

> **½ cup medium** *or* **firm tofu**
> **2-3 tbsp soy mayonnaise (pg. 167)**
> **¼ tsp turmeric**
> **1 tbsp celery, finely diced**
> **1 tsp red** *or* **green onion, finely diced**
> **dash of pepper**
> **4 slices of bread**
> **¼ tsp Dijon mustard (optional)**

In a small bowl, mash together the tofu, mayonnaise, and turmeric. Stir in the celery, onions, pepper, and optional mustard. Spread between slices of bread. You can add sprouts, lettuce, grated carrots, or anything else that tickles your fancy.

Thank you. Thank you very much.

> **margarine**
> **2 slices of bread**
> **peanut butter** *or* **nut butter**
> **½ banana, thinly sliced**

Spread a thin layer of margarine on both slices of bread. On the other side of one slice, spread a layer of nut butter (beware: this gets a little messy). Lay the slice margarine-side down in a frying pan and add banana slices, and top with the other slice of bread, margarine-side up. Fry until golden, flip, and once done, serve. Dip in maple syrup if you like!

RABBIT SHAKE

Hup-sha, hup-sha, quick like a bunny.

½ cup soft *or* **silken tofu**
1-2 cup orange *or* **apple juice**
1 banana (frozen works best)
1 carrot, finely grated

Combine all ingredients in a blender, and blend on high speed until very smooth. Makes 1-2 servings.

TOFUDGESICLES

A sweet, cool treat.

1 cup soft *or* **silken tofu**
½ cup soy milk
⅓ cup sweetener
¼ cup carob *or* **cocoa powder**
2 tsp vanilla extract
¼ tsp cinnamon
1 tsp Inka (optional)
dash of salt
popsicle moulds

In a blender or food processor, blend together all the ingredients until very smooth and creamy. Pour into popsicle moulds and freeze. Remove from freezer 5 minutes before serving. Makes 8-12, depending on moulds.

ORANGESICLES

> ¼ cup soft *or* silken tofu
> 1 cup soy milk
> ¾ cup frozen orange juice concentrate
> ¼ cup sweetener
> 1 tsp vanilla extract
> popsicle moulds

In a blender or food processor, blend together all the ingredients until very smooth and creamy. Pour into popsicle moulds and freeze. Remove from freezer 5 minutes before serving. Makes 8-12, depending on moulds.

SMOOTHIE ICE POPS

The coolest summer dessert you can find.

> 1 cup fruit (e.g., strawberries, blueberries)
> 1 banana, chopped
> 1 cup soft tofu
> ½ cup soy milk
> ½ cup fruit juice (e.g., pineapple, apple, guava)
> popsicle moulds

In a blender or food processor, blend together all the ingredients until very smooth and creamy. Pour into popsicle moulds and freeze. Remove from freezer 5 minutes before serving. Makes 8-12, depending on moulds.

JUICE POPSICLES

Sugar-free and simple to make. My mum used to let me make different combinations, like: grape/apple or orange/papaya. Let them decide! Ⓢ

> various juices
> popsicle moulds

Pour juice into popsicle moulds and freeze. Remove from freezer 5 minutes before serving.

FEEDING KIDS ON THE ROAD

There's a simple rule of the road: feed children when they're hungry. Full tummies make for happier travellers. At rest stops, buy juice and crackers rather than soda, candy, or chips. Avoid salty snacks and sugary drinks. Remember to offer LOTS of water. There may be more pee stops, but it's important to keep hydrated!

Foods to Pack for an Outing or Trip

- dried apricots, figs, prunes, cranberries
- fruit leathers or fruit roll-ups
- small juice boxes or cans of juice
- small soy milk boxes
- small cans of vegetable juice
- jars of natural baby food
- wheat germ or oat bran (add it to cold or hot cereal, on salads, in soups)
- trail mix (pg. 184)
- tofu jerky (pgs. 172-173)
- bottled water

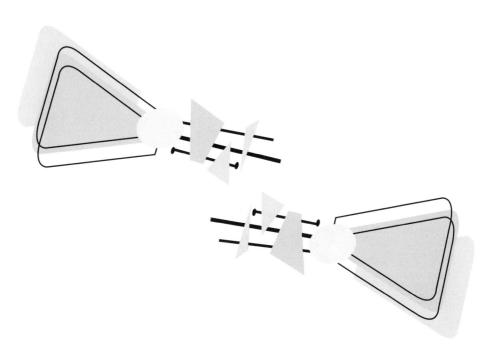

Vegan House & Home

Today's market is saturated with house-cleaning and beauty products. Our ancestors lived for hundreds of years without these kinds of products; their houses looked great, and so did they! Most store-bought products do tremendous amounts of damage to our environment, not to mention all the waste due to over-packaging. Some companies offer goods that are "green" and/or animal cruelty-free, but you still have to deal with all that packaging. With the recipes and ideas offered in this chapter, you can look great and live in a clean and safe home environment without harming the planet.

HOUSEHOLD CLEANERS

If you're looking for alternatives to standard household cleaning products, try some of the following formulas and techniques. They are safer for your home, your children, your animal friends, and the environment. And they cost less!

All-Purpose Cleaner

- Mix vinegar and salt for a good surface cleaner.
- Pour some baking soda and vinegar on a damp sponge. It will clean and deodorize all kitchen and bathroom surfaces.

Deodorizer

- Place partially filled saucers of vinegar around the room.
- Boil 1 tablespoon of vinegar in 1 cup of water to eliminate unpleasant cooking odours.
- Baking soda is excellent for absorbing odours.

Removing crayon marks

- Crayon marks on the floor or table can be removed by rubbing them with some toothpaste on a damp cloth. Don't use this on wallpaper or porous surfaces.

Removing grease spots

- Immediately pour salt on grease spots to absorb and prevent staining.

Removing scratches

- Mix equal parts of lemon juice and vegetable oil, and rub against scratches with a soft cloth until they disappear.

Laundry starch

- Dissolve 1 tablespoon of cornstarch in 2 cups of cold water. Place in a spray bottle. Shake well before using. Make sure to label this so you don't use it for cleaning.

Oven cleaner

- While the oven is still warm, pour some salt on grimy areas. If the areas are dry, dampen with water before applying the salt. When the oven cools down, scrape the grime off and wash clean.
- Spray grimy areas with water or vinegar-water and apply a layer of baking soda. Rub gently with fine steel wool and wipe off. Rinse with water and wipe dry.

Toilet bowl cleaner

- Sprinkle baking soda into the bowl, then drizzle with vinegar and scour with a toilet brush. This combination both cleans and deodorizes. *Note: Do NOT mix this combination with store-bought toilet cleaners. The combination will create toxic fumes.*

Glass cleaner

- Mix equal amounts of water and vinegar in a spray bottle. Wipe the glass with newspaper for a streak-free shine.

1. Kill weeds. Spray full-strength on growth until weeds have starved.

2. Kill unwanted grass on walks and driveways.

3. Increase soil acidity. Use $\frac{1}{2}$ cup of vinegar in 1 gallon of tap water for watering plants such as rhododendrons, gardenias, or azaleas.

4. Deter ants. Spray vinegar around doors, appliances, and along other areas where ants are.

5. Polish car chrome. Apply full-strength.

6. Remove skunk odour from a dog. Rub fur with full-strength vinegar and rinse.

7. Keep cats away. Sprinkle vinegar on areas you don't want the cat walking, sleeping, or scratching.

8. Keep dogs from scratching their ears. Use a clean, soft cloth dipped in vinegar diluted with water.

9. Floor cleaner. Mix 1 cup white vinegar with 2 gallons hot water.

10. Freshen wilted vegetables. Soak them in 2 cups of water and a tablespoon of vinegar.

11. Soothe a bee or jellyfish sting. Dot the irritation with vinegar to relieve itching.

12. Relieve sunburn. Lightly rub on white vinegar. You may have to reapply.

13. Condition hair. Add a tablespoon of vinegar to dissolve sticky residue left by shampoo.

14. Relieve dry and itchy skin. Add 2 tablespoons to bath water.

15. Fight dandruff. See page 200 for recipe.

16. Soothe a sore throat. Pour a teaspoon of apple cider vinegar in a glass of water. Gargle, then swallow.

17. Treat sinus infections and chest colds. Add 1/4 cup or more of vinegar to a vaporizer.

18. Deodorize the kitchen drain. Pour a cup down the drain once a week. Let stand 30 minutes and then flush with cold water.

19. Eliminate onion odours. Rub on your fingers before and after slicing.

20. Clean and disinfect wood cutting boards. Wipe with full-strength vinegar.

21. Remove fruit stains from hands. Rub with vinegar.

22. Cut grease and odour on dishes. Add a tablespoon of vinegar to hot soapy water.

23. Clean a teapot. Boil a mixture of water and vinegar in the teapot. Wipe away the grime.

24. Freshen a lunchbox. Soak a piece of bread in vinegar and let it sit in the lunchbox over night.

25. Clean the refrigerator. Wash with a solution of equal parts water and vinegar.

26. Unclog a drain. Pour a handful of baking soda down the drain, add $\frac{1}{2}$ cup of vinegar, and close with plug for 20 seconds. Rinse with hot water.

27. Clean and deodorize jars. Rinse mayonnaise, peanut butter, and mustard jars with vinegar when empty.

28. Clean the dishwasher. Run a cup of vinegar through the whole cycle once a month to reduce soap build-up on the inner mechanisms and on glassware.

29. Clean stainless steel. Wipe with a vinegar-dampened cloth.

30. Remove stains from pots. Fill the pot with a solution of 3 tablespoons of vinegar to a pint of water. Boil until stain loosens and can be washed away.

31. Clean the microwave. Boil a solution of $\frac{1}{4}$ cup of vinegar and 1 cup of water in the microwave. Will loosen food particles from microwave walls and deodorize.

32. Dissolve rust from bolts and other metals. Soak in full-strength vinegar.

33. Eliminate cooking smells. Let simmer a small pot of vinegar and water solution.

34. Unclog steam iron. Pour equal amounts of vinegar and water into the iron's water chamber. Turn to steam and leave the iron on for 5 minutes in an upright position. Then unplug and allow to cool. Any loose particles should come out when you empty the water.

35. Clean a scorched iron plate. Heat equal parts vinegar and salt in a small pan. Rub solution on the cooled iron surface to remove dark or burned stains.

36. Remove lint from clothes. Add $\frac{1}{2}$ cup of vinegar to the rinse cycle of the washing machine. This also helps to brighten fabric colours.

37. Freshen the washing machine. Pour 1 cup of vinegar in the machine and let it run through a regular cycle (no clothes added). Will dissolve soap residue.

38. Remove tough stains. Gently rub vinegar on the stains before placing in the washing machine.

39. Eliminate smoke odours from clothes. Add 1 cup of vinegar to a bathtub of hot water. Hang clothes above the steam.

40. Remove decals. Brush with a couple coats of vinegar and allow to soak in before washing off.

41. Clean eyeglasses. Wipe each lens with a drop of vinegar.

42. Freshen cut flowers. Add 2 tablespoons of vinegar and 1 teaspoon of sugar for each litre of water.

43. Extinguish fires. Throw on grease fires to arrest flames.

44. Feel good. A teaspoon of apple cider vinegar in a glass of water, with a bit of sweetener added for flavour, will give you an overall healthy feeling.

HEALTH & BEAUTY PRODUCTS

Here are a few beauty products you can make in your own kitchen. It will save you some money, save the animals, and save your skin! Remember: these recipes have no preservatives, so the recipes are for small amounts. Use them up quickly and ALWAYS label your bottles so there won't be any accidents! Also, be sure to test a small area for skin sensitivity before using any mixture. Dab a little on the inside of your wrist or underside of your arm and let sit for 30-40 minutes. Wait 24-48 hours and see if it causes a reaction such as a rash. If not, you're free to use it!

MAKEUP REMOVER

Apply vegetable oil, shortening, or Vitamin E oil to skin and tissue off. This is a simple and effective makeup remover.

NORMAL SKIN CLEANSER

> **2 tbsp lemon juice**
> **6 tbsp vegetable shortening**

In a blender or food processor, blend together the lemon juice and vegetable shortening until well mixed. Apply to your face and tissue off. Store in the refrigerator in a clean, dry jar with a tight-fitting lid.

FRUITY FACE CLEANSER

For oily or combination skin. Tomatoes are highly acidic, so be careful using this cleanser if you have sensitive skin.

> **½ cup apple**
> **½ cup cucumber**
> **½ cup tomatoes** *or* **peaches**

In a blender or food processor, blend together the apple, cucumber, and tomatoes or peaches. Store in the refrigerator in a clean, dry jar that with a tight-fitting lid. Use 1 teaspoon as a cleanser. Apply to face, wait 15-30 seconds, and rinse with warm water.

PARSLEY SKIN TONER

For normal or dry skin. Parsley is a wonderful skin softener and toner.

> **½ cup fresh parsley, chopped**
> **1 cup boiling water**

In a medium bowl, place the chopped parsley and cover with boiling water. Allow to cool completely. Strain and pour into a clean jar with a tight-fitting lid. Apply to skin with a cotton ball.

LEMON TONER

For oily or combination skin. Witch hazel is a natural, non-drying astringent distilled from the witch hazel shrub.

> **½ cup lemon juice**
> **1 cup water**
> **⅔ cup witch hazel**

In a clean, dry jar, combine the lemon juice, water, and witch hazel. Cap tightly and shake well before using. Apply with a cotton ball.

GREEN GODDESS MASK

For dry skin.

> **1 avocado**

In a blender, food processor, or with a fork, blend together the flesh of the avocado into a creamy texture. Massage into your face and neck. Tissue off after 10-15 minutes with warm water and then apply a toner.

HOT MEDITERRANEAN MOMMA MASK

For normal skin.

> **¼ cup mashed, cooked or canned chickpeas**
> **1 tbsp olive or flax oil**
> **¼ tsp lemon juice**

In a blender or food processor, or with a fork, blend all ingredients into a creamy texture. Apply mixture to your face and leave on for 15-20 minutes. Rinse with warm, then cool, water.

CUCUMBER LEMON MASK

For oily skin.

> **½ cucumber, chopped**
> **1 tbsp lemon juice**
> **1 tsp fresh mint**

In a blender or food processor, blend together the cucumbers, lemon juice, and mint until well-mixed. Refrigerate for 10 minutes. Apply mixture to your face and leave on for 10-15 minutes. Rinse with warm, then cool, water.

BLEMISHED SKIN MASK

Again, note that tomatoes are highly acidic so be careful using this cleanser if you have sensitive skin.

1 tomato, finely chopped
1 tsp lemon juice
1 tbsp cooked oatmeal

In a blender or food processor, blend together the tomatoes, lemon juice, and oatmeal until well-mixed. Apply mixture to your face, making sure it is thick enough to stay on blemished areas: cheeks, forehead, or chin. Leave on for 5-10 minutes, then scrub off with a clean washcloth dipped in warm water.

OATMEAL ALMOND FACIAL SCRUB

¼ cup rolled oat flakes
¼ cup almonds
water

In a food processor, grind the oat flakes and almonds to a fine consistency. Slowly add water until it becomes a paste. Apply mixture to your face and massage. Rinse with cool water.

PIMPLE KILLER

Garlic clears out your pores, acting as a remedy for pimples. Peel and mash a garlic clove. Apply the paste to your pimple (being careful to avoid contact with your eyes) and leave on for 15 minutes. Wash off with a warm cloth. Warning: this can be very smelly, and even more so as it rinses off.

POTATO EYE REMEDY

This recipe will lighten dark circles under your eyes and tighten your skin. Wrap a grated raw potato in a cheesecloth and apply to closed eyelids for 15-20 minutes. Wipe off residue with a cloth rinsed in cool water and apply an eye cream.

DIRTY BOY SHAMPOO

For really dirty hair!

¾ cup warm water
½ cup animal-friendly shampoo
1½ tsp salt

2 tsp jojoba oil
⅛ tsp peppermint essential oil

In a clean, dry container add the water, shampoo, salt, jojoba oil, and peppermint oil. Cap tightly and shake until well-blended.

A weak vinegar rinse is the best conditioner you can use after shampooing. It restores the natural acid balance to the hair and takes out any traces of soap and grime.

1 tbsp apple cider vinegar
4 cups water

Place vinegar and water in a clean, dry container and cap tightly. Shake well. After shampooing, work through and rinse. Use 1-2 cups depending on hair length.

SAGE RINSE

2 cups red wine vinegar
2 cups water
¼ cup fresh sage

Combine vinegar, water, and sage in medium saucepan. Bring to a boil and reduce heat to low. Simmer uncovered for 15 minutes, then cover pot, remove from heat, and let steep for 30 minutes. Strain out sage, and once the rinse has cooled, store in a clean, dry container with a tight-fitting lid. After shampooing, pour half a cup over your hair, then rinse.

RINSE FOR DAMAGED HAIR

¼ cup kelp powder
1 cup Sage Rinse mixture (see above)

Combine kelp and Sage Rinse in a clean, dry container. Cap tightly and shake well. Apply generously to freshly shampooed hair. Leave on for 20 minutes, then rinse thoroughly.

HOT OIL TREATMENT FOR DRY HAIR

Not for fine hair.

¼ cup olive oil
¼ cup very hot water

Place olive oil and hot water in a clean, dry container, cap tightly, and shake very well. Massage into dry hair. Put a shower cap or plastic bag over your hair and wrap your head in a towel. Leave mixture on your hair for 15-20 minutes. This is important: when you are ready to rinse, apply shampoo directly to your hair without washing out the oil treatment. Then rinse, apply shampoo again, and condition as usual. (If you apply water before you apply shampoo, you'll have a hard time getting the oil out.)

DANDRUFF TREATMENT

> **2 tbsp apple cider vinegar**
> **2 tbsp water**
> **2 tbsp flax oil** *or* **olive oil**

In a clean, dry container, combine the vinegar, water, and oil. Cap tightly and shake until well mixed. Massage into your scalp and leave on for 15-20 minutes. Shampoo out.

CINNAMON TOOTHPASTE

Forget your toothpaste at home? This spicy toothpaste will help keep your teeth pearly white and your breath fresh. Baking soda neutralizes acids from plaque, helping to prevent gingivitis or gum disease.

> **1 tsp baking soda**
> **¼ tsp cinnamon**
> **1 drop tea tree oil (optional)**

In a cup or small bowl, mix together the soda, cinnamon, and tea tree oil. Place damp toothbrush into the mixture and brush teeth.

PEPPERMINT-CLOVE TOOTHPASTE

> **½ tsp baking soda**
> **½ tsp sea salt**
> **1 drop clove essential oil**
> **1 drop peppermint essential oil**

In a cup or small bowl, mix together the soda, salt, and oils. Place damp toothbrush into mixture and brush teeth.

TEA TREE-PEPPERMINT MOUTHWASH

> **1¼ cup water**
> **6 drops tea tree oil**
> **6 drops peppermint essential oil**

Pour water and oils into a clean, dry container. Cap tightly and shake well. Rinse mouth out, but do not swallow.

2 tbsp fresh rosemary, parsley, *or* **mint**
2 whole cloves
2 cups water

In a small saucepan, bring water and chosen herb to a boil. Reduce heat and simmer for 15-20 minutes. Set aside to cool. Strain into a clean, dry jar and cap tightly. Rinse mouth out, but do not swallow.

½ cup sea salt
1 cup baking soda
1 ½ cup epsom salts
5-10 drops of essential oil (your choice of fragrance)

In a clean, dry container with a tight-fitting lid (or in a sealable bag), combine together all the ingredients and shake until well-mixed. Pour ¼ - ½ cup in bath.

2 tbsp fine sea salt
2 tbsp apple cider vinegar
½ cup flax oil *or* **olive oil**

In a small cup or bowl, mix the salt and vinegar together. Standing in the tub or shower (without water), rub yourself all over with oil. Gently massage in the pre-mixed salt mixture, paying attention to rough spots. Run a warm bath or shower and massage the oil and salt off of your skin.

½ cup cornstarch
2-5 drops essential oil (your choice of fragrance)

In a clean, dry container with a tight-fitting lid (or in a sealable bag), combine ingredients and shake until well-mixed. Dust body, feet, and armpits with powder, using a duster, a soft cloth, or your hands.

> **¼ cup almond oil**
> **3-4 tbsp cocoa butter (solid), grated (the more cocoa butter you add, the harder the salve)**
> **1-2 Vitamin E capsules, pierced and drained**

In a small saucepan on medium-low heat, melt the oil, cocoa butter, and Vitamin E oil together until well mixed. Pour into a small, clean, dry container and let cool. Once cool and set, cap tightly and use as needed. To make this as soft as petroleum jelly, add a bit more oil; to make it harder, add more cocoa butter.

> **1 tsp essential oil (your choice of fragrance)**
> **1 tbsp almond oil**

In a clean, dry bottle, pour ingredients and shake well before using. Good for up to 1 year.

> **¼ cup almond oil**
> **3-4 tbsp cocoa butter (solid), grated (the more cocoa butter you add, the harder the salve)**
> **1-2 Vitamin E capsules, pierced and drained**
> **7-15 drops of essential oil (your choice of fragrance)**

In a small saucepan on medium-low heat, melt the oil, cocoa butter, Vitamin E oil, and fragrance together until well-mixed. Pour into a small, clean, dry bottle and let cool. Once cool and set, cap tightly and use as needed. To make this as soft as petroleum jelly, add a bit more oil; to make it harder, add more cocoa butter.

Here are some scent combinations that you might want to try:

jasmine, patchouli
lavender, spearmint
sandalwood, musk, frankincense
sandalwood, musk, patchouli
lemon, spearmint, grapefruit
vanilla, musk
ginger, cinnamon, clove
strawberry, vanilla

MASSAGE OIL

| ½ cup of oil (olive, almond, apricot, *or* sunflower)
| 10 drops essential oil (your choice of fragrance)

Pour oils into a clean, dry container. Cap tightly and shake well before using.

ALL-PURPOSE SALVE

Use for insect bites, itching, wounds, minor skin abrasions, burns, bruises, tattoos, and on fungal infections. Store salve in a dark-coloured jar so the light doesn't oxidize the herbs' healing properties. You can get these ingredients at health food or herb stores, or pick your own.

| 2 tbsp St. John's wort*
| 2 tbsp calendula*
| 2 tbsp comfrey leaf*
| 2 tbsp plantain*
| 1 cup olive oil
| 1 tbsp Vitamin E oil
| ¾-1 cup cocoa butter (solid), grated (the more cocoa butter you add, the harder the salve)

In a small pot, combine the herbs and oils. Simmer on low heat for about 4 hours to extract the beneficial properties of the herbs into the oil. Do not let oil get too hot. Once done, remove from heat and allow the oil to cool. Strain into a clean dry jar, using a cheese cloth or sieve. Pour strained oil back into pot and add cocoa butter. On low heat, simmer until the cocoa butter is completely melted. Pour back into jar and let cool completely, then cap tightly.

St. John's wort: good for burns, wounds, bites, itching, pain
calendula: anti-inflammatory; aids in healing abrasions; skin soother
comfrey leaf: speeds healing of wounds and skin conditions
plantain: pain relief; antiseptic for stings and bites

BUG REPELLENT

| 1 cup water
| 20 drops citronella oil
| 10 drops lavender essential oil
| 7 drops eucalyptus essential oil

In a spray bottle, combine all the ingredients and shake well. Spray exposed areas, but avoid face and eye area. To avoid possible irritation, try it out on a small patch of skin first.

PEPPERMINT ITCH LOTION

For relief of itching.

> **½ cup water**
> **½ cup witch hazel**
> **3-4 drops peppermint** *or* **eucalyptus essential oil**

In a clean, dry container, combine all the ingredients. Cap tightly and shake well. Apply to your skin with clean hands or cotton ball.

SOOTHING SUNBURN LOTION

Always wear sunscreen and cover up as much as possible when you're outside in the sun. And keep your body well-hydrated by drinking plenty of water.

> **4 tbsp water**
> **2 tbsp witch hazel**
> **1 cup baking soda**
> **2-4 drops peppermint essential oil**

In a clean, dry container, combine all the ingredients. Cap tightly and shake well. Gently apply to sunburned skin and allow to dry. This lotion will leave a fine, powdery film as it dries.

CALENDULA BABY OIL

Calendula is healing and soothing to the skin. It is excellent for massaging your babies, but grown-ups can use this oil too!

> **1 cup of oil (olive, almond, apricot,** *or* **sunflower)**
> **2 ½ tbsp calendula flowers**

In a small pot, combine the oil and flowers. Simmer on low heat for about 4 hours to extract the beneficial properties of the calendula into the oil. Do not let the oil get too hot. Once done, remove from heat and allow the oil to cool. Strain into a clean, dry container, using a cheesecloth or sieve. Cap tightly.

> **¼ cup water**
> **¼ cup animal-friendly shampoo**
> **1 tbsp vinegar**
> **¼ cup aloe vera gel**
> **1 tbsp calendula oil (pg. 204)**
> **1 drop lavender essential oil**
> **1 drop tea tree oil**

In a clean, dry jar, combine the water, shampoo, vinegar, aloe, calendula, lavender, and tea tree oil. Cap tightly, and shake well. Store in the fridge. Use soft but sturdy towels for wipes (flannel, old towels, etc.). Cut them into squares or rectangles and place them in a container with a tight lid. Pour solution over wipes. After using wipe, rinse thoroughly and wash in hot water in the washing machine, dry, and re-saturate with wipe solution. If your baby has a really red, raw diaper rash you might not want to use these wipes, as vinegar may cause a burning sensation.

A N I M A L   T R E A T S

These recipes are not for you, but for the ones who know you the best. They tolerate your tardiness, your mood swings, and your weird idiosyncrasies. They also love you no matter what you look like in the morning. Treat your animal friends well; they deserve only the best.

D O G   &   C A T   B I S C U I T S

> **1 cup whole wheat flour**
> **2 tbsp wheat germ**
> **¼ cup bran flakes**
> **¼ cup soy flour**
> **1 tbsp molasses**
> **2 tbsp oil**

> **1 tbsp kelp powder**
> **1 tsp sage**
> **1 tbsp brewer's yeast**
> **⅓ cup water**
> **2 tbsp textured vegetable protein**

Preheat oven to 350°F. In a medium bowl, combine the flour, wheat germ, bran flakes, soy flour, molasses, oil, kelp, sage, yeast, water, and TVP. Roll out and cut into shapes (for cats, roll out and cut into narrow strips or ribbons). Place on a cookie sheet and bake for 20-35 minutes. Watch the kitty strips, as they will bake faster than the larger shapes. Cats like these biscuits soft, but dogs like them crunchy, so if the biscuits are not hard enough, leave them in the oven with the heat turned off until they reach the desired hardness. Makes 12 large or 24 small biscuits.

½ cup oatmeal flour
¼ cup soy bean flour
1 cup rolled oat flakes
¼ cup carob (do not use chocolate, it is toxic to dogs)
2 tbsp textured vegetable protein
1 tbsp brewer's yeast
4 tbsp oil
¼ cup water (if too dry, add a little more)

Preheat oven to 350°F. In a medium bowl, combine the flours, oats, carob, TVP, brewer's yeast, oil, and water. Roll out and cut into shapes. Place on a cookie sheet and bake for 35-40 minutes. Makes 12 large or 24 small crunchies.

BAD BREATH DOG BISCUITS

For some reason, my niece Heidi loves to eat these biscuits. It's so cute when she smiles and her teeth are green. ⓢ

2 cups whole wheat flour
½ cup cornmeal
⅓ cup fresh mint, chopped
½ cup fresh parsley, chopped
1 tsp spirulina
2 tbsp textured vegetable protein
¾ cup water
6 tbsp oil

Preheat oven to 350°F. In a medium bowl, combine the flour, cornmeal, mint, parsley, spirulina, TVP, water, and oil. Roll out and cut into shapes. Place on a cookie sheet and bake for 35-40 minutes. Makes 12 large or 24 small biscuits.

2 cups whole wheat flour
½ cup cornmeal
2 tbsp textured vegetable protein
1 tbsp brewer's yeast
⅔ cup water
6 tbsp oil

Preheat oven to 350° F. In a medium bowl, combine the flour, cornmeal, TVP, yeast, water, and oil. Roll out and cut into shapes. Place on a cookie sheet and bake for 35-40 minutes. Makes 12 large or 24 small biscuits.

FLEA BUSTERS

Here are some ideas to prevent those nasty fleas:

Brewer's yeast: 1 tsp or 1 tablet a day. Note: some animals are allergic to brewer's yeast; watch for itchy patches. Consult your vet.

Garlic: Most animals love garlic when mixed into food.

Calendula ointment or oil: An excellent repellent that helps with itching.

Vinegar: A ratio of 1 teaspoon of vinegar to 4 cups of water in their drinking water helps to keep your pets free of fleas and ticks.

FLEA HOUSE & PET SPRAY

Here is a natural way of eliminating fleas that is not harmful to humans or pets.

¼ tsp eucalyptus *or* **wintergreen essential oil**
1 cup water

Add oil to spray bottle filled with water. Spray your house with a fine mist-the carpet, furniture, car, pets' beds – everywhere. Fleas hate the aroma and run for cover. Spraying your pet is also a great idea. Spray areas 3 times a week all year round, but especially during summer, the peak flea season.

Trying to figure out what ingredients contain animal products can be a nightmare. We hope this A to Z listing of animal-product ingredients to avoid will help you on your journey to becoming a full-fledged vegan warrior. This list is used with the permission of People for the Ethical Treatment of Animals.

A

Adrenaline. Hormone from adrenal glands of hogs, cattle, and sheep. In medicine. Alternatives: synthetics.

Alanine. (See Amino Acids.)

Albumen. In eggs, milk, muscles, blood, and many vegetable tissues and fluids. In cosmetics, albumen is usually derived from egg whites and used as a coagulating agent. May cause allergic reaction. In cakes, cookies, candies, etc. Egg whites sometimes used in "clearing" wines. Derivative: Albumin.

Albumin. (See Albumen.)

Alcloxa. (See Allantoin.)

Aldioxa. (See Allantoin.)

Aliphatic Alcohol. (See Lanolin and Vitamin A.)

Allantoin. Uric acid from cows, most mammals. Also in many plants (especially comfrey). In cosmetics (especially creams and lotions) and used in treatment of wounds and ulcers. Derivatives: Alcloxa, Aldioxa. Alternatives: extract of comfrey root, synthetics.

Alpha-Hydroxy Acids. Any one of several acids used as an exfoliant and in anti-wrinkle products. Lactic acid may be animal-derived (see Lactic Acid). Alternatives: glycolic acid, citric acid, and salicylic acid are plant- or fruit-derived.

Ambergris. From whale intestines. Used as a fixative in making perfumes and as a flavouring in foods and beverages. Alternatives: synthetic or vegetable fixatives.

Amino Acids. The building blocks of protein in all animals and plants. In cosmetics, vitamins, supplements, shampoos, etc. Alternatives: synthetics, plant sources.

Aminosuccinate Acid. (See Aspartic Acid.)

Animal Fats and Oils. In foods, cosmetics, etc. Highly allergenic. Alternatives:olive oil, wheat germ oil, coconut oil, flaxseed oil, almond oil, safflower oil, etc.

Animal Hair. In some blankets, mattresses, brushes, furniture, etc. Alternatives: vegetable and synthetic fibers.

Arachidonic Acid. A liquid unsaturated fatty acid that is found in liver, brain, glands, and fat of animals and humans. Generally isolated from animal liver. Used in companion animal food for nutrition and in skin creams and lotions to soothe eczema and rashes. Alternatives: synthetics, aloe vera, tea tree oil, calendula ointment.

Arachidyl Proprionate. A wax that can be from animal fat. Alternatives: peanut or vegetable oil.

Aspartic Acid. Aminosuccinate Acid. Can be animal or plant source (e.g., molasses). Sometimes synthesized for commercial purposes.

B

Bee Pollen. Microsporic grains in seed plants gathered by bees then collected from the legs of bees. Causes allergic reactions in some people. In nutritional supplements, shampoos, toothpaste's, deodorants. Alternatives: synthetics, plant amino acids, pollen collected from plants.

Bee Products. Produced by bees for their own use. Bees are selectively bred. Culled bees are killed. A cheap sugar is substituted for their stolen honey. Millions die as a result. Their legs are often torn off by pollen-collection trapdoors.

Beeswax. Honeycomb. Wax obtained from melting honeycomb with boiling water, straining it, and cooling it. From virgin bees. Very cheap and widely used but harmful to the skin. In lipsticks and many other cosmetics (especially face creams, lotions, mascara, eye creams and shadows, face makeup's, nail whiteners, lip balms, etc.). Derivatives: Cera Flava. Alternatives: paraffin, vegetable oils and fats. Ceresin aka ceresine aka earth wax. (Made from the mineral ozokerite. Replaces beeswax in cosmetics. Also used to wax paper, to make polishing cloths, in dentistry for taking wax impressions, and in candle-making.) Also, carnauba wax (from the Brazilian palm tree; used in many cosmetics, including lipstick; rarely causes allergic reactions). Candelilla wax (from candelilla plants; used in many cosmetics, including lipstick; also in the manufacture of rubber, phonograph records, in waterproofing and writing inks; no known toxicity). Japan wax (Vegetable wax. Japan tallow. Fat from the fruit of a tree grown in Japan and China.). Benzoic Acid. In almost all vertebrates and in berries. Used as a preservative in mouthwashes, deodorants, creams, aftershave lotions, etc. Alternatives: cranberries, gum benzoin (tincture) from the aromatic balsamic resin from trees grown in China, Sumatra, Thailand, and Cambodia.

Beer. Most domestic beers use animal charcoal. Drink organic beer or make your own.

Beta Carotene. (See Carotene.)

Biotin. Vitamin H. Vitamin B Factor. In every living cell and in larger amounts in milk and yeast. Used as a texturizer in cosmetics, shampoos, and creams. Alternatives: plant sources.

Blood. From any slaughtered animal. Used as adhesive in plywood, also found in cheese-making, foam rubber, intravenous feedings, and medicines. Possibly in foods such as lecithin. Alternatives: synthetics, plant sources.

Boar Bristles. Hair from wild or captive hogs. In "natural" toothbrushes and bath and shaving brushes. Alternatives: vegetable fibers, nylon, the peelu branch or peelu gum (Asian, available in the U.S., its juice replaces toothpaste).

Bone Char. Animal bone ash. Used in bone china and often to make sugar white. Serves as the charcoal used in aquarium filters. Alternatives: synthetic tribasic calcium phosphate.

Bone Meal. Crushed or ground animal bones. In some fertilizers. In some vitamins and supplements as a source of calcium. In toothpastes. Alternatives: plant mulch, vegetable compost, dolomite, clay, vegetarian vitamins.

Brown and White Sugar. Most refineries use animal charcoal filters. Alternatives: Sucanat (brand name) sweetener, turbinado sugar, concentrated fruit sweetener, rice syrup, maple syrup (after checking up on company to make sure they don't use lard as a de-foamer)

C

Calciferol. (See Vitamin D.)

Calfskin. (See Leather.)

Caprylamine Oxide. (See Caprylic Acid.)

Capryl Betaine. (See Caprylic Acid.)

Caprylic Acid. A liquid fatty acid from cow's or goat's milk. Also from palm and coconut oil, other plant oils. In perfumes, soaps. Derivatives: Caprylic Triglyceride, Caprylamine Oxide, Capryl Betaine. Alternatives: plant sources.

Caprylic Triglyceride. (See Caprylic Acid.)

Carbamide. (See Urea.)

Carmine. Cochineal. Carminic Acid. Red pigment from the crushed female cochineal insect. Reportedly 70,000 beetles must be killed to produce one pound of this red dye. Used in cosmetics, shampoos, red apple sauce, and other foods (including red lollipops and food colouring). May cause allergic reaction. Alternatives: beet juice (used in powders, rouges, shampoos; no known toxicity); alkanet root (from the root of this herblike tree; used as a red dye for inks, wines, lip balms, etc.; no known toxicity. Can also be combined to make a copper or blue colouring). (See Colours.)

Carminic Acid. (See Carmine.)

Carotene. Provitamin A. Beta Carotene. A pigment found in many animal tissues and in all plants. Used as a colouring in cosmetics and in the manufacture of vitamin A.

Casein. Caseinate. Sodium Caseinate. Milk protein. In "non-dairy" creamers, soy cheese, many cosmetics, hair preparations, beauty masks. Alternatives: soy protein, soy milk, and other vegetable milks.

Caseinate. (See Casein.)

Castor. Castoreum. Creamy substance with strong odour from muskrat and beaver genitals. Used as a fixative in perfume and incense. Alternatives: synthetics, plant castor oil.

Castoreum. (See Castor.)

Catgut. Tough string from the intestines of sheep, horses, etc. Used for surgical sutures. Also for stringing tennis rackets and musical instruments, etc. Alternatives: nylon and other synthetic fibers.

Cera Flava. (See Beeswax.)

Cetyl Alcohol. Wax found in spermaceti from sperm whales or dolphins. Alternatives: vegetable cetyl alcohol (e.g., coconut), synthetic spermaceti.

Cetyl Palmitate. (See Spermaceti.)

Chitosan. A fiber derived from crustacean shells. Used as a lipid binder in diet products. Alternatives: raspberries, yams, legumes, dried apricots, and many other fruits and vegetables.

Chocolate. Contains milk/milk products, white sugar eat carob or dark chocolate instead.

Cholesterin. (See Lanolin.)

Cholesterol. A steroid alcohol in all animal fats and oils, nervous tissue, egg yolk, and blood. Can be derived from lanolin. In cosmetics, eye creams, shampoos, etc. Alternatives: solid complex alcohols (sterols) from plant sources.

Choline Bitartrate. (See Lecithin.)

Civet. Unctuous secretion painfully scraped from a gland very near the genital organs of civet cats. Used as a fixative in perfumes. Alternatives: (See alternatives to Musk).

Cochineal. (See Carmine.)

Cod Liver Oil. (See Marine Oil.)

Collagen. Fibrous protein in vertebrates. Usually derived from animal tissue. Can't affect the skin's own collagen. An allergen. Alternatives: soy protein, almond oil, amla oil (see alternative to Keratin), etc.

Colours. Dyes. Pigments from animal, plant, and synthetic sources used to colour foods, cosmetics, and other products. Cochineal is from insects. Widely used FD? and D? colours are coal-tar (bituminous coal) derivatives that are continously tested on animals due to their carcinogenic properties. Alternatives: grapes, beets, turmeric, saffron, carrots, chlorophyll, annatto, alkanet.

Cortisone. Corticosteroid. Hormone from adrenal glands. Widely used in medicine. Alternatives: synthetics.

Cysteine, L-Form. An amino acid from hair which can come from animals. Used in hair care products and creams, in some bakery products, and in wound-healing formulations. Alternatives: plant sources.

Cystine. An amino acid found in urine and horsehair. Used as a nutritional supplement and in emollients. Alternatives: plant sources.

D

Dexpanthenol. (See Panthenol.)

Diglycerides. (See Monoglycerides and Glycerin.)

Dimethyl Stearamine. (See Stearic Acid.)

Down. Goose or duck insulating feathers. From slaughtered or cruelly exploited geese. Used as an insulator in quilts, parkas, sleeping bags, pillows, etc. Alternatives: polyester and synthetic substitutes, kapok (silky fibers from the seeds of some tropical trees) and milkweed seed pod fibers.

Duodenum Substances. From the digestive tracts of cows and pigs. Added to some vitamin tablets. In some medicines. Alternatives: vegetarian vitamins, synthetics.

Dyes. (See Colours.)

E

Egg Protein. In shampoos, skin preparations, etc. Alternatives: plant proteins.

Elastin. Protein found in the neck ligaments and aortas of cows. Similar to collagen. Can't affect the skin's own elasticity. Alternatives: synthetics, protein from plant tissues.

Emu Oil. From flightless ratite birds native to Australia and now factory farmed. Used in cosmetics, creams. Alternatives: vegetable and plant oils.

Ergocalciferol. (See Vitamin D.)

Ergosterol. (See Vitamin D.)

Estrace. (See Estrogen.)

Estradiol. (See Estrogen.)

Estrogen. Estrace. Estradiol. Hormones from cow ovaries and pregnant mares' urine. Considered a drug. Can have harmful systemic effects if used by children. Used for reproductive problems and in birth control pills and menopausal drugs. In creams and lotions. Has a negligible effect in the creams as a skin restorative; simple vegetable-source emollients are considered better. Alternatives: oral contraceptives and menopausal drugs based on synthetic steroids or phytoestrogens (from plants; currently being researched). Menopausal symptoms can also be treated with diet and herbs.

F

Fats. (See Animal Fats.)

Fatty Acids. Can be one or any mixture of liquid and solid acids such as caprylic, lauric, myristic, oleic, palmitic, and stearic. Used in bubble baths, lipsticks, soap, detergents, cosmetics, food. Alternatives: vegetable-derived acids, soy lecithin, safflower oil, bitter almond oil, sunflower oil, etc.

FD&C Colours. (See Colours.)

Feathers. From exploited and slaughtered birds. Used whole as ornaments or ground up in shampoos. (See Down and Keratin.)

Fish Liver Oil. Used in vitamins and supplements. In milk fortified with vitamin D. Alternatives: yeast extract ergosterol and exposure of skin to sunshine.

Fish Oil. (See Marine Oil.) Fish oil can also be from marine mammals. Used in soap-making.

Fish Scales. Used in shimmery makeups. Alternatives: mica, rayon, synthetic pearl.

Fructose. From white sugar, even further refined. (see sugar)

Fur. Obtained from animals (usually mink, foxes, or rabbits) cruelly trapped in steel-jaw leghold traps or raised in intensive confinement on fur "farms." Alternatives: synthetics. (See Sable Brushes.)

G

Gelatin. Gel. Protein obtained by boiling skin, tendons, ligaments, and/or bones with water. From cows and pigs. Used in shampoos, face masks, and other cosmetics. Used as a thickener for fruit gelatins and puddings (e.g., "Jello"). In candies, marshmallows, cakes, ice cream, yogurts. On photographic film and in vitamins as a coating and as capsules. Sometimes used to assist in "clearing" wines. Alternatives: carrageen (carrageenan, Irish moss), seaweeds (algin, agar-agar, kelp-used in jellies, plastics, medicine), pectin from fruits, dextrins, locust bean gum, cotton gum, silica gel. Marshmallows were originally made from the root of the marsh mallow plant. Vegetarian capsules are now available from several companies. Digital cameras don't use film.

Glucose Tyrosinase. (See Tyrosine.)

Glycerides. (See Glycerin.)

Glycerin. Glycerol. A byproduct of soap manufacture (normally uses animal fat). In cosmetics, foods, mouthwashes, chewing gum, toothpastes, soaps, ointments, medicines, lubricants, transmission and brake fluid, and plastics. Derivatives: Glycerides, Glyceryls, Glycreth-26, Polyglycerol. Alternatives: vegetable glycerin-a byproduct of vegetable oil soap. Derivatives of seaweed, petroleum.

Glycerol. (See Glycerin.)

Glyceryls. (See Glycerin.)

Glycreth-26. (See Glycerin.)

Guanine. Pearl Essence. Obtained from scales of fish. Constituent of ribonucleic acid and deoxyribonucleic acid and found in all animal and plant tissues. In shampoo, nail polish, other cosmetics. Alternatives: leguminous plants, synthetic pearl, or aluminum and bronze particles.

H

Hide Glue. Same as gelatin but of a cruder impure form. Alternatives: dextrins and synthetic petrochemical-based adhesives. (See Gelatin.)

Honey. Food for bees, made by bees. Can cause allergic reactions. Used as a colouring and an emollient in cosmetics and as a flavoring in foods. Should never be fed to infants. Alternatives: in foods-maple syrup, date sugar, syrups made from grains such as barley malt, turbinado sugar, molasses; in cosmetics-vegetable colours and oils. Some Vegans choose to use honey.

Honeycomb. (See Beeswax.)

Horsehair. (See Animal Hair.)

Hyaluronic Acid. A protein found in umbilical cords and the fluids around the joints. Used as a cosmetic oil. Alternatives: plant oils.

Hydrocortisone. (See Cortisone.)

Hydrolyzed Animal Protein. In cosmetics, especially shampoo and hair treatments. Alternatives: soy protein, other vegetable proteins, amla oil (see alternatives to Keratin).

I

Imidazolidinyl Urea. (See Urea.)

Insulin. From hog pancreas. Used by millions of diabetics daily. Alternatives: synthetics, vegetarian diet and nutritional supplements, human insulin grown in a lab.

Isinglass. A form of gelatin prepared from the internal membranes of fish bladders. Sometimes used in "clearing" wines and in foods. Alternatives: bentonite clay, "Japanese isinglass," agar-agar (see alternatives to Gelatin), mica, a mineral used in cosmetics.

Isopropyl Lanolate. (See Lanolin.)

Isopropyl Myristate. (See Myristic Acid.)

Isopropyl Palmitate. Complex mixtures of isomers of stearic acid and palmitic acid. (See Stearic Acid).

K

Keratin. Protein from the ground-up horns, hooves, feathers, quills, and hair of various animals. In hair rinses, shampoos, permanent wave solutions. Alternatives: almond oil, soy protein, amla oil (from the fruit of an Indian tree), human hair from salons. Rosemary and nettle give body and strand strength to hair.

L

Lactic Acid. Found in blood and muscle tissue. Also in sour milk, beer, sauerkraut, pickles, and other food products made by bacterial fermentation. Used in skin fresheners, as a preservative, in the formation of plasticizers, etc. Alternative: plant milk sugars, synthetics.

Lactose. Milk sugar from milk of mammals. In eye lotions, foods, tablets, cosmetics, baked goods, medicines. Alternatives: plant milk sugars.

Laneth. (See Lanolin.)

Lanogene. (See Lanolin.)

Lanolin. Lanolin Acids. Wool Fat. Wool Wax. A product of the oil glands of sheep, extracted from their wool. Used as an emollient in many skin care products and cosmetics and in medicines. An allergen with no proven effectiveness. (See Wool for cruelty to sheep.) Derivatives: Aliphatic Alcohols, Cholesterin, Isopropyl Lanolate, Laneth, Lanogene, Lanolin Alcohols, Lanosterols, Sterols, Triterpene Alcohols. Alternatives: plant and vegetable oils.

Lanolin Alcohol. (See Lanolin.)

Lanosterols. (See Lanolin.)

Lard. Fat from hog abdomens. In shaving creams, soaps, cosmetics. In baked goods, French fries, refried beans, and many other foods. Alternatives: pure vegetable fats or oils.

Leather. Suede. Calfskin. Sheepskin. Alligator Skin. Other Types of Skin. Subsidizes the meat industry. Used to make wallets, handbags, furniture and car upholstery, shoes, etc. Alternatives: cotton, canvas, nylon, vinyl, ultrasuede, other synthetics.

Lecithin. Choline Bitartrate. Waxy substance in nervous tissue of all living organisms. But, frequently obtained for commercial purposes from eggs and soybeans. Also from nerve tissue, blood, milk, corn. Choline bitartrate, the basic constituent of lecithin, is in many animal and plant tissues and prepared synthetically. Lecithin can be in eye creams, lipsticks, liquid powders, handcreams, lotions, soaps, shampoos, other cosmetics, and some medicines. Alternatives: soybean lecithin, synthetics.

Linoleic Acid. An essential fatty acid. Used in cosmetics, vitamins. (See alternatives to Fatty Acids.) Lipase. Enzyme from the stomachs and tongue glands of calves, kids, and lambs. Used in cheese-making and in digestive aids. Alternatives: vegetable enzymes, castor beans.

Lipoids. Lipids. Fat and fat-like substances that are found in animals and plants. Alternatives: vegetable oils. Marine Oil. From fish or marine mammals (including porpoises). Used in soap-making. Used as a shortening (especially in some

margarines), as a lubricant, and in paint. Alternatives: vegetable oils.

M

Maple Syrup. Most companies add lard as foam reducer. Buy organic or check with company

Methionine. Essential amino acid found in various proteins (usually from egg albumen and casein). Used as a texturizer and for freshness in potato chips. Alternatives: synthetics.

Milk Protein. Hydrolyzed milk protein. From the milk of cows. In cosmetics, shampoos, moisturizers, conditioners, etc. Alternatives: soy protein, other plant proteins.

Mink Oil. From minks. In cosmetics, creams, etc. Alternatives: vegetable oils and emollients such as avocado oil, almond oil, and jojoba oil.

Molasses. By product of sugar; lard to reduce foam. Use organic Molasses or check with company. Monoglycerides. Glycerides. (See Glycerin.) From animal fat. In margarines, cake mixes, candies, foods, etc. In cosmetics. Alternative: vegetable glycerides.

Musk (Oil). Dried secretion painfully obtained from musk deer, beaver, muskrat, civet cat, and otter genitals. Wild cats are kept captive in cages in horrible conditions and are whipped around the genitals to produce the scent; beavers are trapped; deer are shot. In perfumes and in food flavorings. Alternatives: labdanum oil (which comes from various rockrose shrubs) and other plants with a musky scent. Labdanum oil has no known toxicity.

Myristal Ether Sulfate. (See Myristic Acid.)

Myristic Acid. Organic acid in most animal and vegetable fats. In butter acids. Used in shampoos, creams, cosmetics. In food flavorings. Derivatives: Isopropyl Myristate, Myristal Ether Sulfate, Myristyls, Oleyl Myristate. Alternatives: nut butters, oil of lovage, coconut oil, extract from seed kernels of nutmeg, etc.

Myristyls. (See Myristic Acid.)

N

"Natural Sources." Can mean animal or vegetable sources. Most often in the health food industry, especially in the cosmetics area, it means animal sources, such as animal elastin, glands, fat, protein, and oil. Alternatives: plant sources.

Nucleic Acids. In the nucleus of all living cells. Used in cosmetics, shampoos, conditioners, etc. Also in vitamins, supplements. Alternatives: plant sources.

O

Ocenol. (See Oleyl Alcohol.)

Octyl Dodecanol. Mixture of solid waxy alcohols. Primarily from stearyl alcohol. (See Stearyl Alcohol.)

Oleic Acid. Obtained from various animal and vegetable fats and oils. Usually obtained commercially from inedible tallow. (See Tallow.) In foods, soft soap, bar soap, permanent wave solutions, creams, nail polish, lipsticks, many other skin preparations. Derivatives: Oleyl Oleate, Oleyl Stearate. Alternatives: coconut oil. (See alternatives to Animal Fats and Oils.)

Oils. (See alternatives to Animal Fats and Oils.)

Oleths. (See Oleyl Alcohol.)

Oleyl Alcohol. Ocenol. Found in fish oils. Used in the manufacture of detergents, as a plasticizer for softening fabrics, and as a carrier for medications. Derivatives: Oleths, Oleyl Arachidate, Oleyl Imidazoline.

Oleyl Arachidate. (See Oleyl Alcohol.)

Oleyl Imidazoline. (See Oleyl Alcohol.)

Oleyl Myristate. (See Myristic Acid.)

Oleyl Oleate. (See Oleic Acid.)

Oleyl Stearate. (See Oleic Acid.)

P

Palmitamide. (See Palmitic Acid.)

Palmitamine. (See Palmitic Acid.)

Palmitate. (See Palmitic Acid.)

Palmitic Acid. From fats, oils (see Fatty Acids). Mixed with stearic acid. Found in many animal fats and plant oils. In shampoos, shaving soaps, creams. Derivatives: Palmitate, Palmitamine, **Palmitamide.** Alternatives: palm oil, vegetable sources.

Panthenol. Dexpanthenol. Vitamin B-Complex Factor.Provitamin B-5. Can come from animal or plant sources or synthetics. In shampoos, supplements, emollients, etc. In foods. Derivative: Panthenyl. Alternatives: synthetics, plants.

Panthenyl. (See Panthenol.)

Pepsin. In hogs' stomachs. A clotting agent. In some cheeses and vitamins. Same uses and alternatives as Rennet.

Placenta. Placenta Polypeptides Protein.

Afterbirth. Contains waste matter eliminated by the fetus. Derived from the uterus of slaughtered animals. Animal placenta is widely used in skin creams, shampoos, masks, etc. Alternatives: kelp. (See alternatives for Animal Fats and Oils.)

Polyglycerol. (See Glycerin.)

Polypeptides. From animal protein. Used in cosmetics. Alternatives: plant proteins and enzymes.

Polysorbates. Derivatives of fatty acids. In cosmetics, foods.

Pristane. Obtained from the liver oil of sharks and from whale ambergris. (See Squalene, Ambergris.) Used as a lubricant and anti-corrosive agent. In cosmetics. Alternatives: plant oils, synthetics.

Progesterone. A steroid hormone used in anti-wrinkle face creams. Can have adverse systemic effects. Alternatives: synthetics.

Propolis. Tree sap gathered by bees and used as a sealant in beehives. In toothpaste, shampoo, deodorant, supplements, etc. Alternatives: tree sap, synthetics.

Provitamin A. (See Carotene.)

Provitamin B-5. (See Panthenol.)

Provitamin D-2. (See Vitamin D.)

R

Rennet. Rennin. Enzyme from calves' stomachs. Used in cheese-making, rennet custard (junket), and in many coagulated dairy products. Alternatives: microbial coagulating agents, bacteria culture, lemon juice, or vegetable rennet.

Rennin. (See Rennet.)

Resinous Glaze. (See Shellac.)

Ribonucleic Acid. (See RNA.)

RNA. Ribonucleic Acid. RNA is in all living cells. Used in many protein shampoos and cosmetics. Alternatives: plant cells.

Royal Jelly. Secretion from the throat glands of the honeybee workers that is fed to the larvae in a colony and to all queen larvae.No proven value in cosmetics preparations. Alternatives: aloe vera, comfrey, other plant derivatives.

S

Sable Brushes. From the fur of sables (weasel-like mammals). Used to make eye makeup, lipstick, and artists' brushes. Alternatives: synthetic fibers.

Shark Liver Oil. Used in lubricating creams and lotions. Derivatives:Squalane, Squalene. Alternatives: vegetable oils.

Sheepskin. (See Leather.)

Shellac. Resinous Glaze. Resinous excretion of certain insects. Used as a candy glaze, in hair lacquer, and on jewelry. Alternatives: plant waxes.

Silk. Silk Powder. Silk is the shiny fiber made by silkworms to form their cocoons. Worms are boiled in their cocoons to get the silk. Used in cloth. In silk-screening (other fine cloth can be and is used instead). Taffeta can be made from silk or nylon. Silk powder is obtained from the secretion of the silkworm. It is used as a coloring agent in face powders, soaps, etc. Can cause severe allergic skin reactions and systemic reactions (if inhaled or ingested). Alternatives: milkweed seed-pod fibers, nylon, silk-cotton tree and ceiba tree filaments (kapok), rayon, and synthetic silks.

Snails. In some cosmetics (crushed).

Sodium Caseinate. (See Casein.)

Sodium Steroyl Lactylate. (See Lactic Acid.)

Sodium Tallowate. (See Tallow.)

Spermaceti. Cetyl Palmitate. Sperm Oil. Waxy oil derived from the sperm whale's head or from dolphins. In many margarines. In skin creams, ointments, shampoos, candles, etc. Used in the leather industry. May become rancid and cause irritations. Alternatives: synthetic spermaceti, jojoba oil, and other vegetable emollients.

Sponge (Luna and Sea). A plant-like animal. Lives in the sea. Becoming scarce. Alternatives: synthetic sponges, loofahs (plants used as sponges).

Squalane. (See Shark Liver Oil.)

Squalene. Oil from shark livers, etc. In cosmetics, moisturizers, hair dyes, surface-active agents. Alternatives: vegetable emollients such as olive oil, wheat germ oil, rice bran oil, etc.

Stearamide. (See Stearic Acid.)

Stearamine. (See Stearic Acid.)

Stearamine Oxide. (See Stearyl Alcohol.)

Stearates. (See Stearic Acid.)

Stearic Acid. Fat from cows and sheep and from dogs and cats euthanized in animal shelters, etc. Most often refers to a fatty substance taken from the stomachs of pigs. Can be harsh, irritating. Used in cosmetics, soaps, lubricants, candles, hairspray, conditioners, deodorants, creams, chewing gum, food flavoring. Derivatives: Stearamide,Stearamine, Stearates, Stearic Hydrazide, Stearone, Stearoxytri-methylsilane, Stearoyl Lactylic Acid, Stearyl Betaine, Stearyl Imidazoline. Alternatives: Stearic acid can be found in many vegetable fats, coconut.

Stearic Hydrazide. (See Stearic Acid.)

Stearone. (See Stearic Acid.)

Stearoxytrimethylsilane. (See Stearic Acid.)

Stearoyl Lactylic Acid. (See Stearic Acid.)

Stearyl Acetate. (See Stearyl Alcohol.)

Stearyl Alcohol. Sterols. A mixture of solid alcohols. Can be prepared from sperm whale oil. In medicines, creams, rinses, shampoos, etc. Derivatives: Stearamine Oxide, Stearyl Acetate, Stearyl Caprylate, Stearyl Citrate, Stearyldimethyl Amine, Stearyl Glycyrrhetinate, Stearyl Heptanoate, Stearyl Octanoate, Stearyl Stearate. Alternatives: plant sources, vegetable stearic acid.

Steroids. Sterols. From various animal glands or from plant tissues. Steroids include sterols. Sterols are alcohol from animals or plants (e.g., cholesterol). Used in hormone preparation. In creams, lotions, hair conditioners, fragrances, etc. Alternatives: plant tissues, synthetics.

Sterols. (See Stearyl Alcohol and Steroids.)

Suede. (See Leather.)

Sugar. Most refineries use animal charcoal filters. Alternatives: Sucanat (brand name)sweetner, turbinado sugar, concentrated fruit sweetener, rice syrup, maple syrup (after checking up on company to make sure they don't use lard as a de-foamer)

Syrup, Maple. Most companies add lard as foam reducer. Buy organic or check with company.

T

Tallow. Tallow Fatty Alcohol. Stearic Acid. Rendered beef fat. May cause eczema and blackheads. In wax paper, crayons, margarines, paints, rubber, lubricants, etc. In candles, soaps, lipsticks, shaving creams, other cosmetics. Chemicals (e.g., PCB) can be in animal tallow. Derivatives: Sodium Tallowate, Tallow Acid, Tallow Amide, Tallow Amine, Talloweth-6, Tallow Glycerides, Tallow Imidazoline. Alternatives: vegetable tallow, Japan tallow, paraffin and/or ceresin (see alternatives for Beeswax for all three). Paraffin is usually from petroleum, wood, coal, or shale oil.

Triterpene Alcohols. (See Lanolin.)

Turtle Oil. Sea Turtle Oil. From the muscles and genitals of giant sea turtles. In soap, skin creams, nail creams, other cosmetics. Alternatives: vegetable emollients (see alternatives to Animal Fats and Oils).

Tyrosine. Amino acid hydrolyzed from casein. Used in cosmetics and creams. Derivative: Glucose Tyrosinase. Urea. Carbamide. Excreted from urine and other bodily fluids. In deodorants, ammoniated dentrifices, mouthwashes, hair colorings, hand creams, lotions, shampoos, etc. Used to "brown" baked goods, such as pretzels. Derivatives: Imidazolidinyl Urea, Uric Acid. Alternatives: synthetics.

V

Vinegar distilled (white). Use animal charcoal for filtering use rice, wine, or apple cider vinegar

Vitamin A. Can come from fish liver oil (e.g., shark liver oil), egg yolk, butter, lemongrass, wheat germ oil, carotene in carrots, and synthetics. It is an aliphatic alcohol. In cosmetics, creams, perfumes, hair dyes, etc. In vitamins, supplements. Alternatives: carrots, other vegetables, synthetics.

Vitamin B-Complex Factor. (See Panthenol.)

Vitamin B Factor. (See Biotin.)

Vitamin B-12. Usually animal source. Some vegetarian B-12 vitamins are in a stomach base. Alternatives: some vegetarian B-12-fortified yeasts and analogs available. Plant algae discovered containing B-12, now in supplement form (spirulina). Also, B-12 is normally produced in a healthy body.

Vitamin D. Ergocalciferol. Vitamin D-2. Ergosterol. Provitamin D-2. Calciferol. Vitamin D-3. Vitamin D can come from fish liver oil, milk, egg yolk, etc. Vitamin D-2 can come from animal fats or plant sterols. Vitamins D-2 and D-3 may be from fish oil. All the D vitamins can be in creams, lotions, other cosmetics, vitamin tablets, etc. Alternatives: plant and mineral sources, synthetics, completely vegetarian vitamins, exposure of skin to sunshine. Many other vitamins can come from animal sources. Examples: choline, biotin, inositol, riboflavin, etc.

Vitamin H. (See Biotin.)

W

Wax. Glossy, hard substance that is soft when hot. From animals and plants. In lipsticks, depilatories, hair straighteners. Alternatives: vegetable waxes.

Whey. A serum from milk. Usually in cakes, cookies, candies, and breads. In cheese-making. Alternatives: soybean whey.

White Sugar, Brown sugar. Most refineries use animal charcoal filters. Alternatives: Sucanat (brand name) sweetner, turbinado sugar, concentrated fruit sweetener, rice syrup, maple syrup (after checking up on company to make sure they don't use lard as a de-foamer)

Wool. From sheep. Used in clothing. Ram lambs and old "wool" sheep are slaughtered for their meat. Sheep are transported without food or water, in extreme heat and cold. Legs are broken, eyes injured, etc. Sheep are bred to be unnaturally woolly, also unnaturally wrinkly, which causes them to get insect infestations around the tail areas. The farmer's solution to this is the painful cutting away of the flesh around the tail (called mulesing). "Inferior" sheep are killed. When shearing the sheep, they are pinned down violently and sheared roughly. Their skin is cut up. Every year, hundreds of thousands of shorn sheep die from exposure to cold. Natural predators of sheep (wolves, coyotes, eagles, etc.) are poisoned, trapped, and shot. In the U.S., overgrazing of cattle and sheep is turning more than 150 million acres of land to desert. "Natural" wool production uses enormous amounts of resources and energy (to breed, raise, feed, shear, transport, slaughter, etc., the sheep). Derivatives: Lanolin,

Wool Wax, Wool Fat. Alternatives: cotton, cotton flannel, synthetic fibers, ramie, etc.

Wool Fat, wool wax. (See Lanolin.)

People for the Ethical Treatment of Animals

There are many ways to make your life animal friendly. Reading labels is a good way to start. If you're interested in avoiding companies that test or use animal products, you can contact People for the Ethical Treatment of Animals (PETA)'s website:

peta.org

or

People for the Ethical Treatment of Animals
501 Front St., Norfolk, VA
USA 23510
(757) 622-7382

For a few bucks, they can also provide you with a booklet of animal-friendly and non-animal-friendly companies entitled Shopping Guide for Caring Consumers that you can carry with you while you shop. PETA is an excellent resource for books, products, and other information.

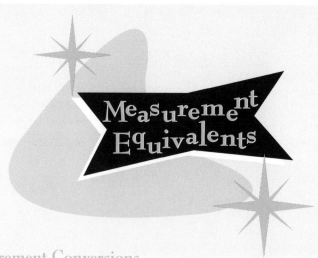

Measurement Equivalents

Measurement Conversions

TEASPOON	TABLESPOON	CUP	FLUID OUNCE
3 tsp	1 tbsp	$\frac{1}{16}$ cup	$\frac{1}{2}$ oz
6 tsp	2 tbsp	$\frac{1}{8}$ cup	1 oz
12 tsp	4 tbsp	$\frac{1}{4}$ cup	2 oz
16 tsp	5 $\frac{1}{3}$ tbsp	$\frac{1}{3}$ cup	2 $\frac{2}{3}$ oz
24 tsp	8 tbsp	$\frac{1}{2}$ cup	4 oz
32 tsp	10 $\frac{2}{3}$ tbsp	$\frac{2}{3}$ cup	5 $\frac{1}{3}$ oz
36 tsp	12 tbsp	$\frac{3}{4}$ cup	6 oz
48 tsp	16 tbsp	1 cup	8 oz

If you don't have measuring spoons, you can always use your hands!

HAND MEASUREMENT	TSP/TBSP/CUP
1 pinch	$\frac{1}{8}$ tsp
3 pinches	$\frac{1}{2}$ tsp
5 pinches	1 tsp
palm of hand	1 tbsp
1 cupped hand	1 cup

POUND	OUNCE
$\frac{1}{4}$ lb	4 oz
$\frac{1}{2}$ lb	8 oz
$\frac{3}{4}$ lb	12 oz
1 lb	16 oz

INDEX